Hit the Job Running

Because landing the job is the easy part

ANDREA DOLPH, LYNDA CLEMENS
and RAY SARNACKI

RISE AND SHINE PRESS • WAYNE, PENNSYLVANIA

Hit the Job Running: Because landing the job is the easy part /
    Andrea Dolph, Lynda Clemens and Ray Sarnacki — 2nd ed.

        p. cm

    Include index.

    ISBN-13 978-0-9774099-1-4

    ISBN-10 0-9774099-1-0

        1. Business / Career

Cartoons reprinted with permission from Randy Glasbergen.

Printed in the United States of America

In the United States and/or other countries:

Microsoft® is a registered trademark of Microsoft Corporation • Wal-Mart® is a registered trademark of Wal-Mart Stores, Inc. • L-3 Communications® is a registered trademark of L-3 Communications Corporation • NYSE® is a registered trademark of the New York Stock Exchange • Nasdaq® is a registered trademark of The Nasdaq Stock Market, Inc. • AMEX® is a registered trademark of the American Stock Exchange, Inc. • Six Sigma® is a registered trademark of Motorola, Inc. • Fortune 500® is a registered trademark of Time, Inc. • ISO® is a registered trademark of the International Organization for Standardization • Toastmasters® is a registered trademark of Toastmasters International • Standard & Poor's® , S&P® are a registered trademarks of the McGraw-Hill Companies, Inc.

RISE AND SHINE PRESS
P.O. Box 11
Wayne, PA 19087

Table of Contents

What Now?   289

Don't become complacent ❖ Commit to continuous learning ❖ Work to build a life ❖ Take initiative ❖ Define and achieve the success you imagine

Foreword

Each year I have the privilege of working closely with approximately twenty five newly-graduated engineers. I see the best and brightest our universities have to offer. As Administrator for the Engineering Development Program (EDP) at L-3 Communications - Communications Systems East Division, it is my job to see that their transition from an engineering student to a professional engineer is as seamless and complete as possible.

My company realizes the development of these engineers is vital to our existence; so much so that they commit an enormous amount of resources toward this end. Our EDP is a nine-month program that develops the engineer in three different areas: technical knowledge, L-3's core business areas and the individual's professional growth. Our new engineers have a solid technical base; this is what they receive from their respective universities. Enhancing this is not a problem. Educating them on our various business endeavors, while a large undertaking, is also a relatively straight forward item. What poses the greatest challenge is educating these young men and women as to the ways of the corporate world. The list of items that need to be addressed (and are not covered in any college course) is virtually endless—planning and completing assignments, group dynamics, asking for and receiving help, communicating with co-workers, workplace behavior, business acumen and so on.

My predecessor in EDP called upon Andrea Dolph and Ray Sarnacki to share their knowledge of the business world with our EDP participants. Highly successful veterans of the corporate world themselves, Andrea and Ray have exceeded our expectations in educating our young engineers with regards to not only what is expected of them, but how to excel in the workplace environment. Andrea and Ray do a wonderful job of sharing their knowledge and experiences with the class. They sprinkle in a nice mix of real-life scenarios which the class always enjoys and will find most useful. Their textbook is an integral part of our class.

Upon taking over EDP, I not only retained the services of Andrea, Ray, and Lynda Clemens but have expanded their role considerably. My end-of-year class survey has them consistently ranked as the top presenters—and for good reason. Their material is top-notch and is presented in such an inspiring manner that previous year's EDP participants often stop by to see them when they return to present to the current class. Probably no better compliment could be received.

The material in this book is not engineering-specific; it applies to any environment or profession. Nor is it useful to only those just entering the workplace. This book is certainly a must read for younger employees; but any person of any age or profession would find this material very useful. I would expect to see a copy on the desk of anyone looking to gain an edge in the corporate world.

—Scott C. Vail

Introduction

If you are like many young adults, you will find the transition from school to work to be a challenge. Why shouldn't it be? The workplace is a vastly different world from high school and college. Consider the following examples:

College	Workplace
• Appearance and etiquette have little bearing on academic performance.	• Appearance and etiquette have significant impact on perceptions of professionalism.
• Fresh start every semester.	• First impressions are often final.
• Assignments have well-defined due dates and outcomes.	• Assignments are open-ended with partial details.
• Relationships have little bearing on grades.	• Quality of relationships can influence appraisals and promotions
• You select your friends.	• No choice of coworkers.
• Assessment and promotion are based on grades.	• Assessment and promotion are based on multiple subjective factors.

To deal with these differences, you may find you need a broader skill set than what you've acquired so far. In addition to your basic mental abilities, the subject matter expertise you gained in your studies, and positive personal traits (such as, attitude and integrity), you need a set of workplace skills—which you may not have developed yet. These skills include the ability to quickly assess and adapt to a new environment, the ability to work effectively with a diverse and changing set of coworkers, and the ability to balance the demands of your professional and private life.

When employers are asked to identify what makes new employees successful, they cite workplace skills—not subject matter expertise. In fact, some companies won't hire new college graduates because they don't have time or funding to train them in workplace skills. If recent graduates do get hired, they are often among the first let go if the company needs to downsize, because they lack these workplace skills. It's not that employers want to see new hires fail. Many companies don't have the resources to provide training in these skills, nor can they afford to wait for new employees to come up to speed—a process that can take a few years! In fact, because workplace skills become second nature over time, it doesn't even occur to many managers that their new hires simply haven't learned these skills.

From a new employee's perspective, a lack of honed workplace skills can be confusing and frustrating. New hires are often unsure about where they fit into their new organization; they are not prepared for the rules, policies and procedures they encounter. Many don't know what skills they are missing. These new hires feel the pressure to perform but don't know how to go about acquiring the knowledge to gain the information they need.

For example, one young man identified by his company as a "high potential" employee said he sat frustrated at his desk for two weeks after receiving his first assignment because he was not sure what he had specifically been asked to accomplish. Another young woman, rather than reading the materials she received in orientation, waited for direction on how to get her relocation expenses paid. It was not until she received a note from personnel reminding her that the six-month window to submit reimbursement claims was about to close that she panicked and asked her supervisor for guidance. The real-life examples are endless.

The purpose of this book is to help you be a successful new employee. "Success" does not necessarily mean getting on a fast track to the top of your organization. It means performing competently in your job so you always have choices about where you want to take your career. You won't be stuck in a job; you're there because you want to be.

This book will expose you to concepts that can jump-start your problem solving and performance levels to those of a more experienced professional. Each chapter helps develop your mastery by explaining why the competency is important, the "theory of the case" for each skill and a process or time-dimensioned set of steps you can take to develop your proficiency. You will also find a set of frequently asked questions at the end of each chapter that describes real-life application of the skills. Return to specific chapters to reinforce your abilities, as you gain more experience.

This book has contributed to the success of many new employees for nearly two decades. May you also find that it helps you to *hit the job running*!

Introduction to the Workplace

The transition from college to your first job as a professional will be like none other you've ever experienced. While going from high school to college required some personal adjustments, you were still essentially a student. Now, with your new job, that's about to change. You are leaving the classroom for the "real world," where you make your own decisions and are in charge of your future. The first section of this book provides you with guidelines for orienting yourself in this new world of work. You will learn how to make a good impression, how to dress and behave, and how to be accepted.

Chapter 1: First Days on the Job—Setting reasonable expectations, dealing with less than ideal circumstances and taking advantage of opportunities early on can have an effect on your longer term job success. This chapter illustrates the value of a positive attitude, even in the face of some disappointments, through true stories about new employees' first experiences.

Chapter 2: Look and Act Like a Professional—Your personal appearance and behavior had little, if any, effect on your GPA. In the work world, first impressions matter. This chapter provides you with guidelines for looking and acting like a professional.

Chapter 3: Learning the Ground Rules—Teamwork is important in the workplace. To be a team player, you have to know the rules. Every organization has its own, unique culture and norms of behavior. In this chapter, you'll learn how to identify your business's written and unwritten rules and adapt to them, in order to become an accepted member of the team.

Chapter 4: Business Acumen—Virtually every decision your organization makes is based on some aspect of finance or accounting—the universal language of business. It's never too early to start thinking like your boss. This chapter introduces the fundamental concepts of profit, revenue and expenses, how they affect your job, and how you can use them to benefit yourself and your organization.

CHAPTER 1

First Days on the Job

In This Chapter

- Challenges you may face in the early days

- Stories about people like you

- How your outlook impacts your success

"Never turn down a job because you think it's too small; you don't know where it can lead."

~ Julie Morgan ~

WHY YOU SHOULD CARE

It was a challenge, but you have landed your first professional job. Congratulations! Hopefully you're excited, eager to start working, and looking forward to new challenges and new learning opportunities. You may also feel a little nervous—that's normal. New employees who say they weren't a little anxious about their first day of work probably aren't telling the truth!

This may be the most difficult transition of your life—or, at least, your life so far. The workplace is very different from the world of education you are leaving. Your personal life may change: No more late nights out during the week; you have to get up in the morning. No more long summer breaks; two weeks' vacation is more the norm. Your coworkers will probably be more diverse than your classmates in many ways. Some may be old enough to be your parents! Aspects of your assignments will probably be less interesting than you'd like, and at times absolutely mind-numbing. And you may not have all the skills you need to succeed initially, which is why you're reading this book.

While you have a whole career to grow into, your first job can set the stage for how easy or difficult the next few years will be. It can affect your professional reputation, your career opportunities, and your attitude toward work. You will do your best if you are happy, so you need to do everything you can to *be* happy. That starts with coming to your first job with the right set of expectations.

WHAT TO EXPECT IN THE FIRST FEW WEEKS

Every job will be different, so it's impossible to say exactly what you'll walk into. Maybe your first day will be like:*

- *Ben's experience with a large defense contractor. Ben was pleased to see he was assigned a large, corner cubicle with a real wall on two sides and a door. The administrative assistant had arranged to have the area freshly painted, the desk drawers were filled with basic supplies, and the phone was connected. She apologized profusely that the computer wasn't hooked up, but the technician was expected that day. Some reading material was stacked on the desk. The administrative assistant had also scheduled a number of meetings with various managers, lead engineers, and coworkers. After a few weeks, the company expected he could start working on a real satellite design project. "This is going to be great!" Ben thought.*
- *Michele's first day. When Michele started work at a glamorous West Coast PR firm, she was thrilled with her upscale work area,*

---

*To find out what happened to these new employees, turn to the end of this chapter.

situated so she could greet and interact with clients as they waited to speak to her boss. Not only was her workspace plush, but a beautifully wrapped present awaited her. "Get yourself situated, and then I have work for you," her boss called to say.

- ***Rohan's new job.*** *Rohan's new work area was a small, half-walled cubicle in the midst of many other cubicles. It was evident that someone in the architectural firm had made an effort to clean up his workspace, but Rohan needed to wash it down again to remove the previous occupant's "palm grime" from the keyboard. An administrator made a point of showing him the new pencil sharpener, tape dispenser, and stapler she had bought. After a short morning orientation, Rohan took a building tour of the coffee area, rest rooms, and supply closet. He was also introduced to his peers and bosses. By 11 A.M., he was working on his first assignment.*

- ***Kendra's miserable start to her job with a mid-sized consulting firm.*** *Her desktop was filthy. Not only were her phone and computer not connected but the computer was missing the keyboard. Her new boss, who had been so friendly in her interviews, was strangely aloof. Her peers ignored her. "What have I committed to?" Kendra sobbed when she got home that night.*

As you can see, anything is possible. Two new employees, working for the same company, may have entirely different initial experiences. You don't need to be overly pessimistic, but don't expect a perfect first day, either. Don't take any disappointments personally. It's not about you. Be flexible and adapt to your situation. It also helps to think through what you might not like and to develop strategies to deal with what might go wrong. Here are some things you might have to cope with in the early days, and some ideas to help you deal with them.

Workspace

Let's face it—your first workspace probably won't be a large private office with a view. Your work area will probably be small. You may sit in a fairly public area that's noisy, with little to no privacy. If you are in an office environment, odds are you'll be assigned to a cubicle.

Why do new employees start out in these conditions? Building space is pricey, so organizations have to use all the space they can. That means that once the window offices are laid out, the interior building space is what remains for other work areas. If you were a manager deciding where your employees will sit, would you give the better areas to your newest employee, or to the employee who has worked hard for the organization for several years? Be honest! Do a good job and show a little dedication, and it won't be long until you're moving to better real estate.

Knowing What's Going On

You may find the first few weeks very confusing—possibly to the point of frustration. You won't know the new lingo and acronyms. You won't know who people are talking about. (You're told to "Remember what Bob says..." Who is Bob, and why should you care? Is he a high level manager? A key customer? Just another new employee?) You won't know anything about office projects—their expected outcomes, current status, or significance to the organization. You won't know where you and your position fit into the organization, what's expected of you, and how to behave.

New employees react in different ways to their lack of knowledge, with varying degrees of success. Some simply tune out: They daydream, text their friends, and avoid leaving their desks. If you saw a coworker behaving this way, what impression would it make on you? Would you consider him motivated and interested in learning about the job?

Rachel took an assertive approach. Confident of her intelligence and good ideas, she spoke up at every opportunity, never hesitating to suggest new ways to do things or to criticize another employee's ideas. Before long, Rachel noticed she was not invited to join in most of the informal discussions coworkers have to solve problems and share status. Why was she shut out? Without much knowledge of her new work environment, Rachel didn't realize her new ideas often weren't as brilliant or implementable as she thought. More importantly, her peers found her criticism arrogant and insulting.

Langston tried a different approach that was a lot more successful. For the first couple of weeks, he didn't contribute much to work conversations, but he actively listened, took notes on things he didn't understand, and asked his coworkers or boss for explanations outside of formal meetings. Eventually, as his knowledge increased, he began contributing in informed and respectful ways. In return, he earned the respect and ear of his coworkers.

Loneliness

In the first couple of weeks, you may be very lonely. You won't have a place in the office social network or a circle of office friends. You may have trouble relating initially to your coworkers—especially if they're a lot older, from different walks of life, or were raised in an unfamiliar culture.

Ellie was miserable in her new job. For the first two weeks, she ate lunch by herself every day. When she finally asked two women in the office to eat with her, they said no. Her initial strategy of running errands and making phone calls at lunch worked for a while, but finally she couldn't stand it any longer. She went out of her way to make personal connections with her coworkers. She asked about photos of their kids or college memorabilia on their desks. She joined in conversations about the local sports teams or popular TV shows. Soon she was busy going out at lunchtime with her peers, and had trouble finding time to run her errands.

A word to the wise: Until you know your office mates well, avoid conversations about office gossip, politics, values, and religion!

First Assignments

It's your first day on the job. There's an opening for you—a project just kicking off. It happens to utilize your skills and knowledge perfectly. You don't need any company-specific knowledge or experience; it doesn't matter that you're not familiar with your industry or your client. You can jump right in and excel. . . Small chance of this!

Eric's experience is probably more typical. After a day of orientation, he was given a pile of documents and a list of links on his organization's internal website and told to read for a while to come up to speed. When he finished reading the stack, Eric was given another. Even though the reading was extremely boring, and Eric wasn't able to do any real work for a while, he applied himself to really learning the material. He started asking intelligent questions and, before long, was able to contribute at staff meetings. Soon he had a real assignment that he was well-prepared to contribute to. Carlos was less patient. He bragged to anyone who would listen about his academic career, complained bitterly about the "incompetent management" that was too stupid to recognize his brilliance, and didn't pay attention in his training courses because he thought he already knew all the material. Carlos never did figure out why his fellow new employees were more accepted by their work teams and, consequently, much happier than he was.

TAKE THE INITIATIVE

There are many things you can do in the first days and weeks on the job to start off successfully. The key is that you take the steps needed. Don't wait for someone else—whether your boss or peers—to do it for you.

Steps for First Days on the Job

1. Be patient
2. Take initiative
3. Ask questions
4. Get a buddy
5. Identify a role model
6. Get a life outside of work
7. Do your best on EVERY assignment

---

1. Be patient

Remember: Things will change faster than you think. It won't be long before there's a newer employee looking up to you as the person with experience. Set reasonable expectations. Ask people who have been around a little longer than you what they experienced at the beginning. Don't make unrealistic demands, like asking for a highly visible or critical assignment. They'll come.

2. Take initiative

Start by getting your office and equipment set up, if they aren't already. Don't wait for it to happen; it might take a few days, if ever. If it's not provided, ask for background reading—and read it! Later, you'll find it's a luxury to have time to come up to speed. Volunteer for "extracurricular" assignments, like helping with the office United Way Campaign or blood drive. These assignments will help you meet other people and show your willingness to work. Attend optional seminars and meetings, such as a lunchtime class. It indicates your interest in learning more. Ask if you can sit in on project reviews, planning meetings, or other business activities so you can find out more about what's going on. Don't take it personally if you're not allowed into customer meetings for a while. That's fairly common.

3. Ask questions

This is your opportunity! No one expects you to know much, so questions (even lots of them) are acceptable and welcomed. Take advantage of this time in your career. "Dumb questions" asked after you've been on board for several months are just that—dumb. Ask about acronyms and business-specific language, who people are, how work gets done, customer demands, your manager's expectations, etc. Even though you're expected to ask questions, be sensitive about when you ask them. The middle of a tense meeting probably isn't the best time. Keep a log of the answers you receive. You don't want to ask the same questions over and over. That's dumb, too. Recording the answers also lets you have a reference to look back on—just in case you forget. There's usually a lot to learn in the early days.

4. Get a buddy

A buddy is someone with experience in your workplace who is responsible for helping you get through your first several months on the job. You may be assigned one as part of your on-boarding process. Take advantage of this resource! Sometimes buddies become career-long mentors. If you aren't assigned one, ask for one. Buddies are best if they are not your managers. They don't need to be your age, or even close. An older, more experienced employee may be much more insightful. On the other hand, it might be easier for you to relate to someone with only slightly more experience than you. He'll remember what it's like being new. The ideal is one of each.

5. Identify a role model

Superstars are easy to spot. Find a few! What skills, knowledge, and behaviors do these people possess that make them successful? Begin practicing these behaviors yourself. But be true to yourself. If you're shy and the role model you've chosen is especially outgoing, don't try to be something you're not. You probably won't appear genuine, and that's annoying. Either try to adapt your style to be closer to that of your role model, or find a role model with a style closer to your own. Avoid emulating the outlying personalities—the office clown, boat rocker, or antagonist—until you understand whether and how these styles are accepted. Few people can pull them off successfully.

6. Get a life outside of work

Yes, it's important that you do well at work, but it's also important that you have balance in your life. You need friends not just for fun and companionship. They're good for your mental health and to come to your rescue when your car breaks down or you're sick. Outside activities—sports, service activities, or an art class—are equally important. They help relieve stress, give you more life experiences (that might be transferable to your work), introduce you to new contacts, and make you a more interesting person. Learn something new; meet someone new; try something new.

7. Do your best on EVERY assignment

It doesn't matter if the task is boring or inconsequential. Do your best! Every job is an opportunity to learn something about your workplace. Look behind the immediate task for the underlying process(es). How does it fit in with the bigger picture? What people are involved? Why is this task necessary? Many successful people attribute their success to their obscure beginnings in the mail room or as a grocery bagger, where they learned how things really get done behind the scenes. Additionally, your early assignments are the beginnings of your track record. First impressions are hard to shake—good or bad. Do a good job, and you'll start building trust in your abilities. Do a bad job, and people will wonder about your abilities. If you can't do the easy work, will you really be able to do the more difficult jobs?

SUMMARY

Starting a new job is a time of excitement, anticipation and change. If you arrive with reasonable expectations, a positive attitude, good manners and a willingness to work hard, you will be able to adapt to whatever situation you face. We have all been in less than ideal situations. It's how you deal with them that gains you the respect and goodwill of your coworkers and boss. Be patient and read this book for tips on handling workplace challenges. You will hit the job running!

FAQs

Q: *Is it OK for my mom or dad to come to my orientation sessions and first day of work with me?"*

A: In a word: NO. Your new organization may allow it, but why would you want to leave that first impression with your new boss and coworkers? Think about the message you'd be sending: "I can't stand on my own two feet." "I'm not mature or confident enough to be here as an adult." Do you think your manager would feel comfortable assigning you any serious responsibility? Yes, it's possible you'll be hit with a lot of information you're not familiar with—401(k) specifics, tax deductions, and insurance options. Do your best to understand, ask questions, and bring the materials home to discuss with your parents outside the office.

Q: *I can't take it anymore! I've been here two months and have had no training on my position, have only the vaguest idea what I'm supposed to do, and never see my manager. I'm depressed and ready to find another job. Is this the right thing to do?*

A: Been there. Yes, this is a depressing situation. There may not be any training for you to take. Your manager may be overloaded with work from her boss. Here are a few things to try, though, before you look for a new job.

- Schedule a meeting with your boss to discuss your job. Don't just ask for a meeting as you pass in the hall and hope that it happens. Do what it takes to get an appointment written into her calendar "formally." Talk to the administrative assistant; use the automated scheduler. Do whatever it takes in your environment. Be clear about what you want to talk about so your boss is prepared. If possible, bring suggestions for what to do next. For example, can she assign you to support a more senior person in the office?

- Make sure you haven't overlooked anything you've been asked to do, like completing background reading or finishing a series of "meet and greet" interviews. Your manager may consider these as prerequisites to a "real" assignment. Get them done! You want to appear motivated, not impatient.

- Ask other relatively new hires what their first months on the job were like. If they had a similar experience, find out what worked for them.

- If you can't get in to talk to your manager, ask a senior person in your unit for guidance. Avoid whining and other negative talk. Express your enthusiasm to start working, and ask how you can start. He or she will probably understand and try to help.

Looking for a new job should be your absolute last resort. You know from just having gone through it, that job hunting is stressful and energy draining. Now it will be tougher, because you'll have to explain why you didn't last in your current position. Even if you're justified, this would be a red flag to most employers.

Q: *Is it OK to try to arrange to talk to my manager once or twice a week? I want to impress him and get a promotion ASAP.*

A: It's reasonable to talk to your manager a couple of times a week, especially in your first few months on the job. Make sure you're not monopolizing his time, if he has a large staff. Make sure you're not wasting his time, either. "Face time" can work against you if you don't have anything important to discuss—like significant progress or a set of well-thought-out questions. As for the quick promotion, you should put your energy into accomplishing an outcome that earns you the promotion. Success in the academic world you just left is based largely on what you know. The work world rewards what you do.

Q: *I'm new to a small regional office and was told the new person is expected to take orders for afternoon snacks, call in the order, and distribute the food and correct change to everyone. In my opinion, this is demeaning, nonproductive and time-consuming. How do I get out of this?*

A: The key to your question: Is this really what is expected of a new person? If so, you'll have to "pay your dues" if you want to be accepted by your team. Can you find a way to have fun with it? Can you use it as an opportunity to build relationships? Define a process that gets everyone fed in the minimum amount of time (and impresses everyone with your resourcefulness). If this isn't how everyone is treated, in a way they're bullying you. The best way to deal with a bully is to laugh off the harassment and not let it show if it bothers you. You could volunteer to get the snacks now and then, but politely say "no" if you don't feel like it. Your coworkers might bother you and make you feel uncomfortable for a couple of days, but soon they'll get bored with their game and move on.

The Outcome of the Stories

The stories are true, but the names have been changed to protect the innocent. What happened to:

Ben?—Ben had interesting work and fun coworkers during his two years with the defense contractor, but his boss turned out to be a tyrant. He yelled and harassed all his employees. Finally, the stress drove Ben to find a new job. As Ben collected his personal items to leave on his last afternoon, the boss called to yell one more time.

Michele?—*Michele starting doing small tasks for her boss the very first day of her employment. But each time she finished one, her boss berated her for the errors she had made. At the end of the first day, Michele left a note on her chair that read: "Thank you very much for the lovely gift, but I cannot accept it. Nor can I keep this job. No one should be treated like I was today." She never came back.*

Rohan?—*Rohan got challenging assignments, received several promotions, and made many good friends at the architectural firm, where he still works after twelve years.*

Kendra?—*Kendra toughed it out at the consulting firm. She did some really outstanding work for a key customer, which gained her much recognition. About eighteen months after Kendra started work, her boss and most of her coworkers were unexpectedly laid off. Kendra was not. She was considered too valuable. However, she resigned about three months later when her new boss yelled at her for not lying to a client.*

CHAPTER 2

Look and Act Like a Professional

> **In This Chapter**
>
> - First impressions make a difference
> - Your appearance counts
> - Your actions reflect your attitude
> - Etiquette is more than knowing which fork to use
> - Polishing your professional image

"It is only shallow people who do not judge by appearances."

~ Oscar Wilde ~

WHY YOU SHOULD CARE

If you're like most people, you're both excited and a little nervous to be starting a new job. You're anxious to get off to a good start and demonstrate you can do the job well. Here's where to start.

Believe it or not, being a professional is as much about looking and acting the part as it is about doing the job well. Certainly skill and competence are essential to success, but your appearance, behavior and manners affect the way you're seen and can make or break your career with the company.

Your image is formed the minute you step in the door. People make assumptions about you within the first 30 seconds of meeting you. They base these assumptions on how you look and act as compared to their accepted social norms. This first impression is often hard to "undo." It can influence how your coworkers judge your future performance, or whether they even want to work with you.

The scrutiny doesn't end with that first impression. Your coworkers will continue to judge you, based on your ongoing appearance and behavior. If you dress or act like you are still in college, they might assume you are immature, irresponsible or even incompetent. Your manager may be reluctant to give you assignments that involve people outside the organization, for fear that your appearance or behavior will reflect poorly on the company. In a layoff situation, your image could affect whether you're the one to go.

Yes, this may seem superficial and unfair; after all, weren't you hired for your ability and intelligence? However, it is a reality you must deal with—and even use to your advantage. Think of your image as part of your personal marketing campaign. Just as a marketing department packages its products to attract customers, you can use your appearance and behavior to project qualities that will make people want to buy what you're selling—you!

WHAT DOES IT MEAN TO LOOK AND ACT PROFESSIONAL?

You have many opportunities everyday to leave an impression on your coworkers, management and customers. The key is to get in the habit of presenting a positive image so that people will want to learn more about you—and will give you the chance to demonstrate your skills and intelligence.

Looking the Part

What style of dress is right for your job? Appropriate dress varies by profession and company. It is also influenced by the type of clients you work with and by the public image your company wants to project.

For example, if you work in a bank or financial institution, you may dress more conventionally, to project an image of conservatism and reliability to your clients. Conversely, if you work in fashion retail or an architectural firm, you may dress with more flair and individuality, to reflect the creativity and style of your business.

That doesn't mean you can't be an individual. We all have our own style and taste in clothing. But if your personal style stands out too much at the office, your coworkers may question what message you're trying to send. Are you making a fashion statement, or do you want to be accepted as a professional? Who are you trying to impress? And are you even aware how you look to others and how they react?

There's more to your appearance than the clothes you wear. Your appearance includes how you groom yourself and what your office space looks like. Carelessness, sloppiness and lack of cleanliness can offend coworkers; they also say a lot about how you view yourself.

Laura, a new systems engineer, rushes into work every morning, looking as if she just got out of the shower. Her hair is wet, and her clothes disheveled. Papers and stacks of folders are strewn on chairs and the floor in her office. She projects a disorganized image—not a good message for someone whose job requires discipline and organization. Laura may be very good at what she does technically, but her boss may limit her level of responsibility until she gets her personal act together and appears more professional.

Acting the Part

Your actions and mannerisms speak volumes about your attitude towards your job and the people you work with. They also reflect your level of maturity. Your coworkers and supervisors will pick up on silent cues and won't hesitate to judge you based on how you treat them. Consider the following employees:

- *Tom is a customer relations specialist who works on crossword puzzles during his manager's weekly staff meetings, rarely engaging in the discussion. To his manager and coworkers, Tom's behavior implies he is bored, uninterested in his job, and would rather be someplace else. Chances are he will be eventually—the unemployment line.*

- *Emily wants to appear capable, positive and friendly. However, she slouches, speaks too softly and fails to look anyone in the eye when speaking—suggesting a lack of confidence. Emily's project leader hesitates to give her any real responsibility for fear she'll crumble under the pressure.*

- *On the other hand, Natalie, a financial analyst who graduated with high honors from a prestigious university, loudly expresses strong opinions about how things should be done in her organization. She quickly dismisses others' ideas, usually sarcastically. Natalie's ideas are often sound, but by shutting down her coworkers, she alienates them so much that her team ostracizes her.*

Etiquette and Social Graces

Contrary to what many people think, etiquette is more than knowing which fork to use at a dinner party. Good manners and social graces are tools to get you through uncomfortable social situations and relationships. Etiquette means recognizing that there are other people in the world and taking their feelings into consideration. Saying "please" and "thank you," speaking politely, and being patient are small gestures that go a long way toward showing people you care. Your good manners make others feel good about you and about themselves—and they will be likely to return the favor.

A Timeline for Polishing Your Image

(0-3 months)

1. Check your personal grooming habits
2. Clean up your work area

(3-6 months)

3. Make over your wardrobe
4. Evaluate your behavior
5. Watch your manners

Consider the case of Ken, who always leaves a mess in the office microwave after heating his lunch and never makes a fresh pot of coffee when he takes the last cup. When the printer jams, he leaves it and finds another to use. His coworkers resent having to clean up after him. Ken's lack of courtesy says he doesn't care about them, so why should they care about him? If Ken doesn't change his habits, they may not come to his rescue when he makes a mistake on the job or cooperate when he needs their help.

TAKE THE INITIATIVE

1. Check your personal grooming habits

Use the checklist in Table 2.1 as a guideline. We don't always know how we come across to others. Ask a trusted friend to help you objectively assess your grooming habits.

Table 2.1: Personal Grooming Checklist

Hair	✔ Washed ✔ Combed and neat ✔ Professionally cut in a maintainable style ✔ Natural-looking color ✔ Don't show up for work with wet hair
Nails	✔ Clean ✔ Filed and trimmed ✔ Women: Avoid garish nail polish and excessively long nails
Teeth	✔ Brush and floss regularly ✔ Keep a tin of breath mints handy ✔ Use mouthwash for bad breath problems
Body	✔ Avoid using perfume/cologne/aftershave with heavy fragrance ✔ During work hours avoid garlic and other fragrant spices ✔ Bathe regularly ✔ Use deodorant ✔ Wear clean clothes and underwear
Other	✔ Posture—stand/sit straight; don't slouch ✔ Maintain weight appropriate for your height and build ✔ Never groom in public

2. Clean up your work area

Your work area is not a dorm room. It should be free of clutter and tastefully decorated. Bring in a few items to brighten up your office and personalize your work space: plants, photo, posters, and other interesting objects that say something about you as a person. Don't overdo it. Use these guidelines:

- *Keep your desktop clear.* Only keep items on your desk that you need daily (for example, in/out baskets, calendar, pad of paper). Keep supplies (staplers, pens, paper clips, etc.) in your desk drawers. When you've completed a task, clear your desktop to help you clear your mind for the next task. See Chapter 15, *Achieving Work-Life Balance*, for more about organizing your office space.

- *Keep your work area clean.* It should be free of coffee, tea and other food stains.

- *Decorate tastefully.* Make sure that posters, calendar, and your computer desktop do not contain sexist, racist or other offensive material. Avoid "overly cute" items.

- *Limit toys and gadgets.* Don't overdo it; one or two novelty items are OK.

- *Get rid of trash.* Make sure your trash can gets emptied every night; put it where the cleaning crew will easily find it.

3. Make over your wardrobe

To determine what's appropriate to wear, read your company's dress code and observe what other employees are wearing. Be careful though—not everyone adheres to dress codes. Next, think about what image you want to convey at work. Most likely, you'll want to drop the "college-look" (for example, T-shirts with slogans or artwork, worn-out jeans, or shorts). Avoid provocative or revealing clothing. If you're not sure where to start, Table 2.2 can help, by providing some general guidelines for *conservative* office attire. Remember the "rules" will vary from one company to the next.

Table 2.2: Guidelines for Conservative Office Attire

	Acceptable	Unacceptable
Suit / Dress / Skirts / Sports Coats / Pants	• Good fit • Classic style, nicely tailored • Well-made • Black, gray, navy or earth tones • Pressed • Clean and unstained • Odor free • Khakis or slacks for casual wear	• Provocative clothing (tight-fitting, revealing or suggestive) • Miniskirts • Hot colors or garish plaids • Shorts • Jeans (may be acceptable in some jobs or companies) • Capri pants
Shirt	• Polo shirts with collars • Long-sleeve dress shirts • Clean, pressed and unstained • Odor free	• Athletic wear • Halter tops • Missing buttons • Holes, tears or stains in fabric
Shoes	• Black, brown or burgundy • Polished • Well maintained • Loafers (but never with a suit)	• Run-down or worn-out • Sandals or flip flops • Sneakers or gym shoes • Hiking boots
Accessories	• Women: colorful scarf or brooch • Men: stylish colorful tie, belt or suspenders that match shoes	• Items bearing cartoon characters or obscenities
Jewelry	• Minimal and tasteful • Watch • Wedding band or engagement ring • Class ring or plain ring • Women: earrings or simple necklace	• Noisy bangle bracelets • Long dangling or large hoop earrings • Extreme body piercing (nose, lip, eyebrow, tongue)
Makeup	• Natural looking • Neutral colors that enhance skin tone and facial features	• Offensive tattoos—especially those that are profane, vulgar or advocate violence. Acceptability varies by company

Tips for Buying a Quality Suit

Even though you are most likely on a budget, remember that a suit is an investment. It should be something that you wear for years. Go with a classic cut that can withstand the years and a durable fabric, such as wool. Think twice about buying the cheapest suit you can find. Look instead for a brand that you can trust to deliver quality and value.

- Steer clear of trendy styles, especially for your first suit. They will become outdated more quickly and will be hard to mix and match.

- Ask if the store or brand offers free or reduced-price tailoring with the purchase of a suit. If it does, ask to see a sample of the tailor's work before buying the suit.

- Bring an honest friend to get a second opinion.

- You want the suit to last. Before buying, check for fabric flaws, pills, pulls or loose treads. Check the seams and lining to make sure that they are strong.

- Women: Opt for both the skirt and the pants, if they match the jacket. It is the easiest way to change the look of a suit: you can wear the pants in the winter and the skirt in warmer weather.

- Try your pants on with the shoes you will be wearing with them to see if they need to be hemmed. You want the pants to hit the top of the shoe, with enough material to create a slight break in the leg.

- When trying on the jacket, put your arms in a "driving" position (as if you are holding the steering wheel). This tests how comfortable the suit will be as you move naturally throughout the workday.

Putting together a basic wardrobe doesn't have to cost you a lot of money. Here are some tips for planning and building a basic wardrobe:

- For jackets, suits and pants (and skirts for women), stick with basic colors: black, navy, gray and earth tones. Sure, it sounds boring, but think of these pieces as a base. You can add color and interest with different colored shirts or blouses, and accessories. Basic color pieces make it easier to match items and update your wardrobe.

- Buy outfits that can be mixed and matched. Ten to fifteen basic pieces can easily become twenty-five different outfits or more. Buy a suit whose jacket can be worn with a different colored pair of pants (or skirt), and whose pants (or skirt) can be worn on its own.

- Even if you work in a casual office, you'll need to have at least one good suit when the occasion calls for "business attire," such as meeting customers or traveling to corporate headquarters to meet with executives. That goes for women as well as men. You can't fake a good suit; if you buy a cheap one, you'll have to replace it sooner.

- Save money on shirts. Many bargain stores have great inexpensive shirts. The less you spend on shirts, the more variety you can have. Plus, it will be easier to update your look.

4. Evaluate your behavior

Use the checklists below to evaluate your attitude, mannerisms, level of maturity and how you treat others. Be honest with yourself. We don't always know the effect we have on others, so you may want to ask someone you trust for feedback. Ask someone who you consider a role model at work to help you identify new behaviors to adopt. Modify your behavior and see if it makes a difference.

Attitude

✔ **Ease up on your ego.** Be self-confident, but don't go overboard. Overconfidence can be interpreted as arrogance. You may have been an A-student and president of your class, but you're just another new employee to your coworkers. Displays of ego will be resented and get in the way of building good working relationships.

✔ **Accept assignments eagerly.** Everyone gets his or her share of low-level assignments. Instead of whining or complaining, show a "can-do" attitude to demonstrate that you can get a job done, and do it well.

✔ **Show your interest and commitment.** Show you are a serious employee by speaking up at general meetings and showing up at office parties. Attendance may be optional, but your absence could be conspicuous.

✔ **Don't be overly cynical.** Give people the benefit of the doubt, unless they have given you a good reason not to trust their motives.

✔ **Deal with issues constructively.** Don't look for someone to blame, and don't whine about problems. Pitch in, even if it's not in your job description, and focus on solving the problem.

✔ **Avoid "us-versus-them" talk.** Whether it's employees vs. management or your unit vs. another, it's divisive and demonstrates that you are not a team player.

✔ **You're there to work.** Personal conversations, office pools, etc., help build rapport with coworkers. But spending too much time socializing will get in the way of your job.

✔ **Show up for work and be on time.** Show you are dependable and committed. Always tell your manager when you will be absent or late. Give advance notice if you plan to take some time off.

Mannerisms

✔ **Don't act like you're back in college.** Avoid too much clowning around or horseplay.

✔ *Keep the volume down.* If you are allowed to play music in your office, be considerate of others. Turn down the volume or wear headphones, if it doesn't present a safety issue. Don't yell over cubicle walls or down the hall to have a conversation.

✔ *Make eye contact.* Look people in the eye when speaking to them. This conveys an honest, open character. If you're shy or this is not your cultural norm, you must learn to do this, no matter how difficult. Remember to break eye contact periodically. Staring too long could be misinterpreted as hostility or confrontation.

✔ *Learn to listen.* Sometimes, we are so worried about what we are going to say next that we don't listen effectively to others. Be an active listener. Make eye contact, paraphrase what was said, and use nonverbal cues to show you are listening, like nodding your head or leaning forward. See Chapter 12, *Spoken Workplace Communications*, for more on this topic.

✔ *Watch your accent.* We all have accents, regardless of where we come from. However, some regional accents are more difficult to understand than others. If someone seems to be having trouble understanding yours, stop and ask, especially if you are speaking by phone. Slow down your speech, if necessary.

Maturity and Judgment

✔ *Admit your mistakes.* We all make mistakes at some point in our career. When you are at fault, admit it, learn from it, and move on.

✔ *Become a low-maintenance employee.* Strive to be someone who can work independently.

✔ *Curb your drinking.* Don't come to work hung over. Drinking too much at office parties or other social events can lead you to do or say something embarrassing that you'll regret later.

✔ *Chill your emotions.* Excessive displays of emotion—either positive or negative—are inappropriate in the workplace. Express your feelings with professionally appropriate comments and behavior. Never take your bad day out on your coworkers.

✔ *Avoid foul language.* Cursing and off-color jokes are offensive to most people. Do not use vulgar or otherwise offensive language in the office.

✔ *Monitor your conversations.* Never hold a private conversation in a public area, such as a washroom, elevator or lounge. You never know who is listening.

Respect for Others

✔ *Individuals are unique.* Not everyone sees things the same way you do. Consider the perspective of others, instead of judging solely from your own point of view.

✔ *Treat everyone with respect.* Show everyone the same respect you would show the president of the company. Secretaries and staff assistants, in particular, are sensitive to whether or not you respect them and their abilities. Treat them well; they have more influence on your career than you may realize.

✔ *Show your appreciation.* Be sure to say "please" and "thank you" in your business interchanges. It creates goodwill among those you work with. When someone gives you personal time (for example, for a special meeting, to give you advice or to take you to lunch) acknowledge the gift with an email or even a "thank you" note.

✔ *Stifle stereotypes.* Do not make assumptions about people; you could be wrong. All managers are not older white males, and secretaries are not necessarily female.

✔ *Use humor appropriately.* Humor can lighten up the office atmosphere and relieve stress. But never tell a joke at the expense of others.

✔ *Keep appointments.* Being late sends a message that you do not respect the other person's time. If you are habitually late, use your favorite electronic device to remind you of appointments. When you must cancel, don't just be a "no show." Give the other person advance notice and ask to reschedule.

✔ *Don't overstay your welcome.* When meeting with someone, stick to business and be aware how much time you are taking. Be sensitive to signs (like shuffling papers, looking at their watch) that it's time to end the meeting—and leave.

✔ ***Don't linger.*** When you stop by to see someone, do not hang in the doorway if he or she is on the phone or with someone else. Unless he or she signals you to stay, leave and return later.

✔ ***Resist gossip.*** You'll learn quickly that the office grapevine is not limited to business rumors. Do not engage in personal gossip about coworkers or your manager.

✔ ***Never ask about someone else's salary.*** Other people's salary and financial matters are none of your business. By the same token, never discuss your personal finances at work.

✔ ***Never snoop.*** Resist the temptation to glance over papers left on a printer, the fax machine or a desk. If you are caught, you will lose the trust of at least one person and risk others' hearing you are a "snoop."

5. Watch your manners

Do you know the basics of etiquette? The checklists below provide some guidelines to help you handle certain work-related situations. A good etiquette book is a valuable investment in your future.

Introductions

✔ ***Shake hands.*** When you meet someone, smile and greet him or her warmly with a firm handshake. (Grasp his or her hand so that the webs of your thumbs meet, then shake from your elbow for about 2-3 seconds.)

✔ ***Be brief.*** If you are introducing yourself, state your name, the company you are with, and what you do. Provide just enough information to interest them in talking with you.

✔ ***Make introductions.*** If you are introducing other people, address the most senior or oldest person first. When introducing someone, say his or her name first and then state your relationship (for example, "This is Kathy, my wife.").

✔ ***Don't use first names.*** When you meet someone new, address him or her as Mr., Mrs., Ms., or Dr. until you are invited to use a first name—especially if he or she is older than you or more senior in rank.

Business Meals

- ✔ *Keep your napkin.* Place your napkin on your lap as soon as you sit down. If you leave during the meal, put it on the chair. When the meal is complete, place your napkin next to your plate.

- ✔ *Think before you order.* When ordering a meal, follow your host's lead. Don't order the most expensive item on the menu. Avoid messy food (for example, tacos, fried chicken) that is difficult to eat gracefully.

- ✔ *Use the correct fork.* If you're not sure which fork or spoon to use first, here's an easy way to remember: Work from the outside in with each course. Your bread-and-butter plate is always on the left.

- ✔ *Don't embarrass yourself.* Don't talk with your mouth full. Don't wave your utensils in the air while you talk, lean your elbows on the table, or pick your teeth.

- ✔ *Pass the butter.* Don't reach across anyone for an item on the table. Ask politely ("Please pass the …") for it to be passed. If the bread or another item is in front of you at the beginning of the meal, it is your responsibility to start passing it.

- ✔ *Hold onto your silver.* Once you start eating, your utensils should not touch the table again. When you finish eating, place your utensils together on the plate at the four o'clock position.

- ✔ *Wait for your host.* Your host will likely signal that the meal is over by placing his or her napkin on the table and standing up.

Dressing for the Occasion

- ✔ *Business or smart casual.* Acceptable clothing includes sweaters, turtlenecks, blazers, golf shirts, khakis or corduroys. Women can wear slacks or skirts.

"I *am* dressed for success! Of course, my idea of success may not be exactly the same as yours."

✔ ***Resort casual.*** Shorts, golf shirts, khakis and sandals are appropriate, depending on the climate. For women, casual skirts or sundresses are acceptable.

✔ ***Business attire.***

- Men: collared shirt and tie with a jacket or suit

- Women: skirt, pants suit, or business dress

✔ ***Black tie optional.***

- Men: tux or dark business suit

- Women: formal gown, dark dress or suit.

Communications

✔ ***Learn the phone system.*** Each phone system has a different way of forwarding calls or setting up conference calls. Learn how to use these features without dropping a caller.

✔ ***Answer the phone courteously.*** If your company has a standard way of answering the phone, use it. Otherwise, simply state your company's name and your own. ("XYZ Company. This is Sally Smith speaking.")

✔ **Use speakerphones properly.** Only use a speakerphone when you are on a conference call with other people in the room, or when you have to look up information while speaking. Be sure to tell the person on the other end that you are using the speaker or that there are others in the room with you. Avoid extraneous noise that can disrupt the call (for example, typing, shuffling papers, eating, side conversations). Don't use a speakerphone to listen to your voice mail.

✔ **Answer voice mail.** Respond to incoming calls within one business day if the caller has a legitimate reason for contacting you. If you are going to be out of the office, leave a recorded greeting that says when you'll be out and an alternate number to call for immediate help. When you leave a message on someone's voice mail, speak slowly and clearly. Repeat your phone number at the end of the message so the person you're calling can write it down.

✔ **Be considerate with cell phones.** Turn off your cell phone or set it to silent mode when you are in a meeting, public event or business lunch. Don't talk loudly in public places where it will disturb others (for example, restaurants, trains, hotel lobbies). If your minutes or battery are running low when you receive a call, ask if you can call back later from a landline phone.

✔ **Use email wisely.** Keep messages short and don't send complicated attachments. Watch what you write because you can't retrieve it once you hit the send button. Remember that the contents of your messages belong to the company and may be monitored. When using a distribution list, direct the recipients to the contents of the message, instead of just "blasting" it out to the world. Don't forward jokes or cartoons. Find out your company's policy on personal use of email. As with voice messages, respond to all business email within one business day.

✔ **Fax documents correctly.** Always include a cover page that identifies the recipient, sender, number of pages being transmitted and a phone contact, in case there are problems with the transmission. Avoid sending anything longer than ten pages. Fax machines are usually shared by others, so don't send private or sensitive information.

SUMMARY

As the saying goes, "You never get a second chance to make a good first impression." How others perceive you the first time they interact with you influences all your future contacts with them. Looking professional and acting the part will help get you "in the door" and make opportunities available to you. Once you're in, make sure to live up to that positive first impression, and never do anything less.

This chapter covered general aspects of how to look and act on the job. You will find that every industry and company has its own "culture" and acceptable norms of appearance and behavior. Chapter 3, *Learning the Ground Rules*, provides guidelines to help you identify what your company expects from you as a new employee.

FAQS:

Q: *People in my office use foul language regularly. Does that mean I can, too?*

A: It's best not to use profanity in the office, but in some businesses an occasional curse word may be appropriate to make your point. Don't get in the habit of swearing like a proverbial sailor. Curse words may start creeping into your vocabulary at inappropriate times where it could prove embarrassing. Avoid the "F-word" at all costs.

Q: *Is it all right to order alcohol when I go out to lunch with my supervisor?*

A: In general, most companies frown on drinking alcohol at business meals. Many will not even reimburse employees for drinks on their expense accounts. Follow your supervisor's lead. If he or she orders a drink or insists you have one, it's probably okay. But limit it to one. No more.

Q: *Several people in my office regularly share gossip. What should I do when they try to include me?*

A: There are two types of office gossip: business and personal. It's okay to engage in gossip that deals with business issues (mergers, acquisitions, changes in the business, new initiatives, etc.). Business gossip can be part of the process for assimilating change in the organization's culture. Of course, always consider your sources, and don't overdo it. On the other hand, don't engage in personal gossip about an individual. Politely say you are not interested, and change the subject.

Q: *Several times a month, someone takes up a collection for a coworker having a baby or retiring. I don't even know these people, and I'm on a limited budget. Should I be expected to contribute?*

A: Gift collections for births, deaths, weddings, retirements, etc., are commonplace in most offices. If you can afford it, give something, even if it's only a dollar. It's a nice gesture that shows you are on the team. If you cannot afford it, politely decline. Be consistent, so that you appear fair and even-handed.

Q: *Is it okay to have a tattoo?*

A: That depends on where you work. Tattoos and body piercings (other than simple earrings) are becoming more acceptable in business. But some companies ban them outright, especially service-oriented industries where employees regularly interact with customers, or where they present a potential safety hazard. Other companies are more open to discreet body art. If you do get a tattoo, place it where it won't show when you're wearing normal business attire. And stay away from profane or vulgar artwork, and anything that advocates violence.

CHAPTER 3

Learning the Ground Rules

In This Chapter

- The importance of fitting in
- Elements of an organization's culture
- The difference between formal and informal rules
- Clues to understanding your organization
- Adapting to your organization's culture

"When you are at Rome live in the Roman style; when you are elsewhere live as they live elsewhere."

~ Saint Ambrose ~

WHY YOU SHOULD CARE

You've been on the job for several days. In that time, you may have attended an orientation session, discussed job responsibilities with your supervisor, met some coworkers, and been assigned a "buddy" to help you learn the ropes. As a new employee, you've been focusing all your attention on immediate tasks—from remembering names to ordering supplies.

Now, step back a moment. It's just as important for you, as a new employee, to learn how you will fit into the "culture" of your new work environment. Misinterpreting an organization's culture and its informal rules is one of the main reasons people are fired or laid off in difficult times. Believe it or not, workers are rarely let go for a lack of technical skills. The ones asked to leave first, regardless of job level, are usually those who violate a formal policy or who did not take the time to understand and integrate into their work world. Why? Because managers believe that employees who fail to fit in prove less productive and upset office dynamics.

Every organization has its own culture—also known as "the way we do things around here." In your first weeks on the job, look around you. Notice your environment, learn the rules and observe your coworkers. Your job satisfaction depends on your appreciation of this culture and how well you adapt. Understanding the rules—both written and unwritten—helps you figure out how to adapt your style to interact with coworkers, and ultimately become an accepted member of the team.

The time to start asking questions is *now*, when you are new and expected to ask questions—and will be cut some slack for any mistakes you make.

WHAT ARE THE GROUND RULES?

Your organization's cultural norms will not be handed to you in a manual or at an orientation session. You'll have to take the initiative to uncover them yourself. The clues are all around you. They're reflected in the company's goals and values, performance expectations and standards, organization structure, informal customs and even the language it uses. No single source will tell you everything you need to know. You'll have to check out several sources for clues. Over time, you'll develop a clear picture of what is expected of you, so you can adapt successfully and be more effective in your new job. Here are the five major areas to investigate:

The Formal Rules

These are the written policies that most companies give new employees when they are hired. Since they are documented, they are the easiest ground rules to learn. They typically address time recording and attendance, dress codes, and eligibility for benefits, as well as standards and procedures for performing your job. The larger the organization, the more formal its policies. You won't be expected to memorize all the rules, but you will be expected to know the policies that routinely apply to you, which policy applies to a given situation, and where to find a policy when you need it. Policies are usually available in print or on a company website. If in doubt, ask your manager or Human Resources Department.

Now comes the tricky part. Sometimes there are discrepancies between the written rules and how they apply in practice. You'll find that some rules are generally ignored, while others can mean different things in different situations. One common example is the definition of a normal workday. While the official policy may be an eight-hour workday, in practice, employees may routinely work (unpaid) overtime. Don't risk violating the rules. If you notice a discrepancy between policy and practice, ask your manager or Human Resources Department.

One consequence of breaking the formal rules is termination, especially if you break a rule that puts the company in jeopardy (like breaking the law or the terms of a contract) or is particularly sensitive (like using company resources for personal gain). Follow the written policies exactly, until you are sure which ones you can safely stretch. Why risk your job for a personal long distance phone call? Don't worry too much about making a mistake, at least in the beginning. Most employers understand there is a lot to learn when you're new and will tolerate an honest mistake with no malicious intent. But that won't last forever, so learn the formal rules.

The Physical Environment

One of the most visible indicators of your organization's culture is the appearance of your working environment. Notice the condition of the building and its décor. They'll tell you what impression your company wants to make on customers and prospective employees. For example, a company that displays the history of its products in the lobby obviously wants to show pride in its heritage and its ability to change with the times, while a company that decorates the lobby with modern art may want to convey an image of forward thinking. Other physical clues to a company's culture can be found in the layout of the building and grounds, the degree of privacy and the quality of accommodations. Look for a more complete checklist later in this chapter.

Style and Norms of Behavior

Every organization has its own personality and style. Your company's style is reflected in its informal rules, or the "norms" of behavior for employees. Some companies are tightly knit communities, where workers socialize after hours. Others are loosely tied groups of individuals who travel or work from home, rarely collaborating or even seeing each other. Some companies are strictly disciplined, with specific performance targets and close oversight of outcomes, while others are more freewheeling and flexible with results. Some organizations promote individualism; others are intolerant of differences.

To succeed at your new job, you'll have to learn these "informal rules." They are harder to identify than formal policies because they are undocumented and represent unstated expectations of how you should relate to others at work and at company functions.

An organization's style is determined by many factors and can change over time. One of the main factors is the executive team at the top. Their values, experiences, personalities, and ambitions all influence what they expect from their employees. Another major factor is the market in which the organization competes. The type of product or service offered, the competitiveness of the market, and customer expectations all affect a company's style. Finally, even the geographic location can make a difference. A business located in New York City, for example, is likely to be more formal and high pressured than a business located upstate.

If you don't learn the informal rules, you just won't "get it." That may sound like you're back in high school, but being accepted is a fact of life in every organization. You will most likely be viewed as an "outsider," and you'll find it difficult to establish the working relationships critical to doing your job. Take the example of Andrew.

Andrew was smart and hard-working. Shortly after Andrew started his new job, his unit moved into a newly renovated work space. His unit manager let her employees decide their seating assignments among themselves. Andrew was adamant about getting a window cubicle—normally, a perk of seniority in this organization. Despite strong resistance from his team, Andrew stubbornly insisted on his prime location. Finally his coworkers gave in, and Andrew got his seat, but not without a price. After that, Andrew's coworkers never accepted him as part of their team. They were uncooperative when he needed help and kept important information from him. Andrew's performance suffered, but more importantly, he was unhappy in his job. About two years later, Andrew resigned from the corporation.

The Organization's Structure

A company's organization structure tells you who reports to whom, the function of each work unit, and the role of each manager. It also clues you in to where the power lies, how work gets done and by whom. Most companies have one of three basic forms: hierarchical, flat or matrix, as illustrated in Table 3.1.

Table 3.1: Three basic organization structures

Structure	Description	What It Looks Like
Hierachical	Multiple layers of management, usually with few people reporting to each manager.	
Flat	Fewer layers of management. Usually each manager has many people reporting directly to him (known as a broad span of control).	
Matrix	Functional managers lead teams of specifically skilled employees and loan them out to project teams as needed. When projects are completed, employees return to their home unit for reassignment.	

Your company's philosophy of management is inherent in its organization structure. For example, in a hierarchical organization, managers tend to exercise more control and review their employees' work more closely. Conversely, in a flat organization, employees generally work more independently and often have more decision-making authority. Employees in a matrix structure often have multiple managers, depending on their current assignments. Matrixed employees can experience conflicting demands for their time, but they enjoy a variety of assignments and experiences.

Conforming vs. Maintaining Your Individuality

Does adapting to an organization's culture mean you have to give up your individuality? Of course not. In fact, successful organizations actively seek a diversity of opinions and ways of thinking as a source of fresh ideas. (Chapter 13, *Managing Office Relationships,* expands on the concept of diversity.) Just realize that organizations need some set of norms to function efficiently and maintain a sense of order. Adapting to fit in does not mean suppressing your identity.

You can't change who you are, nor should you—but you can change how you act. By modifying your behavior to conform to your company's norms, you'll find people will quickly accept you as a new member of the group. If you don't adapt, you'll find it harder to gain acceptance, although certainly not impossible. The choice is yours. If you sense that your company's culture strongly conflicts with your personal objectives, values, work habits and career aspirations, you won't find the job satisfaction you seek and deserve.

TAKE THE INITIATIVE

Asking questions is the best way to learn what the ground rules are in your organization. As a new employee, you're expected to ask questions—just don't overdo it. Your goal is to get up-to-speed as fast as you can, ultimately becoming self-reliant. Don't annoy your coworkers by repeatedly asking for the same information. If you have trouble remembering, get in the habit of recording the answers to your questions someplace you can easily find them again.

A Timeline for Learning the Ground Rules

(0-3 months)

1. Understand the formal policies
2. Take inventory of your physical work space
3. Learn the acronyms and jargon

(3-6 months)

4. Study your organization's structure

(6-12 months)

5. Observe and adapt to the behavioral norms of your organization
6. Identify your organization's vision and goals

You may notice that some coworkers will add their personal bias to the information they give you. Be wary of employees with overly negative attitudes. Some disgruntled employees like to recruit new people to their "anti-establishment" point of view. While their negativity could be well-founded, it could also be the result of some failing on their part. Listen to what everyone has to say, and then weigh it against your own experience to form your own opinions. Now you are ready to start learning the ground rules.

1. Understand the formal policies

Your first step is to get access to the official policies. Policies are usually reviewed in orientation sessions, so don't skip yours, even if it sounds boring. New employees often receive a policy manual or are referred to a website. If you don't get one, ask your manager or Human Resources Department. Then take the time to browse through the policies to become familiar with them. The checklist in Table 3.2 will help you start your search.

Table 3.2: Checklist of some common policies

Policy Category	Examples of what they cover
Time and Attendance policies	• Number of vacation and sick days allowed • Recording time applied to projects or contracts • Start time; working hours
Personnel policies	• Dress codes • Qualification for benefits available to you
Use of company resources	• Use of phones, computers and corporate credit cards for personal purposes
Technical standards and procedures	• Technical codes, design and quality standards that must be met when producing your product
Customer-imposed policies	• Government ethics and privacy rules • Contract terms and conditions
Travel and expense accounting guidelines	• Approvals required to travel • Spending limits • Reimbursement guidelines • Type of accommodations allowed
Decision-making policies	• Who is allowed to make job offers • How much employees are allowed to purchase in the organization's name—if anything
Intellectual property policies	• Ownership of the rights to materials you create on your employer's time
Non-compete rules	• Agreements prohibiting you from working for a competitor for a period of time, should you leave your current employer

You may find that many policies require you to input data using an automated system. For example, you might have to enter your travel expenses or the time recorded for a project. Learn to use the systems that apply to your job as quickly as possible. A mistake in using the system could cost the company time and effort to trace and correct. At worst, you might be breaking company rules. Look for a user's guide, a "lunch and learn" session or an online course, or ask your manager or Human Resources Department for help.

2. Take inventory of your physical work space

Take a walk around your office. Notice your surroundings. What do you see? And what does it mean to you?

- *Quality of Accommodations:* What shape is your office in? Is it clean, freshly painted and in good condition, or worse for wear? From this information, can you guess how you will be expected to dress? Neat and semi-formal, or casual and comfortable?

- *Corporate Décor:* How is your building decorated? Is there a particular style? Is it rich or utilitarian? What might that say about the kind of clients, their expectations and the degree of interaction you will have with them?

- *Physical Layout:* Does the layout of desks, offices and common space (such as conference rooms and social areas) suggest that you will primarily work alone or in teams? Is every work space alike or does it depend on seniority in the organization? From this, can you guess if the organization has a strict hierarchy of authority or if it is egalitarian?

- *Privacy:* Do you see many office doors? Are they open or closed? What might that say about how much information your coworkers share, both personally and about work?

- *Organizational Identity:* Is the organization's logo prominently displayed at the entrance to your building? Does it appear throughout the building on posters, banners or nameplates? Do coworkers own personal objects with the logo on it, such as T-shirts, lapel pins, coffee mugs, briefcases or mousepads? Is there a strong sense of identity with the parent organization, or do most employees just show up to receive a paycheck?

- **_Employee Décor:_** How do your coworkers decorate their individual work areas? What does that say about what is important to them? Do pictures of families, pets or vacations suggest that personal time is valued? Or do you see awards and commendations, suggesting that achievement and advancement are valued? What is the meaning of other items you see in your coworkers' work areas?

3. Learn the acronyms and jargon

After one week on the job, many new employees are reeling from the new jargon and acronyms thrown at them. You will be at a disadvantage until you master your organization's "language." Keep a list of terms you don't recognize and find out what they mean. The best, and least embarrassing, way to learn is through informal discussions with your coworkers. Some companies do keep a list, so ask.

4. Study your organization chart

Ask for a copy of your organization chart. An organization chart is a graphical illustration of the reporting relationships within your company; it identifies the name of each manager and the function for which he or she is responsible. Knowing who the key executives are will save you the embarrassment of not recognizing their name or face when you meet them. Imagine the impression made by a new hire who, when introduced by name only to the president of his firm at a company picnic, asked, "What do you do for a living?"

Start by finding your position and immediate work unit on the organization chart. Then ask yourself these questions: How does your job function relate to the responsibilities of the other employees in your work unit? How does your unit support the objectives of the business? To learn more, talk to your supervisor, coworkers, mentor or buddy. Read company publications (for example, newsletters, their website). Once you understand your immediate unit, study the chart to learn the function of other units, the names of key individuals, whom they report to, and how they fit into the larger scheme. Use the checklist in Table 3.3 as a guide.

Table 3.3: Learning your organization's structure and what it means to you

Questions to Ask	What to Look For	Analyzing the Implications
How is the organization defined?	By function, product or region Hierarchical, flat or matrix	• Do you think this organization requires narrow specialization or "jack-of-all-trades" skills? • Who will evaluate your performance and determine your salary increase? • Is this the same person who oversees your daily work activities? • Does this structure present any possible obstacles to your advancement?
What is each unit's function?	Tasks and responsibilities of each unit and their relationships	• How well do they seem to work together? • What are the potential sources of conflict with this reporting arrangement?
How many subordinates report directly to each superior?	Number and type of people reporting to them	• The more people who report to your supervisor, the less time he or she has to advise or train you, requiring more initiative on your part. • How much interaction can you expect to have with your immediate manager? Daily? Weekly? Monthly? • In general, to what degree do you expect your superiors to review your work?
Who manages each unit, and who reports to each supervisor?	Names of key people associated with each unit, as well as their general duties, background and experience	• Which of these people will you interact with regularly? • Who are the recognized experts that you can go to when you need help? • Who are the team or project leads?
How is work accomplished?	Well-defined units with clear charters Cross-functional, self-directed work teams A combination of both, depending on the situation	• Will you be expected to work independently, or will a senior person need to sign off on each milestone you accomplish? • What is the probability you will work in a team? • How visible will your work be to upper management?

5. Observe the behavioral norms of your organization

Every organization has its own way of doing things. It is difficult to create an all-inclusive checklist that will cover every possible behavior in your organization's culture. In very large organizations, norms may even vary by physical location. Your best bet is to become a people watcher. Some things to observe are:

- *How do your peers dress and behave?* Is this different at higher levels in the organization? If so, how? Which style is most appropriate for you, given your own aspirations? Is it appropriate for you to dress or behave any differently from your peers?

- *How do your peers' work spaces look?* How are they different from work spaces at other levels in the organization?

- *What hours do your peers keep?* What do they do on their personal time, like lunch? Do they come in during the weekend or take work home? Is working at home during office hours acceptable?

WHITE COLLAR CRIMES

- *Who gets promoted, and who doesn't?* What trends do you see? What kinds of behaviors get rewarded in your company?

- *What are the perks of seniority?* A reserved parking place? A private office with a window? An invitation to the annual management meeting in a posh resort? Does your company have unspoken rules for approaching senior employees?

- *What do people complain about when they socialize?* Are the complaints serious, or just general grumbling?

- *What is discussed at staff meetings?* What does your manager seem strict about, and what does she or he shrug off? What topics and issues are generally raised?

If you pay attention to the answers to these questions, you will start to see trends emerge that will serve as guidelines for your own behavior.

6. Identify your organization's vision and goals

Successful organizations communicate their vision and goals in a variety of ways. Common themes are "top quality," "customer satisfaction," "productivity" and "family friendly." These slogans may sound idealistic or over-simplified, but don't underestimate their power. They reflect the goals, values and directions that company executives consider critical to the business. Chapters 4, *Business Acumen*, and 8, *Mastering Your Job*, discuss the ways in which these goals affect your performance. For now, concentrate on what they say about your company's leadership and its values.

- *Start reading company publications.* Read the mission statement, annual report, memos describing goals and objectives, company newsletters and the website. What are the common themes?

- *Why do you think these themes were selected?* To increase competitiveness? To address a particular problem? To respond to a change in the market? To attract more employees?

- *How does your company support these themes?* Have any initiatives have been put in place, such as a Six Sigma® effort, a fundraising drive, or an initiative for a Malcolm Baldridge quality award or ISO 9000 certification?

> ## How to Get a Copy of Your Company's Annual Report
>
> All companies that offer their stock on a major exchange (NYSE, AMEX or NASDAQ) are considered to be "publicly traded" and required to publish an annual report to the shareholders. The easiest way to get a copy is through the Investor Relations section of your company's website. It can often be downloaded directly to your PC in electronic form. Or ask your Human Resources representative or your manager where you can get a copy.

- *What do these themes say about your management team?* Are they people oriented? Financially oriented? Product oriented?

- *What are the implications for you?* How should you prioritize your work? What skills do you need?

The goals of your organization can change abruptly in response to a sudden problem, a competitor's move or a swing in market conditions. You will find it invaluable to pay attention to your organization's goals and initiatives, not just as a new hire, but throughout your career. Who knows? Maybe someday *you'll* be the leader setting goals for the rest of the organization.

SUMMARY

Uncovering the clues to your organization's culture can be fun. It is also vital to your survival and success. Learning the ground rules of your workplace requires initiative and effort, but think of the rewards. If you know how your company works and how you fit into the scheme of things, you will experience a smoother transition and better performance appraisals, and improve your visibility in the organization. Above all, you will gain more satisfaction from your work.

FAQs:

Q: *I just went on a business trip with several coworkers who told me to pad my expense account. Is this an acceptable "stretch" of the rules?*

A: No, it is not! In fact, getting caught falsifying an expense account is one of the fastest ways to get fired. Your coworkers may have gotten away with this for years, but that doesn't mean it's the right thing to do. Stay honest and it will pay off in the long run.

Q: *Most people in my company work alone in their offices all day long, hardly ever talking to each other, and when they do, it's about work. I want to have fun on the job, talk about last night's ballgame or share a couple of jokes. How do I get everyone to lighten up?*

A: Chances are you find yourself in a workplace where collaboration and sociability are not part of the culture. In highly competitive environments, some people worry that their conversations will expose a weakness or distract them from their work. Other businesses are so cost-conscious that any time spent not working is considered wasteful. Some employees are puzzled by the idea of having "fun" at work. If you can figure out why your culture is the way it is, you may come up with ways to change it. But you're probably fighting an uphill battle. Fortunately, there are probably other people like you in the organization. Find them and have fun—as long as it works within your culture.

Q: *My new company feels like one big family. It seems there's always something going on after hours: a cookout, company meetings followed by a cocktail party, or a trip to see a ball game. I like the people in my office, but I value my privacy and want to spend some of my personal time doing things unrelated to work. What should I do?*

A: Sounds like you've joined a highly communal culture, in which employees have eliminated the line between work and personal life. Work cultures like this tend to be fun and low pressure, with the employees showing a high degree of loyalty and trust in one another. However, employees who want more separation of work and personal life may resent the intrusion on their privacy. You need to assess how much of your private life you want to share, and figure out the consequences of not attending these after-hours functions. Will you still be an accepted member of the team? Will you jeopardize good work assignments or promotions? You can determine this through trial and error, or talk to someone with more experience whom you trust and respect.

CHAPTER 4

Business Acumen

In This Chapter

- Finite resources force choices

- Revenues, expenses and profits

- The language of business

- Understanding how decisions are made

- Developing your business acumen

"Show me the money."

~ Rod Tidwell, character in
the film, "Jerry Maguire" ~

WHY YOU SHOULD CARE

"Business acumen". You may have heard the term from your college advisor or job recruiter, as in: "Be sure to develop your business acumen if you want to succeed in business." But what does it mean? And why is it important?

Business acumen is often defined in terms such as "quickness and accuracy of judgment" or "keenness of insight." In the first three chapters of this book, you learned how to look sharp and act sharp on the job. In this chapter, you will learn how to become a sharp business person.

Getting hired is just the first step. Once you're in the door, you want to show you have the right stuff—the business acumen—it takes to contribute to your company's success. You are here to benefit your company; the smarter your contribution, the more your organization will value you as an employee, and help your career.

Business acumen means understanding how your organization makes its business decisions. To be more specific, it means knowing how and why your company allocates its limited resources to achieve its goals. Every organization has limited resources—whether financial, personnel, equipment or inventory—and must constantly make choices about how to best use them to benefit customers and increase profits. For example, an engineering firm might require product designers to use standard rather than customized parts in order to reduce costs. A retail business determines which merchandise to stock at certain locations based on anticipated demand. A non-profit organization won't launch or expand a service unless it has the resources to deliver it economically.

In each of these cases, the executives in charge had to consider financial or economic factors and their impact on the organization. At some point, you will be asked to participate in your company's decision-making process, most likely on a team with workers from other departments. The recommendations you and your teammates make will require perspective and judgment that go beyond your individual disciplines (for example, engineering, marketing, sales, IT). While office politics can sometimes play a role, more often than not, you'll find most decisions are made based on economics, strategic choices, regulatory requirements and other factors that you may not be familiar with yet. If you can think in business terms and interact with your bosses on a business level—rather than strictly technical or emotional terms—you will:

- Better understand how decisions are made;
- Increase the likelihood of getting your recommendations heard and approved;
- Become recognized as a valuable contributor;
- Realize greater satisfaction from your career.

This chapter provides a basic introduction to get you started developing your business acumen so you can successfully launch your career.

WHAT IS BUSINESS ACUMEN?

Ask several people for a definition of business acumen and you will likely receive as many answers. While no standard definition exists, for new college hires business acumen involves an understanding of the rationale behind the decisions an organization makes in allocating its finite resources to enhance the prospects of achieving its goals. Therefore, instead of a definition, consider the following criteria as essential elements of business acumen for a new employee's first year on the job to lay the foundation for future development:

- Familiarity with basic financial and accounting concepts and terminology.
- Application of these concepts to the decisions about allocating resources.
- Understanding how strategy and external factors play a role in making choices.

Some Basic Finance and Accounting Concepts

Every move an organization takes—whether it's introducing a new product line or investing in a new piece of equipment—has financial and accounting implications. Here are three basic questions to ask when making any business decision:

1. How much will it increase revenue?
2. What will it cost?
3. Will the increase in revenue be sufficient to offset the cost?

To answer these questions, you must know the meaning of these terms—*revenue, expenses* and *profit*—as well as *their fundamental relationship to each other,* as expressed by the equation:

Profit = Revenue – Expenses

Every organization—whether it's a for-profit business, nonprofit organization or government agency—requires *revenue* to operate. Revenue is the money a company receives in exchange for its services or products. The source of an organization's revenue depends on which sector is involved.

- **Private sector businesses** rely on revenue from the sale of products and the fees they charge for services.
- **Nonprofit organizations** (for example, charities, social organizations) rely on donations and grants from individuals, foundations or government agencies. Some nonprofit organizations are set up to be self-sustaining (for example, hospitals and private schools), which means that in addition to donations they bring in revenue by charging fees for services.
- **Government agencies** are funded by taxes, as well as fees for various services (for example, tolls, licenses, recording mortgages and property ownership).

Organizations require revenue to pay for the *expenses* of operating the business. Expenses are the costs incurred in delivering a service or making a product. Some expenses (for example, raw material and labor) are directly related to the manufacture of products or delivery of services. Others are the "overhead" costs of managing the business (for example, accounting, IT, human resources, or legal).

To be fiscally healthy, an organization must take in more revenue than it spends. In the private sector, this is known as making a *profit;* in the nonprofit and government sectors, it is known as a *surplus*. The reverse situation is known as a *loss* or *deficit*.

Profit is a generic term for the money a company has left after taking out all costs associated with running the business. You may hear the terms *net income* or *earnings* used synonymously with profit. The difference between these terms is largely technical, from an accounting perspective.

What a company decides to do with its profits depends on its overall objectives and the financial attractiveness of its options. Growth-oriented companies will likely put most of their profits into research and development to create new products or acquire new companies. Companies in mature markets with few attractive investment alternatives might decide to pay a dividend to their owners.

When an organization incurs a loss, it must either reduce expenses or borrow money to make up the revenue shortfall. If it takes on so much debt that it can't repay its lenders, it faces bankruptcy. To avoid bankruptcy, the company might renegotiate its loans and sell some of its assets for cash. If those efforts fail, the organization must stop operating, liquidate (sell) everything it owns (its assets) and cease to exist when the bankruptcy process is complete.

How Investment Decisions are Made

Now that you understand the basics of **Profit = Revenue – Expense**, let's practice applying it in real life. Imagine a large hospital, Suburban Hospital, as it faces a decision whether to invest in a new CT scan machine.

Like all hospitals, Suburban Hospital depends for most of its revenue on payments from private insurers and the federal government (through Medicaid and Medicare). The hospital feels constantly squeezed between its limited revenue and the high cost of running a modern medical center (for example, purchases of expensive medical technology, building expansion and improvements to facilities). Consequently, Suburban Hospital must constantly choose among its competing needs.

As they consider buying the new CT scan, hospital executives must look at their revenue and the cost of the machine, and then determine if it will be worth the investment. Here is the process they might follow, using the three questions mentioned above:

1. *How much will it increase revenue?* A team estimates the expected revenue to be produced from the CT scan over a period of time, usually several years.

2. *What will it cost?* Next, they consider, not only the initial outlay to buy and install the item, but the recurring annual cost of operating and maintaining it.

3. *Will the increase in sales or profits be sufficient to offset the cost?* By subtracting the annual costs of the CT scan from the expected revenues, the team arrives at an estimate of the financial benefit it will produce for the hospital. This estimate is then analyzed to determine how long it will take for the financial benefit to equal the initial cost (or *payback period*).

Most organizations set a ***minimum return*** for investments to eliminate projects with less than desirable financial returns. If the return on an investment significantly exceeds the minimum return threshold, management will probably go ahead with it—provided it has enough cash and no better alternatives. The financial techniques that management will use to analyze the return on an investment are based on an important concept called the ***time value of money***. To understand how it works, see the insert, The Time Value of Money.

The Time Value of Money

Before making a major investment, organizations use several methods to evaluate whether the financial benefit sufficiently offsets its cost. All of these methods are based on a concept called the ***time value of money***. The principle is simple: A dollar earned today is worth more than a dollar earned at some future date. Why? Because the ***present value*** of a dollar is exactly $1.00. But if you invest that dollar at a guaranteed annual rate of interest of, say, 8%, then the ***future value*** of that original dollar in two years (using the compound interest formula: $\$1.00 \times 1.08^2$) will be approximately $1.17. In other words, $1.00 earned today is the equivalent of $1.17, if earned two years from now.

How does this affect business investment decisions? Suppose you were given a proposal to invest in a project that would pay $1.20 after two years. How would you compare that to the opportunity described above, where you were guaranteed an annual return of 8% for the same period? You would use a technique called ***discounting*** to figure out the ***present value*** of the cash you will receive at the end of the project, or what it is worth today. In this case, the ***present value*** of the $1.20 is $1.03 ($1.2 / 1.08^2). If the project costs more than that amount, the return is not worth the investment, and you would be better off investing your money at the guaranteed 8% annual interest rate.

The Role of Strategy and External Factors

If every investment decision were as simple as plugging some numbers into a formula, decision-making would be pretty easy. In reality, it is not that simple.

First, an organization must choose what customers, or market, it wants to serve and how to best serve them, while still achieving its financial goals. To do this, management analyzes various factors, including demographics, competition, and supply and demand. Next, management uses its best judgment (and sometimes gut instinct) to determine how to best compete in the markets it serves. This helps prioritize the allocation of limited resources.

For example, Suburban Hospital might choose to emphasize the treatment of cardiac patients from around the world. Meanwhile, a neighboring hospital, City Hospital, might choose to emphasize patient care. Suburban Hospital would spend a high percentage of its financial resources hiring the top cardiologists and buying the most advanced equipment. City Hospital, on the other hand, would concentrate on training its staff and upgrading its facilities to make the hospital experience more comfortable for patients and their families.

Sometimes, an organization's choices are limited by factors beyond its control. Factors like government regulations, legal requirements, economic conditions that affect customer behavior, and changes in technology can limit an organization's flexibility.

Take hospitals. Most hospitals today are losing revenue because of reduced payments from private insurers and Medicare. So they would probably rather fund projects that increase patient revenue (for example, operating rooms, surgical suites, medical and diagnostic equipment) and defer projects that don't bring in money, like new administrative systems or facility renovations. However, hospitals may be forced by new government regulations to spend that money on less profitable projects. A good example is what happened when the federal government passed the Health Insurance Portability and Accounting Act (HIPAA) of 1996. HIPAA was adopted to guarantee patient confidentiality, but it required massive paperwork. Hospital administrators were forced to allocate a portion of their budget to comply with the new regulation. Another, even more dramatic example, is the 'Y2K' scare at the turn of the last century. Many organizations had to spend valuable resources to adapt their computer systems so they would function after midnight of December 31, 1999.

You may be thinking that this is a lot to learn and worry about—especially for a new hire who has no control over financial decisions. But as you progress in your organization, your role will grow. You need to start developing your business acumen now, so you can understand why decisions are made, relate to people in higher positions than yours, and rise to the challenge when the time comes—and it will.

TAKE THE INITIATIVE

Learning how your organization operates from a financial perspective won't happen overnight. The process may seem overwhelming, especially if your undergraduate degree did not expose you to the world of finance and accounting. At this point in your career, you

---

A Timeline for Building Your Business Acumen

(0-3 months)

1. Learn about your organization's revenue source: Can you influence it?
2. Learn about your organization's expenses: Where do you spend money?

(3-6 months)

3. Assess the financial impact of your professional decisions

(6-12 months)

4. Learn your organization's plans for its profits

(0-12 months and beyond)

5. Develop your understanding of key financial terms and concepts

should start becoming aware of the business decisions made by people at higher levels in the organization. To make this task less daunting, break the process into smaller components. Concentrate on the individual elements of the profit equation presented earlier in this chapter (Profits = Revenue – Expenses). Become familiar with some basic business terms and concepts.

The following steps will help you get started.

1. Learn about your organization's revenue source: Can you influence it?

Start building your business acumen by concentrating on the 'R' in the equation *Profit = Revenue – Expenses*. What is your organization's primary source of revenue? The source of revenue will depend on what type of organization you've joined. Is it a for-profit company? A nonprofit organization? A government agency? If you don't know, you can easily find out by asking.

Depending on your job, you may not have much direct contact with your revenue source. For example, as a new architect in a large firm, it is unlikely you will interact with the client purchasing your company's services. However, if you work in sales or customer service, you will meet your customers daily.

Now, try to walk in the shoes of the people who fund you—your customers or clients. What would you think about your organization? What would you like? Dislike? What would cause you to spend more money? (Fast and reliable service delivery? Major contributions

Type of Organization	Primary Revenue (Funding) Source
For-Profit	CONSUMERS via sales of a product or service
Nonprofit	DONORS via gifts or donations
	CONSUMERS in the case of a for-sale product or service (for example, hospital, private school)
Government	CITIZENS via taxes
	CONSUMERS in the case of self-sustaining services based on usage (for example, water, sewer, tolls, postal delivery)

toward a humanitarian cause? Lower cost?) What would cause you to spend less money? (A competitor offers a better or more affordable product? Too high a percentage of donations spent on administration versus program services? Incompetence or rude customer service?)

Now that you've looked at your organization from the standpoint of your funding source, what can *you* as a new employee do to influence it? Can you:

- Put more energy and creativity into the sales or fund-raising aspects of your job?
- Treat customers with more care, so they come back to your establishment?
- Pay more attention to the quality of your product or service, so you can beat out the competition?

Remember: If your funding sources go away, so do you. What can you do to influence them in a positive way?

2. Learn about your expenses: Where do you spend money?

You may not realize it, but you are costing your company money. The most obvious expense is your salary and benefits, but there are also other, hidden costs, like the time you spend in "nonproductive" activities, or the supplies you may waste.

The goal of most organizations is to increase profits or surplus. The more profit or surplus an organization has, the more it can do: For example, it can provide more aid to people in need, invest in new products or send more employees to training. Remember that **Profit = Revenues – Expenses**. As an employee, you can increase profits by minimizing the expenses that involve you. In general, that includes labor costs, materials, supplies and purchased services, like paid consultants. Obviously, these resources are necessary to get the job done. The key is to use them efficiently.

These are some expense categories you may contribute to:

- Labor
- Benefits
- Travel expenses
- Supplies and materials
- Production costs
- Equipment

How you spend your workday can cost your company money. Your productivity is the percentage of time you spend creating goods and services that produce revenue. For example, how much of the day do you spend building a widget or talking to customers versus attending a training course or reading email? All these activities are expenses, but some contribute directly to producing the organization's goods and services, while others contribute only indirectly. Attending meetings, sick leave, and other absences are examples of indirect expenses. These activities are often called "overhead," which most organizations try to minimize.

Some organizations actually require employees to record their time as "direct activity" and "indirect activity," so they can keep track of their productivity. Employees may be "coached" if they spend more time on indirect activities than what has been budgeted. You'd be wise to monitor your own time so you never need one of these "coaching" sessions. Make note of how you spend your workday to see if you are truly focusing on getting the job done.

Supplies and equipment are another type of expense you may incur. Personal use of computers and computer peripherals, cell phones, pagers, paper and ink cartridges all fall into this category. Obviously, to be effective, you must incur some expenses; but try not to waste resources. How many times do you need to send a draft of a memo you're writing to the printer?

3. Assess the financial impact of your professional decisions

Our equation **Profits = Revenues – Expenses** looks simple. But how these three variables relate to each other is complex. Sometimes, increasing revenues doesn't necessarily mean greater profits. And cutting expenses in one area can increase total expenditures in others. Here are some examples:

- *As a product designer,* you have an idea for a "hot" new product feature (revenue up—new sales and potential new buyers), but the cost to produce, package and market it is high (expenses up).

- *As a salesperson,* you win a new customer by selling a great deal (new revenue), but you didn't leave enough room to cover expenses (profit down).

- *As a human resources professional,* you fill several job positions quickly so customer commitments are met (revenues up), but you compromise on the quality of the new hires and have to replace them a year later (expenses up).

- *As a financial analyst,* you recommend against upgrading to a new version of business software (expenses down), but the old system is so antiquated that it becomes cumbersome to operate and maintain (expenses up).

The cause and effect of actions you take may not be readily apparent. As you build your business acumen, you will become more adept at assessing how your decisions affect revenue, expenses and profit. Start developing your awareness now, so you are prepared to make the difficult choices for your company later.

4. Learn your organization's plans for its profits or surplus

You may be thinking that a new employee like you has no say in what your organization does with its profits or surplus, so why bother talking about it? The fact is that many of your company's spending decisions most likely do affect your job area, and eventually you will be asked for input. So start learning the rationale behind business decisions that affect you. Look beyond the "politics" in controversial decisions for the trade-off that was made. Try to guess where your organization's budget will be tight and where there is room for spending, so you know what resources are reasonable to ask for. Your recommendations are more likely to be considered and approved if you make your case in terms of your organization's goals and plans

If you haven't already, get a copy of your company's annual report. (Chapter 3, *Learning the Ground Rules*, tells where you can get one.) Usually there is a statement in the beginning that summarizes the organization's accomplishments over the past year and its major goals for the upcoming year. These goals will give you a clue as to how the organization will spend available funds. For example, if the theme is creativity or innovation, you will probably see spending in research and development, new technology or employee training. If the theme focuses on doing more with less, you may see spending on process improvement, or little to no discretionary spending at all.

5. Develop your understanding of key financial terms and concepts

The language of business can be confusing. Take the time to become familiar with a few simple concepts. Doing this will give you confidence and let you communicate more effectively when the topics come up. Here are some ways to develop your financial literacy:

- *Ask questions.* Executives and managers frequently use business or financial terms their employees don't understand. Don't be afraid to speak up and ask for an explanation. Most managers and executives will be more than willing to share their knowledge.

- *Make a habit of reading business periodicals.* Read newspapers like *The Wall Street Journal* and *Investors Business Daily* and magazines like *Business Week, Forbes and Fortune.* This will increase your exposure to financial terms and give you additional insights into the business world. Concentrate on articles about your company or its industry, especially articles on how the relationship between revenue, expenses, and other factors affect your company's profitability.

© 2000 Randy Glasbergen.

GLASBERGEN

"Now that we've celebrated our diversity, embraced a new spirit of creativity, made a fresh commitment to excellence, and given something back to the community, *does anyone here remember what it is we're supposed to manufacture and sell?*"

- ***Buy an introductory or overview book on business.*** Pick up a used text from an introductory finance or accounting course. Most bookstores have good books on the subject. Ask for a recommendation from someone who exhibits good business acumen.
- ***Consider taking a course in finance for nonfinancial managers.*** Many colleges and universities have offerings like this. There are also many non-credit seminars, online courses and workshops that can give you a concentrated overview. Your company may sponsor or recommend a program.

SUMMARY

Many business professionals who did not major in accounting or finance find the terminology and concepts daunting. Yet the terminology of these functions is truly the universal language of business—large and small. Accounting and finance provide the framework measuring an organization's fiscal activity and describing the relationship between critical elements of its business model. As your career progresses, you will find it more and more important to be literate in the terms and concepts used in the financial world.

By the same token, professionals who work in non-finance departments, like Sales and IT, often believe that the money aspect of their organization is someone else's job. It's not. Managing an organization's money is everyone's job. Act like an owner of the business and find ways that you *personally* can help to increase revenue, reduce costs and help your bottom line. Show that you understand how financial decisions are made, and you may one day be the one who makes those decisions for your company.

FAQS

Q: *My request for training to learn a new programming language was turned down. My manager told me it was too expensive. I really want to take this course. Isn't it in my organization's best interest to keep enhancing my skills? What can I do?*

A: Managers must constantly choose between critical business needs and employee development. It's not always easy. Find out why your manager made the choice he did, and change your approach. What did he mean by "too expensive"? Remember that the expense to your company includes the time you spend in training. Look for an alternative course that takes less time and costs less. Maybe the problem was timing. Are you needed in the office to work on a project milestone or to deal with a customer crisis? If this is the case, work with your manager to reschedule the training. Maybe your manager meant that the course wasn't in the training budget this year. If so, ask again later in the year, in case training runs under budget. Or make a strong business case for putting the course in next year's budget, by showing how it would help the business. Find out if the course is eligible under your company's tuition refund plan, or consider paying for it yourself.

Q: *I have an undergraduate degree in electrical engineering. Should I also get an MBA?*

A: This is a common question, with no easy answer. In some industries, an advanced technical degree is more valuable than a business degree. In others, an MBA can enhance your long-term career potential by developing your business skills—especially in financial analysis, strategic planning and leadership—beyond the level of an undergraduate degree. It will also offer greater opportunities to network with business leaders and expand your contacts outside the company. Keep in mind that most business schools prefer to admit people with at least three years' experience in the business world. Choose the right program (full-time, part-time, executive) for the career track you choose to pursue, your personal life and your financial situation. Many schools now offer executive MBA programs, which offer classes on weekends over a two-year period. Once you've identified your needs, look for the right program and learn how it evaluates candidates for admission.

Q: *Whenever I attend a presentation by any of our executives, they speak in a language I don't understand—ROI, ROS, EBITDA, etc. Why do they talk like this? Are they trying to impress us? Are they trying to hide what's really happening? Or are they just out of touch with what the rest of us do for a living?*

A: Managers, especially executives, have a unique perspective. Financial and accounting terms define their world. Regardless of the type of business, an executive's main job is to maximize and balance resources in order to achieve organizational objectives. Wall Street analysts and shareholders hold them accountable to measurements based on financial and accounting terms. Sometimes they forget that many employees, especially recent college grads, may not be familiar with business terms and concepts that come naturally to them. When you find yourself in this situation, ask for an explanation. Most executives will be happy to help you develop your understanding of the business, because it makes their job easier in the long run. If the forum for the presentation doesn't lend itself to asking questions, make a note and talk later to the presenter or someone else with business knowledge.

Q: *I enjoy the technical aspects of my job and have no intention of becoming a CEO or even joining the ranks of management. Why should I learn about finance or accounting?*

A: Learning the business side of things will make you more effective in your job. It will also lead to greater job satisfaction, because you'll have a context for the technical aspects of your work. For example, you may want to recommend a project (for example, buying new equipment, launching a new product, conducting research) that will require a business case to justify the investment. If you don't know how to make that case, you will have to rely on others who may not understand your idea as well as you do, or may not share your passion to get it through the approval process. Besides, you may find that you enjoy the business aspects once you learn them. Why shut down your options this early in your career?

Performing Your Job

In the workplace, performing well means much more than it did when you were in school. Your success in college usually depended on how well you demonstrated your understanding of the subject matter of each course. Doing poorly may have affected your grade point average, but you could always start anew the next semester. In your new job, success is about making things happen—efficiently and effectively. Failure to do so affects your entire career; it can mean missed opportunities for new assignments or advancement, if not outright job termination. Section II, Performing Your Job, provides you with guidelines for hitting each task running, and then benefiting from feedback so you keep the momentum going.

Chapter 5: Understanding Your Assignment—Why waste time and energy doing the wrong thing? This chapter shows how to make sure you know what outcome is expected of you.

Chapter 6: Planning Your Assignment—Chances are your work assignments will be more complex than those you faced in school. In this chapter, you'll learn how to plan your tasks and manage your resources and risks so you can complete assignments successfully.

Chapter 7: Performance Feedback and Compensation—For every job you do, you will get some kind of response, ranging from criticism to a promotion. This chapter shows you how to benefit from both positive and negative feedback.

CHAPTER 5

Understanding Your Assignment

In This Chapter

- Establishing a common understanding of what the job entails

- Taking the initiative to avoid false starts

- Asking the right questions

- Reporting status of your work

"The educated person is someone who knows how to find out what he doesn't know."

~ George Simmel ~

WHY YOU SHOULD CARE

Your first assignment may be the most important of your career. Your manager and teammates form their opinion of your competence based on how well you perform on your first projects. This perception can last for as long as a year. You want to show that you can hit the job running—you can get started and show results quickly. To do this, you must know exactly what you have to do, so you don't waste time going down the wrong track.

This may sound obvious, yet many new employees confess that one of the biggest hurdles they face is figuring out what their assignment involves and how to accomplish it. Some sit paralyzed at their desks for days or even weeks, uncertain how to begin, yet afraid to ask questions for fear of appearing incompetent. Others plow ahead, only to be embarrassed when they find out they didn't do the right thing.

Avoid "new assignment paralysis" or wasted effort by learning and applying the mechanics of accepting an assignment. Once you learn how to fully scope out the task, define the final product and locate the resources you need, you'll be able to focus your energy on doing the job well.

ASKING THE RIGHT QUESTIONS

You have just received your first assignment on the job. Before you throw yourself into the task, make sure you, your manager and your teammates are all on the same page. Do you all share a common understanding of the assignment and what is expected of you? To find out, just ask your manager those well-known reporter's questions: *what, why, how, who, where* and *when*. By the end of your first discussion with your manager or team, you must have all the answers you need for your assignment, or know where to find them. Here is what to ask:

> **WHAT have you been asked to do?** Make sure you know the expected outcome of your assignment, including the level of completion and the format. For example, if you've been asked to write a report, ask your boss if he or she expects a finished document ready for distribution, or just a draft document to serve as the basis for discussion and review? This information helps you plan and schedule your work.

> **WHY have you been assigned the work?** The answer to this question may seem obvious: because it needs to be done! The point is to find out how the task fits into your organization's overall goals. If you see the relationship between your assignment and your company's goals, you can better decide which aspects to emphasize and where to put the most effort. Let's say you're writing a report: Are you expected to defend a specific

position? Explain specific facts to a select group? Or present a specific recommendation for consideration and approval?

HOW should you accomplish this task? Every work environment has its own way of doing things. Your assignment has to follow documented standards and procedures. Your manager may not know every detail that relates to your assignment, especially if he or she supervises a large group of employees. So it's up to you to determine how to accomplish the task. Start by asking to see an example of a similar task that was successfully completed. For complex assignments, you may be expected to create a project plan; if so, refer to Chapter 6, *Planning Your Assignment*.

WHO is involved with this task? Are you part of a team? Who else is on the team? Do you need information from someone working on a related task? If you work in a large organization, make sure to get the last name of anyone involved; you don't want to spend time looking for "John in production."

WHERE are required resources located? Know what you need and where to get it to save time in tracking them down. Resources include the materials, people and the knowledge you need to accomplish the task. Here are things to look for:

- Are the standards you need located in a specific manual?
- Is there a library or database of historical data you need to perform an analysis?
- Do you need special equipment?
- Do you have access to the equipment you need, or is acquiring it part of your task?
- Do you have access to other resources, such as the key to a storeroom or someone's computer access code?
- If you need to talk to an expert, do you know where to find him or her?

WHEN is the assignment due? Avoid surprise due dates. Ask exactly when you must complete the assignment, as well as when and how to report the status of your progress. You can plan your work better if you're sure of your deadlines and interim milestones. It also helps your teammates plan their work, if it is dependent on your results.

Now let's apply these questions to a hypothetical assignment: an office move. Let's say your work group is preparing to move into new office space, with new office furniture and better computing resources. Everyone is looking forward to the move, but senior management is concerned that moving now might jeopardize completing a critical customer project on time. As your group's coordinator, you've been asked to present a brief report to management on the status of the move. What do you need to know in order to complete this assignment successfully? Table 5.1 shows how the six questions discussed in this chapter might apply to this situation.

Table 5.1: An Example of a Completed New Assignment Checklist Involving an Office Relocation.

WHAT are you being asked to do?	• Prepare and give a 10-minute presentation on the status of your group's move to new office space. • Provide presentation slides, as well as hardcopy handouts for the meeting.
WHY has this work been assigned?	• Senior management is concerned that the move will jeopardize completion of a significant project. • If management perceives the risk as high, they will postpone the move up to six months.
HOW are you to accomplish the task?	• Use the department's slide templates for accepted fonts, layouts, etc.
WHO else is involved in this task?	• You need input from facilities, IT and the administrative planners before giving the briefing. • Your manager wants to review the presentation prior to the briefing. • Your manager's administrative assistant can help with logistics, typing, etc., if needed. • The audience includes the head of your department and her staff.
WHERE are any required resources located?	• The briefing will be in the executive conference room (3rd floor, Room 312). • Does this room have a digital projector compatible with your laptop or an overhead slide projector?
WHEN is the assignment due?	• The presentation is next Thursday (a week from today) at 1:30 p.m. • You need to show your manager a draft of your presentation by Monday afternoon.

TAKE THE INITIATIVE

Assignments can come to you in different ways. Your manager may set up an appointment to assign you a new task, stop by your work area, or catch you in the hallway. You may be part of a self-directed team that decides what your assignment will be. Your first discussion about your assignment is critical; it is here that you will learn most of what you need to do the job.

Accepting Your Assignments

1. Prepare and ask the questions you need answered before starting the new task

2. If your manager can't answer the questions, find out where you can get the answers

3. Take notes during the discussion.

4. Summarize the assignment in your own words

5. Set up a specific follow-up meeting to discuss your approach and progress

---

Here are some pointers to make the most of your first assignment meeting.

1. Prepare and ask the questions you need answered before starting the new task

If you have advance notice of the meeting, prepare your questions ahead of time. Bring along your "New Assignment Checklist," and don't be afraid to refer to it during the discussion to make sure you've covered all points. Table 5.2 has a list of detailed follow-up questions you might consider asking. Your advance preparation will leave a good impression with your manager or teammates. If you don't have time to prepare a "New Assignment Checklist," just remember to ask: what, why, how, who, where and when.

Table 5.2: New Assignment Checklist

WHAT are you being asked to do?	✔ What is the expected outcome? To what degree of completion (draft or final product) is the work to be done? ✔ What is the outcome of the task to look like? ✔ Are results to be reported in the form of an informal status discussion with your manager or a formal presentation?
WHY is this work being assigned?	✔ What are the objectives of the task? ✔ How does this assignment relate to the objectives of the organization? ✔ How does this assignment relate to work other people are doing?
HOW are you to accomplish the task?	✔ Are there defined procedures you must follow? ✔ Are there existing tools you can or must use? ✔ Do standards exist for formatting the outcome? ✔ Is there an example of a similar task you can follow? ✔ Is a project plan warranted or expected?
WHO else is involved in this task?	✔ Who is the ultimate audience for the outcome? ✔ Are you supposed to work on this with any other individuals or teams? ✔ Who are the "experts" who can help you if you have questions? ✔ Can you get advice from someone who has done similar work? ✔ Is there someone outside your immediate organization you should coordinate with? ✔ Will any customers be involved? If so, is there anything you should know about them before you contact them?
WHERE are any required resources located?	✔ Where are they (including people) located? ✔ Do you have to do anything to gain access to the resources?
WHEN is the assignment due?	✔ When exactly is the assignment to be completed? ✔ Are there any interim tasks that are due before the final product?

Try to have all your questions ready at the first meeting to avoid bothering people repeatedly. However, if you do think of additional questions, don't hesitate to go back and ask them. You don't always have to arrange a formal meeting to get your answers. Often an email or brief discussion in the hall will work.

2. If your manager doesn't have the answers, find out who does

Your manager may not be familiar with the details of your task. If so, ask him or her who might be able to help you further. Your office "buddy" or other coworkers can also be a source of information.

3. Take notes during the discussion

No one has a perfect memory. Don't feel that you'll appear incompetent if you take notes. It actually demonstrates organizational skills and maturity. If you don't, you may miss some important points. You may realize halfway through the assignment that some points you thought were unimportant are critical to successfully completing the task. Having detailed notes can help you avoid this problem.

Copyright 2002 by Randy Glasbergen.
www.glasbergen.com

"You just spent 45 minutes explaining why you're too busy to do something that would have taken 2 minutes."

4. Summarize the assignment in your own words

Sometimes two people can interpret the same words differently, so summarize and repeat what you hear to make sure you understood correctly. Your manager might clarify a point or even add new information he or she overlooked. Don't use jargon or acronyms unless you are sure you know what they mean. If your manager uses a term you don't understand, ask for an explanation.

5. Set up a specific follow-up meeting to discuss your approach and progress

At your first meeting, arrange a follow-up meeting to review your approach and progress. The purpose of this second meeting is to make sure you really understand the task and are working correctly toward the solution. Discuss what you will cover at the follow-up meeting and how formal it will be. Be specific about the date and time; if you accept a vague answer like "sometime next week," chances are your manager's calendar will fill up and you won't be on it. Know what you will be expected to have completed by then, and bring either the work or a status report with you.

Note: You will receive feedback on your work during this meeting both positive and negative. Be receptive to it. Feedback offers you an opportunity to learn and improve on future assignments, so don't ignore it. To make the most of this experience, refer to Chapter 7, *Performance Feedback and Compensation*.

SUMMARY

Learn to ask the right questions so you clearly understand your assignments and your overall responsibilities. The techniques outlined in this chapter will help you avoid false starts due to misunderstandings or, worse, paralysis from not knowing what to do. Starting with your very first assignment, you will be able to focus on completing the task, instead of worrying about what it entails and how to go about it. Most importantly, you will be able to identify the overall objectives that will be used to evaluate your performance resulting in a better job evaluation.

FAQS

Q: *Everyone here knows more about what's going on than I do. Yet they seem too busy to answer my questions. I'm too embarrassed to ask what I'm supposed to be doing.*

A: This is a common concern for employees in their first year on the job. Most people are afraid to ask questions because they think it makes them look incompetent. Think of the alternative. Wouldn't it be more embarrassing to do something wrong because you didn't ask for help? Remember that experienced coworkers know more about the job because they've been there longer. Most will be happy to help you, as long as you don't make a nuisance of yourself. If you need help from someone who appears busy, let him or her know what you need and ask when it would be more convenient to talk.

Q: *My manager knows very little about the details of how to get assignments done. Aren't managers supposed to know more than their employees? How can I work for someone so incompetent?*

A: Before judging your manager as incompetent, consider that a manager's main responsibility is delegating responsibility to others. Much of a manager's time is spent on things like staying on budget, meeting goals, obtaining and allocating needed resources, reporting status to senior management, maintaining employee morale, and resolving various issues to keep the organization moving forward. This leaves little time to think about the specific details of how tasks are accomplished. For example, an accounting manager must be familiar with an organization's account structure, but not necessarily with the details of how to input journal entries to the accounting system. For specific guidance, turn to senior staff who are experts on the subject.

Q: *I feel like I'm being yanked around! It seems like every time I start an assignment, my manager changes his mind and tells me to do something else. How can I be expected to get anything done?*

A: You need to assess why this is happening. Talk with coworkers about what may be affecting your manager's frequent change in direction. Your organization may be going through a period of change or experiencing financial difficulties. If so, the situation may be out of your manager's direct control. This is common when a shift in the marketplace, like a new competitor or emerging technology, requires a change in a company's strategy or product line.

On the other hand, your manager may truly be indecisive. One strategy is to talk with him or her about the reason for changing direction and its ramifications, as you see them. Ask your manager to help prioritize your current list of assignments and write it down for future discussions, if needed. If you are both reasonable, you'll each walk away from the discussion with a new perspective on the issue. In the end, you may not change your manager's behavior and will just have to live with the decisions he or she makes. If the situation becomes intolerable, you may consider changing departments, or even jobs.

Q: *I just found out someone else in the office has been given the same assignment as me. What's with that? Are we in competition?*

A: Perhaps. This is an "old school" management technique that some managers use occasionally to identify which employees are "true performers." Call it a "survival of the fittest" mentality. Other managers use it to identify alternative solutions to a problem, so they can choose the best one. When you find yourself in this situation, try collaborating with the other employee and presenting a joint solution to your manager. However, be aware that this approach may not work if your corporate culture fosters competition.

CHAPTER 6

Planning Your Assignment

> **In This Chapter**
> - The benefit of working from a plan
> - Steps for writing an effective plan
> - Identifying and managing risk
> - Your role in planning your assignments

"If you don't know where you're going, you might not get there."

~ Yogi Berra ~

WHY YOU SHOULD CARE

Planning your work assignments is a critical skill in business. Unfortunately, too many people learn this the hard way. You'd be surprised by how many employees aren't good at planning and don't even see the value of it.

It takes a little time to write a detailed plan before you begin a project, but it is worth the effort. A plan will save you missteps and aggravation, and maximize the odds that you achieve your goals on time.

Let's take the sample assignment we used in the previous chapter: Your manager has asked you to give a presentation on the status of your work group's move to a new office space. You receive the assignment on Thursday afternoon, and your boss wants a draft by Monday afternoon. You decide to wait until Monday morning to start working on it, because you have plans to go out of town and want to leave early Friday to beat traffic.

On Monday morning, you arrive refreshed and ready to go. There's just one problem: All the people you need to collect status data from are tied up in staff meetings until after lunch. There's no way you can gather the information and complete the draft by the 1 p.m. review with your manager. Now what? Big problem!

If you had taken the time to plan your assignment, you might have avoided this situation. Planning forces you to think through all the tasks, risks and resource requirements ahead of time so you can anticipate any possible problems. That's not all. Planning also allows you to:

> ✔ **Concentrate on your work**, rather than worry about what comes next

> ✔ **Communicate your approach** and assumptions to your manager and others involved

> ✔ **Track what has been accomplished** and what remains to be done

> ✔ **Demonstrate when an assignment is not achievable** within the given time and resources

> ✔ **Analyze how to perform similar tasks** better next time

A well-written plan is a road map to successful completion of your assignment. Not having one is like traveling to a destination without a map or directions. If you're lucky, you'll get there, but you may end up someplace else entirely.

WHAT IS A PLAN?

A plan is a *detailed approach*, worked out beforehand for accomplishing a *defined outcome*. In a well-written plan, the detailed approach consists of the following elements:

Define & Order Tasks	Create an ordered set of steps with a milestone or marker of completion identified for each task.
Identify Resources	Identify materials, equipment, other people's effort and your own time requirements for each task.
Schedule Work	Map each task to a calendar date, identifying a specific completion time.
Assess Risks	Identify threats to the success of each plan, as well as mitigation plans for the more significant risks.

Before you can start this process, you must understand exactly what you need to accomplish, including the due date, the level of completeness (draft vs. finished product) and procedures you must follow. If you haven't already read it, Chapter 5, *Understanding Your Assignment,* explains what questions you need to have answered before you can start your plan.

Many new employees find it difficult to break down an assignment into all its tasks and subtasks, and then put them in sequential order. Here's how to organize your tasks: Start with the obvious tasks, like gathering information or making slides. Add to those, your "enabling" tasks. These are tasks that add to the quality of the product, like reviewing your draft with your manager. Now put the tasks in the order in which they must be performed.

Planning Tip: Define tasks using action-oriented verbs that focus on producing a specific result. For example: if you need to attend a meeting to get information for a presentation, define the tasks as "get information at xyz meeting." Identify success criteria for each task and state what will be accomplished at the completion of each task.

The next step is to break your major tasks down into smaller, more manageable "subtasks." Keep breaking your steps into smaller bites until you have a list of tasks that you can handle without feeling overwhelmed. Table 6.1 shows what a completed list might look like for our assignment.

Table 6.1: A list of tasks and subtasks for a presentation on the status of moving your work group to a new office space

Sample Project Plan

Task and Subtasks

1. Collect and organize information and key points you will present
   a. Create outline
   b. Gather Status info
2. Draft the charts
   a. Hand-write or type initial text
   b. Find missing data, verify points that are not clear
   c. Add graphics (if needed)
3. Review draft charts
   a. Facilities managers (phones, IT, movers, admin planners)
   b. Manager review
4. Finalize presentation slides
   a. Make corrections noted in reviews
   b. Create finished copy
5. Rehearse
6. Get presentation logistics in order
   a. Make slides
   b. Make copies of handouts
   c. Make sure equipment and room are set up as needed
7. Give presentation

Assumptions

1. Only one review is required with the manager
2. The conference room has a computer with projection that connects to the company network

Now that you have your list, identify which tasks are dependent on others. For example, you may not be able to start some tasks until others have been completed; this includes tasks you can't start until a coworker does his or her share.

Other tasks can be done at the same time as others.

Finally, write down all the assumptions you've made when identifying tasks. For example, you may assume a task is

> **Planning Tip:** When planning a work assignment, include tasks that may improve the quality of your performance or product. For example, identify appropriate places to give your supervisor interim status of your progress. Identify draft products that can be reviewed by someone else to improve their quality; then include that review as a task in the plan. Don't have time for these quality tasks? Will you have time to re-do the work if you find out well down the road that what you've done is wrong or not up to standards?

within your job scope or part of a required process when it really is not. By writing these down, you'll be ready to explain the reasoning behind your plan, and ensure you're on the same page with everyone else involved.

Identify
Resources

Your next step is to identify the resources required for each task in your plan. Resources include effort (the amount of time involved), as well as materials, supplies, equipment or facilities. You need to do this for a number of reasons:

- Identifying upfront the resources you'll need lets you know what it will really take to get the job done—and whether your due date is reasonable. For instance, if you need someone with a special skill and no one with that skill is available, can you realistically expect to get everything done in the allotted time?

- You may need to schedule some resources to make sure they are available, such as reserving a conference room or scheduling a meeting with a busy person. This is so important that you may want to list scheduling resources as a separate task in your plan.
- You may want to apply more resources to a task to get it done faster.

Figuring out the physical resources you need is fairly easy; just look at each task on the list and decide what you need to get it done.

Estimating effort (time) is harder. First, you have to decide if you will do all the work yourself, or if you need the help of others. If others are involved, you must estimate their time as well as your own. By the way, you'll find that if you involve others in the planning process, you are more likely to get their commitment.

Here's how to estimate how much time you'll need. Start with the tasks that are fixed in duration or that you have experience with. Your estimate for these should be fairly accurate. Then estimate tasks you're unsure of. Take your best guess—and be generous.

> **Planning Tip:** Every task has a minimum, maximum and average amount of time required to complete it. For instance, in Table 6.1, making corrections to the presentation based on the review (Step 4a) might take less than five minutes if the draft presentation is well done. On the other hand, it could take a few hours if you have to rewrite the presentation. In general, use the average amount of time when drafting your schedule.

As you estimate, record your assumptions, such as when resources will be available and how long you'll need them. In Table 6.2, you'll find a plan with resources and time estimates.

Table 6.2: A sample project plan with resource requirements identified

Sample Project Plan	
Tasks	*Resource Requirements*
1. Collect and organize information and key points you will present	**Total: 1.5 hours**
a. Create outline	30 minutes
b. Gather Status info	Facilities managers (phones, IT, movers, admin planners): 15 minutes per manager
2. Draft the charts	**Total: 3.5 hours**
a. Hand-write or type initial text	1.5 hours
b. Find missing data, verify points that are not clear	Subject matter experts, as needed: 1 hour
c. Add graphics (if needed)	1 hour
3. Review draft charts	**Total: 1.5 hours**
a. With facilities managers	Facilities managers (phones, IT, movers, admin planners): 15 minutes per manager
b. With manager	Your manager: 30 minutes
4. Finalize presentation slides	**Total: 1.5 hours**
a. Make corrections noted in reviews	30 minutes
b. Create finished copy	Your manager's administrative assistant: 1 hour
5. Rehearse with your roommate	**Total: 1 hour**
6. Get presentation logistics in order	**Total: 1.75 hours**
a. Make slides	Administrative assistant: 30 min
b. Make copies of handouts	Administrative assistant: 1 hour
c. Make sure equipment and room are set up as needed	15 minutes
7. Give presentation	**Total: 15 minutes**

Assumptions

1. Only one review is required with the manager.
2. The conference room has a computer with projection that connects to the company network.
3. None of your resources will be on vacation.

Schedule
Work

Now that you know how long each task will take, get out a calendar. It's time to map out the tasks in "calendar time." Calendar time means the actual number of days the work will be spread over versus the number of hours it would take if you did the work non-stop. For example, you may have identified a task that will take sixteen hours to complete. Rather than scheduling two eight-hour days, you might spread the task over four calendar days because you're busy with other things during that time.

As you map the tasks on the calendar, be sure to include any time constraints, like a scheduled holiday or unavailability of a resource. Try to add extra time for unexpected events or redoing a task.

In Table 6.3, a calendar schedule has been added.

If you can't schedule everything by the project's deadline, don't panic! Try the following:

- ✔ **Make sure you didn't double-count effort.** For instance, in task 3b, the meeting with your manager will take 30 minutes of your time and 30 minutes of the manager's time. The total effort is one hour, but the elapsed time is only 30 minutes.

- ✔ **Look for opportunities to do things in parallel** (that is, at the same time). For example, the administrative assistant can be working on tasks 6a and 6b, while you work on tasks 5 and 6c.

- ✔ **Think of feasible alternatives.** For example, you can extend the schedule, reduce the scope of your work, or get someone else to help.

The one thing you should NEVER do is cut your time estimate to meet your deadline. If you really think a task is going to take three days but schedule it for only one day to meet your deadline, you are doomed to failure. If you can't reasonably meet the due date, sit down with your supervisor or project lead and discuss ways to get the work done in time, like reducing the scope of the job or extending the due date.

If your schedule has you finishing the project before the deadline, don't relax just yet. Check your plan to make sure you haven't

Table 6.3: A sample project plan with calendar schedule added

Sample Project Plan		
Tasks	*Time Needed*	*Completion Date*
1. Collect and organize information and key points you will present	**1.5 hours**	**Friday morning**
a. Create outline	30 minutes	Thu pm
b. Gather Status info	15 minutes per manager (4)	Fri am
2. Draft the charts	**3.5 hours**	**Fri close of business**
a. Hand-write or type initial text	1.5 hours	Fri pm
b. Find missing data, verify points that are not clear	1 hour	Fri pm
c. Add graphics (if needed)	1 hour	Fri pm
3. Review draft charts	**1.5 hours**	**Mon afternoon**
a. With facilities managers	15 minutes per manager (4)	Mon am
b. With manager	30 minutes	Mon pm
4. Finalize presentation slides	**1.5 hours**	**Tues close of business**
a. Make corrections noted in reviews	30 minutes	Tues am
b. Create finished copy	1 hour	Tues am
5. Rehearse	**1 hour**	**Wed night**
6. Get presentation logistics in order	**1.75 hours**	**Wed afternoon**
a. Make slides	30 minutes	Wed am
b. Make copies of handouts	1 hour	Wed am
c. Make sure equipment and room are set up as needed	15 minutes	Wed pm
7. Give presentation	**15 minutes**	**Thurs afternoon**

Assumptions

1. Only one review is required with the manager.
2. The conference room has a computer with projection that connects to the company network.
3. None of your resources will be on vacation.

missed any tasks and your time estimates make sense. If the schedule still looks good, enjoy a stress-free assignment!

Risk is anything that might go wrong with your plan. And you can be sure that, despite the most careful planning, something will go wrong. The key to avoiding problems is to anticipate them and to be prepared to deal with them.

You can spot potential risks in your plan before you start working. Ask these questions:

✔ What might go wrong?

✔ How likely is it to happen?

✔ What would the negative impact be?

Focus on the risks that are most likely to occur and which would have the most impact. Then develop a contingency plan. Your risks can change; one risk may never arise, while a new risk pops up unexpectedly. So continue to review your plan periodically for any changes.

Additional Considerations

A plan is never set in stone. As you handle your assignment, you'll probably find that you left out a task or need to change the estimate of a resource. Even experienced planners go through the steps several times before they have a solid plan.

As you write your plan, you may wonder how detailed it needs to be, or how formal. Should you stick to a few, high-level tasks or include every possible subtask you can think of? Can you get away with scribbling your plan on notepaper or should you be prepared to present it to your project team? These are all judgment calls, based on the amount of work involved in the project, its complexity, how critical it is, and the number of resources, including people, involved. You don't want to spend two days writing a plan for a four-hour task. On the other hand, you'll obviously want to thoroughly plan an assignment that could cost your organization thousands of dollars if you are not successful.

TAKE THE INITIATIVE

Planning Your Assignments

1. Be absolutely clear on what you need to accomplish (see Chapter 5).
2. Write your plan.
3. Present your plan to those who need to buy into it.
4. Execute the plan and note the status of your progress.
5. Revise your plan, if necessary
6. When the task is complete, capture your lessons learned.

1. Know what you need to accomplish before you start planning

Before you start any planning, make sure you understand your assignment and its expected outcomes. Be sure you know all your deadlines, too. Follow the steps outlined in Chapter 5, *Understanding Your Assignment*, if you haven't already done so.

2. Write your plan

Draft your plan following the steps described in this chapter. Don't be nervous if you've never done a work-related plan before. You may not realize it, but you've probably planned something similar before, outside of work. For example, planning an off-site business meeting is similar in many ways to planning a big party for friends and family. Coordinating a facilities move involves many of the same steps as moving from your dorm to an apartment. If you are really stuck, ask for help from someone who has done this before. A similar plan may exist that you can use as a model. Try drafting your plan first, and then get your manager or an experienced coworker to review it. Make sure you have something on paper to show him or her; it is much easier for a busy manager to review your draft plan than to help you from scratch. Even if your plan is wrong, your manager will be impressed that you've taken the initiative. Don't forget to note the assumptions behind the steps in your plan. You can refer back to them if questions arise during your assignment.

3. Present your plan to those who need to buy into it

Depending on the scope of the assignment, you'll probably need to review your plan with your manager, your team leader and anyone else involved. How formal this review is depends on the size and significance of your project. Start your review by summarizing the expected outcomes, as you understand them. This is your last good opportunity to make sure everyone agrees on what you're supposed to accomplish. Any misunderstandings that come up later will probably require rework. Next, discuss the high-level tasks in your plan. Be prepared to go into more detail, if asked. Review your assumptions. Identify the risks, or what could go wrong with your plan. And finally, agree on how to report the status of your progress. Don't be surprised if this discussion uncovers a few surprises and requires some changes to your plan. After all, that's the purpose of this review: to make sure the people who care about the outcome of your work agree with your approach and commit to supporting it.

4. Execute your plan and report the status of your progress

Now you can finally start the work—according to your plan. Don't put that plan away once you start; it is your roadmap. As you execute your plan, communicate with others involved. It is good work etiquette to politely give them a heads up if you are expecting something from them soon. People get busy and don't always remember their commitments. Provide regular status reports to the appropriate people.

As you work on your assignment, you may notice that a task is running behind schedule or using more resources than originally planned Do this quick analysis to determine why this task is deviating from your plan:

> ✔ *The cause of the deviation:* Is it the result of a bad assumption? Incomplete information? Events totally out of your control?

> ✔ *The impact on your plan:* Does the deviation threaten your deadline? The number of resources you need to finish the work? The quality of the work?

✔ ***How you can get back on track:*** Can you do the job a little differently? Can you get help? Can you do two separate tasks at the same time? Can you produce a slightly different outcome that will still meet your objectives? Or does it make sense to just extend the due date?

Elements of a Good Status Report

- **Accomplishments**—What was completed within this reporting period, including progress toward a longer-term goal.

- **Issues**—Difficulties that arose and require some help, such as asking your manager to ask another department for overdue input.

- **Upcoming events**—A look at what's expected during the next reporting period. This can include the next set of tasks in your plan, or a problem you sense brewing.

Always let the appropriate people know *as soon as possible* if there is a significant problem—managers don't like surprises! When reporting a problem, don't blame others. Be upfront about what was truly under your control and what was not. You may take a little heat for a mistake, but in the long run that honesty will win you the support of your manager and coworkers. Not all deviations are bad. Sometimes an opportunity arises to do things faster, cheaper or better. If you're following a plan, you'll be more likely to spot these opportunities.

5. Replan, if necessary

Sometimes you'll find that an assumption you made when developing your plan turns out to be wrong. Or things come up that totally change the objectives or constraints on which your plan was based. Determine if you need to update your existing plan, or start from scratch writing a new one. In either case, apply the same planning rules. Remember to review your revised plan with your manager and coworkers, so they are aware of the change.

© Randy Glasbergen, 1996.

"This project is extremely important, but it has
no budget, no guidelines, no support staff and
it's due tomorrow morning. At last, here's
your chance to really impress everyone!"

6. When the task is complete, capture your lessons learned

Many employees are eager to rush off to their next assignment once
the old one is done. Take the time to review your completed plan for
lessons learned. This will help you improve your performance in the
long run. Some organizations schedule formal lessons-learned sessions at the end of their projects. Or you may just want to look over
and assess your completed work on your train ride home from work.

Ask yourself these questions:

✔ *What worked?* What did you do well?

✔ *What didn't work?* What could you have done better?

✔ *What should you remember the next time?*

SUMMARY

Working from a plan does not guarantee a successful outcome, but it
significantly increases your chances of success. Planning doesn't
come easily to most new employees. However, this is one of the most
valuable skills you can learn. Stick with it. Once you start using the
planning process, you will find it easier to do. You'll also find it easier to work with others—and they will find it easier to work with
you.

FAQS

Q: *This seems like a lot of work. Do I need to write a plan for everything I do?*

A: No, it is not necessary to write a plan for each and every task you are assigned. The first thing to consider is your office's policies. Some organizations require a plan for any project lasting two weeks or longer; others never require a plan. If a plan isn't required, it's your judgment call. Usually it's a good idea to draft a plan if:

- You've never done an assignment like this before;
- You are relatively new to planning and need to hone your skills;
- You need to coordinate the efforts of many people or resources;
- It is critical that you complete the task as specified;
- You've been assigned several tasks or projects simultaneously, and an integrated, overall plan would help keep them all on track.

Even if you choose not to write down a plan, you should mentally work through the process described in this chapter.

Q: *How can I write a plan if I've never done the job before?*

A: One way or another, you'll have to figure out what to do to get your job done. You may as well develop a plan of action before jumping in and possibly wasting time and resources. It is particularly important to draft a plan if you haven't done a job before—and commit it to paper. Before starting the assignment, review your plan with more experienced coworkers. Revise your plan if they show you a better way to get the job done. Always draft your plan before you ask for help. That not only shows initiative on your part, but also makes you work through the process so you'll be better at it the next time.

If you're planning an assignment you've never done before, here are a few tips that can help you get started:

- ***Start with the end result and try to figure out what tasks are needed to produce it.*** Then figure out what they require. Keep working backwards like this until you're at the beginning.

- *Think of similar activities you've done in other settings*— at school, around the house, or while participating in a club or hobby. Take the basic steps you used there and adapt them to your current assignment.

- *Find out if a plan exists for similar work* and use that as a model.

Planning is a skill that doesn't come easily to most people. If you work at it, you'll find you can plan quickly and proficiently—even for assignments that are brand new to you.

Q: *I'm nervous about telling my manager bad news, especially if I'm the one who messed up. What should I do?*

A: You're not alone—who likes to admit they've made a mistake? Nevertheless, the sooner you give your manager the bad news, the easier it will be.

If you've kept up with identifying the risks in your plan, chances are you anticipated at least part of the problem and warned your manager about the possibility of a problem. If so, the bad news won't be a big surprise, and you'll probably be advised to execute your back-up plan.

If the bad news is a complete surprise, there are still a few things you can do. First, tell your manager as soon as possible. Managers don't like surprises – especially bad ones! Sooner or later, he or she will find out. You'll appear unprofessional, possibly even secretive, if the news comes from someone else. Second, remember that everyone makes mistakes. Accept the blame for any failings on your part, but avoid pointing the finger at others, even if they messed up. You don't want to look like a tattletale. Finally, try to deliver the bad news as completely and factually as you can. State what happened and its impact, then propose a way to recover. Proposing a way to recover will show initiative and creativity, as well as demonstrate you are responsible and motivated to achieve successful outcomes.

CHAPTER 7

Performance Feedback and Compensation

> ### In This Chapter
>
> - Feedback is a chance to improve
> - Formal vs. informal feedback
> - Getting the most out of an appraisal
> - Disappointing reviews—now what?
> - Compensation is more than a raise

"Once you embrace unpleasant news, not as a negative but as evidence of a need for change, you aren't defeated by it. You're learning from it."

~ Bill Gates ~

WHY YOU SHOULD CARE

Jayne excitedly anticipated her first performance review and salary discussion. The salary increase should be substantial. Of the new hires, she had been No. 1 in sales. Jayne's customers liked her, and she got along well with her boss. But her performance rating was average, as was her salary increase. Why? Jayne's boss explained that Jayne's peers and the office sup-

port staff thought she was unfriendly because she never stopped to talk to anyone when she was in the office. This made the staff uncomfortable around her. They perceived her as arrogant, a non-team player and unappreciative of the support they gave her. Despite all of her positive accomplishments, Jayne was rated as an average employee. Jayne's reaction at the time: "Why didn't anyone tell me I'd be evaluated on that?"

Whether through a formal review process or informal comments made by supervisors and peers, your performance will be rated throughout your career. Unlike notes on coursework from your professors, this feedback cannot be ignored or dismissed; it could determine the future course of your career. To make the most of the feedback you receive, approach it with a positive attitude and an open mind, even when it is critical of your performance.

Both positive and negative feedback offer you an opportunity to learn and do better in the future. Being told what you did well helps you to continue doing what works. Hearing that some areas need improvement helps you correct your performance. Feedback also tells you what areas your manager thinks are most important, so you can focus on them in your next assignment. That's the theoretical importance of feedback. It also has a practical benefit; your formal performance appraisal often determines the size of your raise, your eligibility for a promotion and, in bad economic times, whether or not you keep your job.

WHAT IS PERFORMANCE FEEDBACK?

You can expect to receive performance feedback two ways: informally, as verbal or written comments on your work, and formally, in a documented performance appraisal.

Informal feedback can come at almost any point in your work. A seemingly off-handed comment can be feedback. Your manager may suggest ways to improve your writing style after reviewing a letter you have written. A customer may call your boss to say you performed your job well. Once you have established a track record, your manager's feedback will be more substantial. While this type of feedback does not go on your record, take it seriously. You're learning what you're doing well and where you need to improve.

Formal feedback is a documented assessment of your work, typically called a "performance appraisal." Most organizations use a standardized appraisal template that provides consistency among all managers. New employees typically receive an appraisal after six to twelve months on the job. *Ideally*, your manager will give you a set of performance objectives early on, including evaluation criteria. In some organizations, the manager will base the appraisal on his or her observations of the employee's work, along with informal comments from project managers or experienced coworkers. Many organizations have embraced the concept of "360 degree appraisals." Here, the person writing the appraisal—who may not even be the manager—collects input from the employee's coworkers, peers, customers, other supervisors and even the employee. The writer organizes all of this input into common themes and then communicates it to the employee.

New employees are often surprised by their evaluations. Why? Unlike college professors, most organizations evaluate their employees on more than just what they know. In addition to an employee's knowledge and technical skills (often a small part of the evaluation), organizations also look at:

- ***Accomplishments:*** what outcomes the employee has achieved
- ***How the accomplishments were achieved:*** "soft skills," such as effective communications skills, planning skills, good teamwork and leadership
- ***Adherence to company policies:*** security, use of company resources, tardiness and absenteeism, and others specific to your organization

Exhibit 7.1 is an example of an actual performance appraisal template used by a Fortune 500® company. Would you guess from the evaluation criteria that this company is highly technical?

Recognition and compensation systems—corporate perks, raises and bonuses—are another source of feedback. They show how your work compares to the work of others in your office. How does *your* company reward the contributions of its employees? Many new employees assume that salary increases are the most significant reward. However, while raises are important, in your organization

communications

Communication Systems-East

PERFORMANCE APPRAISAL

The annual Performance Appraisal formally assesses how individuals contribute to the objectives of the organization. It is intended to be a vehicle for documentation of performance, clarification of expectations and exchange of views.

The immediate manager retains the completed appraisal and a copy is provided to the employee and Human Resources.

Procedure

STEP 1

The manager meets with employee to discuss the upcoming performance appraisal. Discussion should include an overview of the forms, process, and target completion dates. Self-Assessment form is handed out to employee. If 360-degree assessment format is to be used, employee and manager should discuss and agree on who will be providing input/feedback on employee performance.

STEP 2

If 360 degree assessment (optional) is being used a letter and form is sent out to each evaluator (see attached sample letter). The evaluator's input will remain confidential and be destroyed after the manager has reviewed the document. Regardless of the amount of input from other sources, the manager retains ownership of the performance appraisal. If 360-degree assessment is not being used, proceed to Step 3.

STEP 3

After receipt and review of employee self-assessment and 360-evaluator input (optional), manager completes Manager's Assessment of employee.

STEP 4

Manager and employee meet to discuss appraisal results. The goal of this meeting is to ensure understanding of performance review, emphasize areas of strength, and discuss areas for improvement. Both manager and employee sign Manager's Assessment form. A copy is provided to employee and to Human Resources.

It is also strongly recommended that this discussion be used to discuss performance objectives/goals for the upcoming year. Objectives/goals should be prioritized and be as specific as possible to allow for measurable results. Performance plans should be documented and mutually agreed upon by manager and employee. A sample form (optional) is enclosed. The employee and manager should retain copies. A follow-up meeting may be necessary to formalize objectives/goals for the upcoming year.

Exhibit 7.1 An example of an actual performance appraisal template.

L3 communications

Communication Systems-East

PERFORMANCE APPRAISAL

Employee Self-Assessment

Employee Name	Title	Clock #

Manager Name	Activity #	Period Covered

Major Accomplishments/Performance Against Objectives:

Strengths:

Developmental Needs:

Demonstrated Success Criteria (see definitions):

E = Exceeds Expectations M = Meets Expectations NI = Needs Improvement NA = Not Applicable

Analytical Ability	Communication	Process Focus
Problem Solving	Leadership/Coaching	Interpersonal Skills
Initiative	Ownership	Integrity
External Focus	Team Player	Professional Growth

Comments/Examples:

Employee's Signature_____ Date _____

NO ATTACHMENTS

Exhibit 7.1 Continued

communications

Communication Systems-East

PERFORMANCE APPRAISAL

Definitions and Instructions

Major Accomplishments:	State how employee performed over the past 12 months. Be concise, specific and quantify information where appropriate (i.e. projects on time within cost, quality, customer satisfaction).
Strengths:	List major traits, qualities, knowledge, training, and abilities that make employee effective.
Developmental Needs:	List areas employee needs to improve upon. Be specific, concise, clear and concrete.

Demonstrated Success Criteria:		
	Analytical Ability:	Perceptiveness, ability to understand and assess.
	Problem Solving:	Ability to resolve complex problems, mental toughness.
	Initiative:	Anticipates what needs to be done and does it. Looks for ways to do things better.
	External Focus:	Monitor, listen and respond to needs of customers, suppliers.
	Communications:	Verbal/Written - presentation skills, ability to be understood.
	Leadership:	Provides sound leadership. Communicates vision and goals. Effectively develops people.
	Ownership:	Takes responsibility for a task and is accountable for how and when the task is done.
	Team Player:	Supports the goals of the organization, willingness to share and participate.
	Process Focus:	Understands how things fit together. Looks at the overall system and how it could be improved.
	Interpersonal Skills:	Ability to effectively deal with coworkers/customer.
	Integrity:	Maintains the highest standards of business and personal ethics.
	Professional Growth:	Continuously seeks self-improvement and opportunities for furthering education. Ability to accept criticism and grow from feedback.

Comments/Examples:	Provide examples of above mentioned Success Criteria. (i.e., employee demonstrated strong "leadership" on last proposal effort)

Exhibit 7.1 Continued

other perks, such as a special training course, may have more value for your career. Ask your manager or an experienced, objective coworker about the types of recognition used in your company. Ask about the criteria, as well as the limitations, for receiving them. Table 7.1 contains a brief summary of some common performance-based compensation.

Table 7.1. Some common forms of performance based compensation.

Salary increases. The size and frequency of raises depend on how well the company is performing, as well as inflation and other general market conditions. How much you receive and how often you get an increase can fluctuate from year to year.

Bonuses. Bonuses can be one-time payments awarded to exceptional employees or pre-negotiated payments for contributions to the company's bottom line.

Awards. Awards can take on a wide variety of forms, such as a cash payment, a dinner or vacation paid for by the company, or a plaque and write-up in the company newsletter.

Training. Training may be an indication that you are an employee whose potential is worth cultivating, especially if you are offered tuition reimbursement for an advanced degree. Not all training is a "reward"—some organizations offer routine training to all employees and some offer training strictly on a seniority basis.

Special assignments. Many managers reward employees for good performance by giving them special assignments that afford them increased visibility and an opportunity to display their talents to other senior people.

Increased responsibility. This might include adding more tasks to your job description or having you perform the same tasks on a more critical assignment, perhaps for a demanding customer or on a more complex problem.

Promotions. Promotions usually involve a change in title and responsibilities. They may or may not include a salary increase. Sometimes a promotion also includes a larger office or new privileges. Regardless of the money and privileges involved, your promotion can provide exposure to new departments, functions and people, grooming you for future career growth.

TAKE THE INITIATIVE

A Timeline for Performance Feedback

1. (1-2 Months) Learn what is expected of you

- Find out what you are expected to do and how you will be evaluated. Ideally, get your objectives documented
- Get a copy of your organization's performance appraisal template.

2. (As You Work) Assess your performance

- Track your accomplishments.
- Assess your own performance regularly.
- Get informal feedback along the way.

3. (Just Prior to the Appraisal) Prepare

- Identify your accomplishments.
- Do a self-evaluation.

4. (During the Appraisal) Get the most out of it

- Stay calm and listen well.
- Take good notes.
- Ask for specific examples of your performance.
- Ask for specific areas where you can improve.

5. (After the Appraisal) Act on the feedback

- Take time to get over any emotional response.
- Schedule a follow-up meeting with your manager if:
  - The feedback was unclear.
  - You think key accomplishments were overlooked.
  - You need to coordinate corrective actions.
  - Assess your compensation.

1. 1-2 Months into the new job: Learn what is expected of you

Determine as soon as possible what you are expected to do and how you will be evaluated in this role. Don't let your formal appraisal be a surprise. Find out about your organization's appraisal process by asking your supervisor, someone in Human Resources or an experienced coworker you respect.

Ideally, your supervisor will give you a set of objectives when you start the job. In reality, busy managers, with full schedules of their own, often overlook this detail. Set up an appointment with your supervisor to discuss your objectives; let him or her know in advance what you want to talk about. You may not get the objectives in writing, but at least you have initiated this important dialog with your manager. For more information about defining your performance objectives, see Chapter 8, *Mastering Your Job.*

Next, get a copy of your organization's performance appraisal template. Read it for the qualities and competencies your organization expects from all its employees. This template, combined with your specific objectives, should give you a comprehensive description of how you will be evaluated.

2. As you work: Assess your own performance and get informal feedback

Keep notes of your accomplishments throughout the year to gauge your own progress. Keep a file of written feedback you may receive from others. Have you been invited to participate in more special tasks than most of your peers? Or does your writing come back to you with more red marks than anyone else's? To avoid surprises, periodically ask your manager, teammates and mentors for informal feedback. Keep the discussion brief—five minutes can be long enough. After completing a major project or presentation, ask immediately for specific reactions and ways to improve. Always be alert for unsolicited feedback, like a comment made during a meeting. It is less traumatic to get a little negative feedback along the way than to get a lot at the end. More importantly, you can correct the problem immediately, resulting in a better formal appraisal when the time comes.

3. Just prior to the appraisal: Prepare

Anticipating a performance review can be a nerve-wracking experience. You may be surprised to hear that the experience can be just as stressful for your manager! Even an excellent employee can put a manager on the defensive if he or she is resistant to feedback. If you are receptive, your manager or teammates are more apt to speak candidly and offer you support. Focus on the appraisal as a chance to learn more about yourself, so you can grow to your full potential. Keep in mind that appraisals are not a judgment of you as a person, but of the quality and value of your contribution and how you accomplished it.

Prepare for your appraisal by determining the most important challenges you faced during the year. Evaluate how you handled challenges. Review your performance objectives and any notes you have made. Then, write down how you think you performed against each goal. Do not focus just on your accomplishments; also consider any problems you had and be prepared to discuss ways to avoid them in the future.

Do not prepare a litany of excuses or blame others for your difficulties. Your appraisal meeting should focus on how *you* performed and what *you* plan to do to avoid repeating problems. This self-review will help you put your past performance in perspective. Surprisingly, when asked to evaluate themselves, most employees are fairly accurate. An honest self-evaluation prepares you to keep an open mind during the appraisal. In fact, some organizations require a self-evaluation as the first step in the appraisal process.

4. The appraisal: Get the most out of it

Consider these pointers to get the most out of your appraisal:

- *Bring your self-evaluation to the meeting.* You will probably be a little nervous during your appraisal discussion, so bring your self-appraisal with you as a reference, along with the list of objectives you established with your manager or team. Also bring any significant indications of your performance, including examples of your work or letters of recognition for your achievements. Don't be afraid to refer to these items.

**"Before we begin your performance review,
I took the liberty of ordering you some comfort food."**

- *Take notes.* Most people tend to focus on and remember the negative. Listen carefully during the appraisal discussion and jot down key points. These notes will be invaluable in putting your manager's comments into perspective after the appraisal.

- *Ask for specific examples of your performance.* All feedback, whether positive or negative, should include specific examples. Do not be satisfied with generalities such as: "You showed initiative," or "I think you're very innovative." Ask for specific examples: "In your opinion, when did I show initiative?" or "Are there other areas where I could have been more innovative?" Specific examples are important because language is subjective. "Innovative," for example, can mean something different to a manager than it does to an employee.

Take the case of Kathy's appraisal discussion. Her manager has just told her that she needs to be more "innovative." Kathy considers herself extremely innovative because she reads trade journals to stay current and is eager to try the latest software products or techniques. Her manager, on the other hand, expects her to find "innovative" ways to improve the work process, such as using less costly methods. Clearly they are talking about two different things.

Without specific examples, both Kathy and her manager will leave the meeting with different ideas of what was said. The manager believes he made it clear to Kathy that she needs to improve her process, and he will look for results at next year's appraisal. Kathy feels unfairly criticized. She will work even harder to make known her familiarity with and desire for the latest software at work. If the budget for software is small, her manager may keep denying her incessant demands for "innovation." At her next appraisal, Kathy will have to deal with two negatives: her failure to demonstrate process improvement and her insistence that new technology is a priority. A downward spiral begins, caused by miscommunication. You can easily avoid this by asking for specific examples of what your manager means.

- *If the feedback is positive:* Thank your manager (and other reviewers or teammates, if they are part of the formal appraisal process) and feel proud! Many people find it difficult to hear good things about themselves and deny the compliment. Resist the urge to say the accomplishment "wasn't a big deal." Be sure to get specific examples of what you did well so you can repeat your performance.

Most people find it hard to tell others where they need to improve, so many managers or teams will limit the appraisal to the positives. Probe for any areas where you can improve. On the other hand, in some organizations even great employees commonly get less than a perfect rating. Even the best employee can become a better one.

- *If the feedback is disappointing:* Remember that negative feedback is not the end of the world. It is an opportunity to learn and do better in the future. Don't get defensive. Do not counter with angry words like "It was someone else's fault," or "I don't care—this place is unprofessional, anyway."

Emotional outbursts will not help. Ask for examples of where you did poorly. Sure, it's painful to explore a poor aspect of your performance; no one wants to hear how he or she failed to measure up. However, you must ask for enough examples to fully understand what your manager or teammates mean. This will also indicate whether you are dealing with a single incident or a pattern.

Discuss in detail the ways in which you can improve. Ask for examples of good performance you can emulate. Offer your own solution to the problem, making sure you can live with what you propose. If your manager suggests going back to night school, don't agree unless you can do it. If you can't, suggest an alternative. Be sure your manager agrees that it is an appropriate solution. Ask for a chance to apply the solution immediately if your current assignment does not offer one. You must show your manager or teammates that you are willing to address the problem, even if it means investing your own time. Set up a follow-up meeting to discuss your progress.

- **If you disagree with your evaluation:** You may be able to provide information that your manager and teammates are not aware of. For example, your manager may think you're unapproachable, when you are really painfully shy. Most managers will reconsider if you can calmly provide new data. Since appraisal discussions can be emotional experiences, it is usually best to ask for a follow-up meeting, when you can be more objective. Note any areas where you and your manager or teammates differed on the importance of an action or assignment. Did you overestimate the significance of a certain assignment? Part of your learning experience is finding out what your company values. It will help you set priorities in the future.

5. After the appraisal: Act on the feedback

Review your notes after the appraisal and check them against your self-evaluation. If the appraisal did not go well, you may want to give yourself a day or more to get over any emotional response so you can be more objective. Is the feedback clear to you after thinking about it for a while? If not, don't hesitate to schedule a follow-up meeting to clarify your understanding.

- **If the criticism is valid, are you willing to change?** For example, you may have been ten minutes late each morning due to the train schedule. Your team is unwilling to accept your staying ten minutes later at night to make up the time. Are you willing to get up in time to catch an earlier train? Are you willing to accept the consequences of using the later train? Poor or average appraisals often result in lower salary increases in the future. If you are unwilling to change and unwilling to accept the consequences, you may need to look for another job.

- **Do others see you differently than you see yourself?** Perception equals reality. No matter what you think of yourself, you must deal with the perceptions others have of you. For example, do you see yourself as friendly and upbeat, but your teammates say you have a negative attitude? You must analyze this discrepancy. When joking with your colleagues, do you put down management and complain about the workplace? Consider what others may think of this behavior. In every negative appraisal, there is usually a grain (or more) of truth. Discuss the discrepancy with a coworker whose opinion you respect. Be willing to listen, and consider changing your behavior.

- **Why others may think your strengths are weaknesses.** Because you are proud of your strengths, you may find it hard to recognize any downside to them. But what we consider strengths can become weaknesses if they are taken to extremes. Table 7.2 is a list of character strengths and their counterpart weaknesses. Look objectively at your own list of strengths, and see how they could be perceived as weaknesses.

6. Assess your compensation

Your salary increase is based on more than performance. Many companies use a formal process to determine raises. First, the average salary increase is determined for the upcoming 12 months. Managers then rank their employees from highest to lowest performer.

Table 7.2: Strengths Can Become Weaknesses When Taken to Extremes

Strength —— becomes a ——▶	Possible Weakness
Helpful	Over commits time – can't deliver
Attentive to detail	Can't see the big picture
Thorough	Over-engineers the solution
Considerate of others	Afraid to take position for fear of alienating others
Assertive	Aggressive, pushy, a 'bulldozer'
Not afraid to ask for help	Hasn't learned to work independently
Likes teamwork	Can't work alone
Keeps manager informed	Needs too much manager attention
Makes decisions promptly and decisively	Rash, shoots from the hip, impulsive

Employees at the midpoint of the ranking usually receive an average raise. Those ranking above the midpoint get a slightly higher percentage; those falling below the midpoint receive less than the average or nothing at all.

- ***Find out the specifics of your company's process,*** including how it works and where you fall within the guidelines. Many employees become angry over smaller-than-anticipated raises because they don't understand the process.

  For example, Joan's roommate got a ten percent salary increase this year, during a boom in her industry. Joan received an above-average (for her company) salary increase of seven percent, indicating that she was performing very well. Nevertheless, Joan was furious because seven percent was lower than her roommate's ten percent. She complained to her manager, who had no power to change the company's salary directives. Refusing to understand and accept the company's policy, she continued to complain to her manager. This eventually became a performance issue in her manager's eyes, and the following year, her increase percentage dropped below the company average.

- ***How do you find out your company's salary process?***

  Your manager should be willing to explain the basics to you, including the average percent increase, the percentage of employees participating and the time frame for receiving salary increases. Most managers will not tell you what you can expect, because the figure could change based on your performance appraisal or a change in economic conditions. Don't ask for salary information that cannot reasonably be shared with you. To protect your coworkers' privacy, your manager will not tell you what salary increase other employees receive.

  Your Human Resources department and experienced coworkers will also have information on salary planning. If you choose to talk to a coworker, make sure he or she is knowledgeable and objective. Fellow employees may not fully understand the process, and if they are not satisfied with their own raises, they may inject a negative bias into the information they give you.

  The size and frequency of raises will fluctuate year to year, depending on how well the company is performing, inflation and other market conditions. Companies will occasionally adjust the percentages to fit special situations. For instance, an architectural firm may discover that it is paying its interior designers less than those at other local firms. To retain their design talent, the company may give the entire interior design department an above-average raise that year.

SUMMARY

The performance appraisal is designed to help you reach your full potential. If you don't receive a formal appraisal by the end of your first year, ask for one. Without a formal appraisal, you might never be aware of your bad work habits, or have the guidance to improve your performance before you damage your career or lose your job. This may not be fair, but it does happen.

Although your formal appraisal will probably stay in your personnel file for years, it will not necessarily hurt your future with the company. If you respond to a poor appraisal by showing a genuine interest in improving, you are likely to impress your manager and win his or her support. Conversely, an outstanding appraisal does not ensure smooth coasting in the future.

FAQs

Q: *My boss isn't located geographically near me. What can I do to make sure he evaluates me fairly?*

A: This is a common situation in an era of globalization, "hoteling," telecommuting and distributed organizations. In this case, it is vitally important that you understand your objectives and how to achieve them. Try to set up a face-to-face meeting or phone call with your boss to discuss the outcomes you are expected to achieve and what is important in accomplishing them. Should you try to cut costs? Improve processes? Contribute to building office morale? Be sure that your efforts clearly contribute to these objectives. Once you start the work, keep your manager informed on interim accomplishments, potential obstacles and any bad news. Find out how your manager prefers to receive this information. Phone? Email? Finally, use good judgment in how often and what you communicate. You need to provide sufficient information without being a nuisance.

Be sure you know the process your boss follows in writing your evaluation. Ideally, your boss will solicit input from people with whom you work closely: the team/project leader, coworkers and even customers, if appropriate. If that's not the case, tactfully request that he or she does get that input.

Finally, if you are still not comfortable with the evaluation process, you can offer to draft your own appraisal, with emphasis on your tasks and accomplishments. Even if your manager doesn't use your self-evaluation as the "official" appraisal, this still gives you the opportunity to identify what you think deserves recognition.

Q: *My manager doesn't give me informal performance feedback. What should I do?*

A: Look for opportunities to ask for brief feedback, preferably one-on-one. You could ask on the way back from lunch, at the conclusion of a meeting or presentation, or on the way to visit a client. If you still don't get useful feedback, try to determine why not. Is your manager too busy to make the time? Or is he or she just uncomfortable giving it? If your manager is just too busy, schedule a time to talk. Set up a brief meeting (ten to fifteen minutes max), and let him or her know what you plan to discuss. You could even email a few questions ahead of time, asking how you did on a particular task or whether you are developing required skills at the expected rate and quality. Keep the meeting brief and to the point; you don't want to waste the opportunity.

If you're still not getting informal feedback, or if it isn't meaningful, solicit feedback elsewhere. Ask a senior coworker, your project lead or, if appropriate, a customer. Again, keep the discussion brief, focus on listening and be sure you understand by paraphrasing or offering examples.

Finally, while you need to get informal feedback periodically, don't solicit it too frequently. You don't want to become a pest!

Q: *My manager never set up-front performance objectives with me. I don't know what I will be evaluated on. What should I do?*

A: Despite the best of intentions, managers often don't get around to setting up-front objectives. Early on, try drafting your own set of prioritized, measurable objectives, with evaluation criteria. Give them to your manager for concurrence, stating in a cover letter or note that this is what you think you are working toward. Request a brief meeting to get feedback, including any changes your manager wants to make. If your work situation changes significantly after writing them (for example, you get a major new task or priorities change), redraft your objectives and approach your manager again.

Q: *I don't get along with all the people who provide the input to my appraisal. How can it be fair?*

A: Performance appraisals, despite many corporate and academic attempts to make them otherwise, are highly subjective. Unfortunately, if the people evaluating you don't like you, they probably won't give you a stellar appraisal. To some degree, that's how it should be, since part of "success" on the job is working well with the rest of your team.

If just one person doesn't like you but you get along great with everyone else, chances are he or she has an issue with interpersonal skills. Your manager probably knows this, but may still challenge you to figure out how to deal with this person. If you don't get along with the majority of your coworkers, then you are most likely the one who needs to make some changes. Give yourself a critical self-evaluation without making excuses, or ask your manager for feedback. You'll probably find the results painful, but it will give you the opportunity to make important changes critical to your career success.

Q: *I know a lot more technically than my manager. How can she accurately evaluate me if she doesn't understand what I do?*

A: Are you sure your manager doesn't share your technical skills? Maybe she just doesn't know the details of your particular assignment. A statement like "I don't understand any of this" could mean either. Your manager might have related knowledge that will help her assess how you get your work done.

There may be times when your manager has little or no technical expertise in your field. True, a less technically savvy manager may not understand or appreciate the effort or talent that a knowledgeable employee demonstrated to achieve a particular outcome. However, that doesn't matter if other factors like teamwork, leadership or customer satisfaction are more important in your job than technical ability. As always, make sure you know what is expected of you and how it will be evaluated. In most cases, if technical competence is a critical part of the evaluation, either your manager will have the capability to evaluate you, or input will be solicited from others. Ask your manager to let other, technically proficient employees who are familiar with your work weigh in on your appraisal. They can either submit written input or have a discussion with your manager.

Q: *A large part of my evaluation will be based on how well my team performs. One of my teammates never pulls his own weight. What should I do if I am penalized for someone else's poor performance? Will my contributions be recognized?*

A: This situation seems to especially worry new employees who are used to being evaluated individually or who had a bad team experience at school. There are a number of possible reasons for your teammate's behavior. First, teams require various roles to be successful; maybe your teammate is just contributing differently than you. Perhaps extenuating circumstances, like an illness in the family, are temporarily affecting his or her performance. If you do extra work to get your team and teammate through this difficult time, your efforts will probably be recognized. Or, your teammate may just be stuck on some part of the task, but is afraid to ask for help. Maybe you can share some information or skill to get him or her moving. Of course, your teammate may just be a slacker, in which case, make sure *you* are doing everything you can to ensure the team's success. If you notice he or she isn't performing, it's likely others do, too.

No matter what, don't blow the whistle on him or her. Employers complain that new employees are often quick to point out their team members' failings, without acknowledging their own mistakes. Handling this problem professionally will win you a better performance appraisal, and the ongoing support of your teammates.

Q: *I don't think I'm paid enough for what I do. I feel that I should have been given a bigger raise this year, but I can't find out what anyone else in the organization makes. How can I be sure I'm paid fairly for what I do?*

A: Many employees, especially new ones, worry they aren't paid enough. Before you react emotionally, look at the situation constructively. Remember that most companies consider sharing information about other employees a breach of privacy.

1. ***Understand the rules.*** Your Human Resources department can explain the details of your compensation process, including salary ranges for various positions, average raises/bonuses across the company, and criteria and timing for receiving them. Make sure you understand these rules. If your company doesn't give bonuses, there's no point in getting upset that you didn't receive one!

2. ***Did you deserve a raise?*** Often, when new employees feel undercompensated, they have overrated their contribution. It's hard to evaluate yourself objectively. Look at your accomplishments and shortcomings as if you were preparing for a performance appraisal. Do you meet or exceed the guidelines? How do your accomplishments compare with those of your peers? This is not easy. A senior worker may be able to give you perspective and an objective assessment.

3. ***Deal with the results.*** If you conclude you are fairly compensated, focus on improving your performance. You may decide that you're fairly paid for your organization, but you want more. It's unlikely you'll change the system. You must decide whether you like your job enough to accept the lower pay, or want to look for a higher-paying job.

If you conclude you're unfairly compensated, think hard about your course of action. People who challenge the system are sometimes seen as troublemakers and may suffer longer-term consequences like low salary increases or limited job opportunities. If you want to take drastic measures like a court battle, be aware that it can be expensive and emotionally draining. Sometimes, the best move is to wait until the next raise or bonus cycle and see what happens. You may be surprised. Very often, the system corrects itself when an employee is truly under-compensated. Of course, your final option is to look for a new job. If you work for an organization that tries to get away with paying you as little as possible, it probably has other objectionable practices, so you won't be happy staying.

Mastering Your Position

Having mastered assignment planning and execution, you can begin to assume more responsibility, take the initiative and look for more challenging "stretch" projects to work on. Key to getting ahead will be knowing how to think creatively and critically, and excel in problem finding and solving.

Chapter 8: Mastering Your Job—Doing a good job means doing more than exactly what you are told. This chapter describes different levels of job mastery, why they are important and how to achieve them.

Chapter 9: Problem Solving Part 1: How to Think!—Creative thinking and critical thinking are skills that can be learned and honed over time. This chapter explains the basics and offers concrete steps and tips to improve your thinking.

Chapter 10: Problem Solving Part 2: A Process—Successful problem solving relies on the important thinking skills covered in Chapter 9, but the solutions can be significantly improved by following a clear, step-by-step process.

CHAPTER 8

Mastering Your Job

In this Chapter

- Just doing your job isn't enough

- Efficiency vs. effectiveness

- Measuring your progress

"The person who knows how will always have a job.
But the person who knows why will be the boss."

~ Carl C. Wood ~

WHY YOU SHOULD CARE

Many new employees make the mistake of thinking that "just doing their job" is good enough, or that they deserve to be rewarded for putting in time and effort. When things are going well for your organization, you might get by with "just doing your job." But who do you think will be the first person let go if the company hits a rough spot and has to cut back, or outsource work to reduce expenses? Will your company keep those employees who "just did their job," or those who made the extra effort and noticeably contributed to their organization's success?

How do you become a valuable employee? What worked in school won't get you ahead in the workplace. In school, you were graded on what you knew and how well you demonstrated your grasp of the subject matter. In the business world, it's not what you know—it's what you do for the company. Your value as an employee is measured by how well you apply your knowledge and skills to produce results that not only meet your job performance standards, but contribute to the company's success.

Whether you want to advance in your organization, become an expert in your field, or just avoid being laid off, mastering your job is key. In the process, you'll gain valuable experience that will lead to greater job satisfaction and more job opportunities in the future.

WHAT DOES IT TAKE TO MASTER YOUR JOB?

Your manager is looking for two things in a valued employee: efficiency and effectiveness.

Being *efficient* means *doing things right* in these important ways:

- *Quantitative:* achieving measurable targets (for example, sales volume, productivity, cost reduction, generating code) on time and within budget

- *Qualitative:* producing complete and accurate work

- *Behavioral:* exhibiting the personal characteristics that are valued in your organization (for example, attitude, initiative, innovation, teamwork)

Being *effective* means *doing the right things*. You are effective if you take the initiative to solve problems or find ways to further the organization's goals. Knowing the right things to do comes with experience. Here's an example of the difference between just doing your job and making the effort to be both efficient and effective:

A retail clerk in a home products store keeps shelves orderly and well stocked, and rings up sales accurately. A second clerk is orderly and accurate, but also knows the capabilities of other employees and where things are located in other departments. A third clerk demonstrates the same skills and knowledge as the first two clerks, but also helps customers by inquiring about their projects, answering their questions and suggesting alternative products. The first sales clerk is efficient and fully satisfactory. The second clerk is becoming more effective because she can help customers find what they need. The third clerk is the most effective and exceeds expectations. With excellent customer service skills, she is helping to increase sales and win repeat customer business.

Mastering your job won't happen overnight. The more complex your job, the longer it will take you to become both efficient and effective. How well you succeed will be reflected in your formal performance appraisal, as well as in raises, promotions and other forms of compensation. Chapter 7, *Performance Feedback and Compensation*, deals with performance appraisals and how to get the most out of them. In general, most job appraisal systems have basically three levels of performance: *fails to meet expectations, fully satisfactory* and *exceeds expectations*. See the diagram below for a description of these categories.

General Performance Categories

"Fails to Meet Expectations"—Employees in this category are not performing at the level expected for the position, and need to improve substantially. Most organizations cannot afford to spend a lot of resources helping a poor performer improve, nor can they afford to keep paying the salary of a person who is not delivering results. These employees face a high risk of termination.

"Fully Satisfactory"—These employees consistently deliver everything asked and may even excel at times. During good economic times, they are welcome on the payroll. They help get the job done. However, during times of economic hardship, they risk losing their jobs in favor of employees who outperform them.

"Exceeds Expectations"—Employees with this rating consistently go "above and beyond" what is asked of them. They master their jobs and make a difference to their organizations with the insight they have gained. These employees are the future of the organization; employers don't want to lose them and often reward them with incentives to remain with the company.

In practice, most companies use a rating scale with at least 5 classifications roughly equal to school letter grades (A, B, C, D and F). Earning less than a "B" leaves you at some risk. The evaluation process is often highly subjective. Ask for periodic feedback from your supervisor so you can make adjustments and avoid surprises when it comes time for your formal performance appraisal.

TAKE THE INITIATIVE

It may take a full year to master your new job and become recognized as a valuable contributor.

A Timeline for Mastering Your Job

(0-3 months)

    1. Know your responsibilities

    2. Define your performance objectives

(0-6 months)

    3. Master the mechanics of your job

(6-12 months)

    4. Develop a sense of ownership

    5. Determine your organization's objectives
       and strategies

The following steps will help you focus your energy and evaluate your progress.

1. Know your responsibilities

Start by reading your job description carefully to get a feel for the scope of your position. Identify the responsibilities for which you are held accountable. Consider the case of Nick, who didn't pay attention to his job description.

Nick, a bright computer-engineering student from a reputable university, was hired by a large corporation to assist in IT strategy definition for one of

its business divisions. However, when some of the network engineers dis-
covered Nick's outstanding network design talent, they kept him busy
answering network questions—not working on strategy, as outlined in his
job description. It wasn't a happy day when Nick's manager finally learned
what was keeping Nick from his assigned responsibilities.

2. Define your performance objectives

It is critical to sit down with your manager as early as possible to discuss your specific performance objectives. If your organization has a
formal process for defining objectives, follow company procedures. If
there is no formal process, and you have not had a discussion with
your manager by the end of your first month, ask for one. Focus your
discussion on the questions and process outlined in Chapter 5,
Understanding Your Assignment:

- *Ask the questions "why, what, how, who, where, and*
  when," as they relate to your job responsibilities. Make sure
  you know the quantitative (product goals, deadlines, and
  resources), qualitative (degree of thoroughness and accuracy)
  and behavioral (personal qualities) expectations of your job.
- *Translate your notes into a list of performance objectives.*
- *Review the list with your manager to make sure you both*
  agree on the expected outcomes. Revise the list when needed.
- *Refer to your list of objectives throughout the year and ask*
  for feedback on how you are doing.

Don't expect your manager to specify every detail you need to follow. Part of being a professional is showing initiative and exercising
good judgment. To fill in the gaps, observe how coworkers handle
their responsibilities and follow their best examples.

3. Master the mechanics of your job

Become competent in the tasks involved in your job, including procedures and when to perform them. Your goal is to consistently complete your assignment on time and within budget, and to meet
quality standards. The following checklist will help:

- *Become technically proficient.* Learn the tools of your trade,
  from paperwork to automated tools. For example, an accountant must become familiar with the chart of accounts used by

the company and the necessary journal entries to record certain transactions. This includes knowing how to input them to the accounting system, as well as how to reconcile problems when the accounts don't balance.

- *Identify the constraints on your work.* Are there specific standards, guidelines or procedures that you must follow? Are there limits on your decision-making authority? If so, become familiar with them and how they affect your tasks. This is especially important if you work as a government contractor or in a highly regulated industry, like banking or financial services.

- *Develop your interpersonal skills.* Learn not only what to do, but also how to go about doing it. This includes the ability to function in a team environment, build customer relationships, and communicate effectively.

- *Understand the theory behind your tasks.* A valuable employee knows not only how to do things, but why they are done a certain way. This in-depth understanding helps you figure out alternative steps when something goes wrong. For example, it is one thing to know how to drive a car, but when

© 1999 Randy Glasbergen.   www.glasbergen.com

"I'm sending you to a seminar to help you work harder and be more productive."

your car doesn't start, it helps to know something about how an engine works so you can find the problem and maybe even fix it.

- **Wean yourself from the experts.** Relying on coworkers or managers for a "quick fix" to problems can be a hard habit to break. As a new employee, you may lack the confidence to work independently. If so, ask yourself what's the worst that could happen if you made a mistake. If the consequences are minor, try working without help. If, after several months, you still find yourself relying on experts, it's time to help yourself. Identify the gaps in your knowledge or skills and find a way to fill them (for example, an after-hours course, reference book, company training, etc.).

4. Develop a sense of ownership

We all know people who say, "It's not my problem," when issues arise outside their direct responsibility. That attitude is the surest way to limit your effectiveness and ultimately handicap your career. Develop a sense of ownership for the success of your organization. Organizations want and need people who are willing to go beyond their job descriptions, especially when a problem or crisis arises. This doesn't mean you have to do someone else's job; but you should make sure that the problem is referred to the appropriate person.

5. Determine your organization's objectives and strategies

The surest way to become a valued employee is by aligning your personal efforts with your organization's goals. If you are in a high-profile position, this can make the difference between losing and keeping your job.

Consider the case of Mark, who graduated with a degree in accounting and was hired to manage the accounts receivable function for a large retail operation. Significant process problems had existed for almost 20 years, causing issues with the company's financial statements. Mark chose to address the problem by fixing the flow of information that is required from departments outside of accounting in order to process amounts due from various companies. While Mark made significant improvements that virtually eliminated the source of the problem, he lost his job after 12 months. Why did this happen?

Mark failed to understand the context of his job assignment. He failed to take into account that executive management planned to take the company public within the next two years and was more concerned about cleaning up their financial statements than eliminating the root cause of the problem. While technically correct, Mark's solution failed to produce the results desired by management at that time.

To avoid finding yourself in Mark's situation, take these actions:

- *Learn your organization's strategic themes.* What are its key goals, and what initiatives has it chosen to pursue? Why were these strategies chosen? How are they expected to position the organization for future success? Ask your manager or coworkers these questions. Listen to discussions in staff meetings. Read memos from your executive team. Sometimes, organizations post signs or run motivational campaigns to promote a strategy initiative. By showing your interest in these strategies, you will not only gain valuable knowledge, but will demonstrate initiative and commitment to your organization.

- *Determine how your job contributes to your organization's goals.* Let's say you are a software programmer at a discount retail chain whose objective is reducing cost. Instead of creating the next "killer app," you should focus on applying existing software technology to streamline the ordering process and reduce warehouse inventory storage costs. There is a purpose for every job in an organization. Find out the purpose for your job, and how it supports your organization's goals.

- *Improve the skills that will most benefit your organization.* How might the organization's goals and strategies impact your individual actions? Professionals are expected to take the initiative to advance their career. Your company's goals and strategies will tell you what actions to take. This could mean signing up for a night course to pick up a new skill, or volunteering for an "extracurricular" assignment that requires some hours of unpaid overtime. Because your time is limited, be selective in choosing what actions will put you most in line with your organization's direction. Table 8.1 below shows how various strategic themes might impact you and the actions you can take.

Table 8.1: How to Be More Valuable Using Strategic Themes

Strategic Themes	Implications for you:	Potential Actions:
Technology Leadership	Emphasize *innovation* by applying your technical knowledge in new ways. Innovation can have different meanings. For a company like Microsoft®, it could mean developing new or improved products for its customers. For a company like Wal-Mart®, with lower profit margins, it might mean finding ways to improve operating efficiency and get products to the market faster.	• Identify technologies critical to your company's growth strategy. • Assess your skills in this area. • Fill any gaps through formal course work or self-directed study. • Look for ways to apply technology on your assignments, consistent with the company's objectives. • Identify company initiatives to drive innovation and find a way to participate.
Service Orientation	Services are a highly profitable segment of today's economy. Generating growth through new services, or increasing profitability through improved service, requires you to understand how your customers measure their success, and to solve the problems they are experiencing. Service and customer satisfaction go hand-in-hand.	• Understand your company's service model and policies. • Identify how customers measure the value of your services. • Know their needs and anticipate changes in them. • Manage their expectations. • Communicate openly, encouraging a dialog to solve problems and improve your value. • Inform them of developments and problems affecting them.
Global Expansion	Many companies grow by taking their products to new markets in other countries. This may require you to interact with people from different cultures and with different values, not to mention different languages, than yours.	• Identify countries or regions where your company is expanding. • Research the culture, history and customs of these countries. • Learn to speak the language or at least some basic phrases. • Take a vacation trip to the region to get some first-hand knowledge.

Table 8.1: How to Be More Valuable Using Strategic Themes (continued)

Strategic Themes	Implications for you:	Potential Actions:
Low Cost Provider	Providing products and services at the lowest price is essential to the survival of many companies. As an employee, you need to constantly look for ways to reduce cost.	• Understand how your organization categorizes expenses. • Identify the largest categories. • Find ways to reduce costs for items you directly influence. • Make specific proposals to your manager to implement changes.

You'll know that you've mastered your job when you can describe your accomplishments not only in terms of *what you did* and *how well you did it,* but in terms of the *results you produced* that contributed to achieving specific organizational goals. For example:

What you did ...	How well (efficiently) you did it ...	Results you produced (effectiveness) ...
• Implemented an inventory control system	• Ahead of schedule and within budget	• Reduced inventory carrying costs by 38%
• Expanded contact list of prospective clients	• Doubled number of qualified sales prospects	• Increased sales revenue for services by 20%
• Analyzed problems in accounts receivable function	• Eliminated cause of missing data leading to payment delays	• Increased cash flow by $500,000 in first quarter

Fully Satisfactory ⟶ *Exceeds Expectations*

SUMMARY

Mastering your job requires more than just doing your job well. It requires seeing the big picture and how you fit into your company's future. A valued employee is both efficient in performing tasks and effective in producing results that help the organization achieve its goals. Take the initiative to understand how your organization works and what it is trying to accomplish. Work with your manager to define your performance standards and objectives, keeping your company's goals in mind. Then use them to gauge your progress in the company.

Do not become complacent with either your level of understanding or your performance. Remember that an organization's goals can change quickly in today's fast-paced business environment. You may also find that, as you demonstrate your capabilities, your bosses will expect more of you and will raise the standards by which your performance is measured. View this as an opportunity. Don't resist your new responsibilities. Be flexible and adapt to the new situation. By doing so, you will continue to grow with your organization.

FAQS

Q: *I need help learning a particular aspect of my job, but my manager doesn't make time to work with me. What's going on? What should I do?*

A: Managers don't always know the details of work they supervise, and may not be able to help you. Most simply don't have the time. Or, this may be a tactic to get you more involved with others in the organization. Regardless of the reason, get the help you need elsewhere. Every organization has subject matter experts who can help you with the more difficult aspects of your job. You can identify them by observing and asking others who they go to for answers. Most experts will respond favorably to a reasonable request for help. Don't waste their time; approach them with well thought-out questions, and take notes.

Q: *I feel like I'm not using all of my skills. How can I get my manager to recognize that I have more abilities and to give me some meatier assignments?*

A: Remember that you have not established a track record yet, so your first assignments are likely to be mundane, even boring. Your manager may feel that a key project is at a phase where he can't risk adding a new, unproven team member with little experience or corporate knowledge. Or perhaps your manager doesn't have the time right now to coach you through a complex assignment. In the meantime, apply yourself to mastering your job, no matter how dull it may seem. By proving you are a competent and reliable employee, you'll open the door to more interesting and challenging opportunities.

Q: *My company doesn't use formal written job descriptions. How can I find out what my job responsibilities are?*

A: It sounds as if you work for a small organization that is very informal. Chances are the lines of responsibility for jobs are not very well defined, and everyone pitches in to get things done. Nevertheless, you still need to understand what your primary responsibilities are. Try writing your own job description. Once you've defined the performance objectives for your position (described above in **Step 2**), write down what you need to do to achieve those objectives and what you must rely on others to do. Review the document with your manager and adjust it accordingly.

Q: *I work in a support job that doesn't affect the finances of our company. How do I align my efforts with the organization's financially based objectives?*

A: Either directly or indirectly, you affect the financial success of your organization by using resources (for example, time, material, travel) in doing your job. Each of these resources costs the company money; the key is to use them reasonably. Remember that **Profit = Revenues - Expenses**. You can help improve your company's profits by working more efficiently, avoiding waste and minimizing expenses. If you haven't already done so, read Chapter 4, *Developing Business Acumen*, for more on this topic.

CHAPTER 9

Problem Solving Part 1: How to Think!

In This Chapter

- What is creativity?

- Obstacles to creative thinking

- What is critical thinking?

- Obstacles to thinking critically

- The role of knowledge

"Intelligence is something we are born with.
Thinking is a skill that must be learned."

~ Edward de Bono ~

WHY YOU SHOULD CARE

If you've glanced at some of the other chapters in this book, you've already figured out that the criteria for success in the workplace are a little—perhaps a lot?—different than in school. Success in school is about demonstrating what you know or have learned, and showing that you can reason about or debate the topic at hand. Success in the workplace is about achieving results—making things happen, removing obstacles and dealing with a rapid rate of change. Some academic knowledge will be needed, but the degree you'll use will depend on your job.

Success in the workplace is also about appealing to the people who provide your organization's revenues—your business clients, non-profit donors or taxpayers. (See Chapter 4, *Business Acumen*, for a more in-depth discussion of revenue providers.) You can attract revenue providers with:

- Products and services that are interesting or unique
- Pricing your product or service lower than your competitors'
- Superior quality of your product or service
- Outstanding customer service

Producing great products and services doesn't happen accidentally. It requires creativity, critical thinking and problem-solving skills. Granted—getting good grades also required some degree of these skills. In the workplace, however, you're expected to apply these skills more actively and more extensively than you've had to up until now.

This chapter will introduce two modes of thinking essential to effective problem solving: creative thinking and critical thinking. Numerous books have been written on each of these topics. The goal of this chapter is to start you on the road to enhancing your skills. The next chapter provides a paradigm or set of steps you can follow to enhance your problem-solving abilities.

HOW TO THINK

Most great problem solvers are mentally agile. They can think in different ways, know when each thinking mode is most appropriate, and move smoothly from one way of thinking to another. Problem solving generally involves moving back and forth between creative thinking and critical thinking.

Creative thinking looks at a matter or situation from different angles and finds new ideas and points of view. It generates possibilities. When it comes to problem solving, creative thinking is necessary to:

- *Generate possible reasons why a problem exists.* The true cause of a problem is not always what appears on the surface. For example, let's say you started running seriously six months ago and you've started experiencing a lot of pain in your knee. The obvious cause of the problem is that somehow you injured yourself from the exercise. The real root cause may be that you have just worn out your running shoes and it's time to buy a new pair.

- *Generate possible solutions to a problem.* As you will read later in this chapter, the immediate solutions that come to mind may be adequate, but adequate is not usually innovative and exciting.

- *Generate possible ways to implement a solution.* In the workplace, there is rarely a single way to implement a solution. Thinking creatively may uncover ways to do things faster and cheaper, improve quality, or reduce stress.

Critical thinking applies measures to new ideas to determine if they are workable and will produce the desired results. It narrows possibilities to the best choice. When problem solving, critical thinking may be used to:

- *Identify facts.* Which facts associated with a problem are relevant, and which can be ignored?

- *Assess possible causes.* Which causes of a problem contribute most significantly, and which have little to no true impact on the situation?

- *Apply evaluation criteria.* Which of many possible solutions is best?

- *Communicate preferred solutions.* Communicate solutions in a structured way so that your audience can follow your reasoning and more readily accept your recommendations.

Both creativity and critical thinking are essential to good problem solving. Imagine trying to solve problems using only creative thinking. You would generate many ideas but would not do the work of evaluating whether the ideas were useful or viable. Additionally, you'd never converge on a single option. Conversely, if you only used critical thinking without thinking creatively first, your problem solving would lack originality and interest. The key is to become skilled in both thinking modes and to learn how and when to switch from one to the other.

What is Creativity?

Often when people think of creativity, they think of the arts. Music, dance, drawing and painting are definitely forms of creative expression. In the workplace, advertising and new product design may also come to mind as creative work. But what about less obvious applications for creativity? For example, in manufacturing—how about a new innovative production process that manufactures items faster or with fewer flaws? In insurance—how about innovative uses of information technology that provide claim information to policy holders more efficiently, more accurately and with less human involvement? In food services—how about new menus that are healthier, with items that taste great and are visually appealing?

A lot of people say they aren't creative, because they can't think up brand-new ideas. But that's not exactly what creativity is. A generally accepted definition of creativity is the ability to combine two ideas that have never been put together before, resulting in something usable or interesting. With a little practice, you can learn to do that. Here's an exercise you can try. It works even better if you try it with a few friends.

Creativity Exercise

Think of two (seemingly) unrelated objects or concepts—let's say "candle" and "mailbox." Combine these two objects in ways you've never heard of before. Go for as many as you can. Here are a few examples:

1. A candle-shaped mailbox
2. A mailbox-shaped candle
3. A fireproof mailbox
4. A mailbox that lights up when you open it
5. Seasonally decorated mailboxes using scented candles

Your first several ideas are likely to be the obvious solutions; they're not particularly new or creative. A lot of people stop here in the creative process—accepting their ideas as "good enough." Press yourself to keep going. Here are more ideas:

6. A flame-throwing mailbox that deters mailbox vandals
7. A flame-throwing mailbox that destroys junk mail
8. A mailbox that waters the lawn
9. Scented mail and mailboxes that make the mail carrier happy
10. Using smoke signals to communicate

After you get past the obvious, the next set of items is usually silly or way-out. This is the next point at which many people give up, thinking, "This isn't very productive. I'm only coming up with dumb ideas." Actually, now is when you're climbing out of your box. Don't judge the ideas—use the way-out ideas as a springboard to ideas that are more workable. Also, allow yourself to stray from the strict combination of the two concepts you're connecting. For example, item 8 above really has nothing to do with candles. That's OK. You're in the world of innovation and originality. Keep going.

11. A multi-purpose mailbox that can receive many items
12. A temperature-controlled mailbox
13. A heated mailbox that holds your pizza delivery if it arrives before you get home from work
14. A way to sort mail according to scent applied by the sender
15. A way to transmit scents electronically

If you've persisted this far, you've probably discovered some really interesting and workable ideas. Ideally, in a real brainstorming session, you should try for a minimum of 75-100 ideas. Initially this may be difficult for you, but the more you practice creative thinking, the easier it will be. "Creative people" think this way all the time. In fact, sometimes they can't stop themselves, and find it hard to get anything done.

Need more inspiration to help enhance your creative thinking skills? Read these thoughts from two very talented dancers and choreographers:

"I am not sure what makes me creative, considering neither of my parents or my siblings are involved in the arts. I always just try to look outside the box—taking a normal idea and flipping it around and thinking about different ways to relay my message. I am inspired by ideas from everyone around me, even from hearing a song in passing or on a TV commercial. It is always a challenge to keep your work fresh and to keep challenging yourself to try new things and push forward. If I get stuck, I usually think of a different way to do something than I have done before. And it always inspires me to go take a class or be in a rehearsal to see other choreographers' work and their process. Usually that can give me a different perspective and jumping off point. Creativity is a process, and one that can always be expanded upon."

—Christa Campbell

"Often what makes me creative is limitations. Having certain things unavailable like funding or top-notch dancers forces me to get creative within my given parameters. Also, very often other art … music, paintings, poems … inspire me. A trick that helps is to introduce random things that make things difficult. Often ideas just come randomly to me at night when I am TRYING to sleep. It's somewhat of a curse, but I'm glad I get the ideas!"

—Michelle Wurtz

Along with practice, here are some other tips to help creative thinking become second nature to you:

- ***Try to maintain an open-minded, non-judgmental attitude*** toward new situations or problems you face.

- ***Persist!*** Don't just accept the first solution that comes along, but push yourself to keep identifying new alternatives, no matter how unusual or "way-out."

- ***Embrace change,*** which is hard for most humans! You don't believe that? Once students establish their seats in a classroom, how often do they relocate to another part of the room?

Conversely, here are some obstacles to creativity you want to avoid.

- Deciding an idea won't work before exploring the possibilities
- Fear of letting go of comfortable or known ways of doing things
- Accepting the status quo and not having the energy or inclination to look for better ways
- Feeling threatened by another person or organization that might have a different or better way of doing things—the "not invented here" syndrome
- Adopting the mindset that "this is good enough"
- Similarly, accepting the first solution you come up with
- Falling into the trap of saying, "We've always done it this way"
- Deciding there isn't enough time to think out of the box
- Fear of looking silly

You will see benefits from enhancing your creative skills, both at work and in your personal life. Creative thinking helps create new opportunities. By thinking outside the box, you can see new ways of using resources, including your time and talents that will open up new paths for you. Additionally, others will be more likely to offer you opportunities, when you demonstrate an ability to innovate. Creative thinking can also make it easier to deal with change. A creative mind sees change as an opportunity rather than a threat, and helps you more readily identify ways to deal with any challenges introduced by the change. And finally, you will be a more interesting person whom people will enjoy being with. All these benefits can contribute to increasing your confidence and your trust in your abilities. So have fun with your creativity, and see where it takes you!

What is Critical Thinking?

Let's start by defining what critical thinking is not. It is not how much you know, although you must have knowledge of the subject matter to be an effective critical thinker. However, there are a lot of people who know a lot of facts, yet are lousy thinkers. You may know some. Another thing critical thinking is not, is constant criticism. You probably also know people with negative attitudes who always find fault with anything you do or any new idea you share. Critical thinking may uncover faults, but it also identifies what works. Finally, critical thinking is not robot-like thinking, lacking emotion and compassion. Good critical thinkers can separate emotions from facts, and allow emotion to factor in when appropriate.

So what is critical thinking? Critical thinking has two parts to it. It is a structured approach to processing information that produces well-reasoned conclusions. It is also a mode of thinking in which the thinker continually improves his or her thinking by constantly evaluating his or her thought process. Let's look at these two requirements a little more closely.

- *A honed set of information processing and reasoning skills:* This dimension of critical thinking requires that you have strong logical thinking and reasoning skills. These skills are the mental tools you need to solve problems. You may have worked on honing yours if you studied for the SATs or ACTs. Figure 9.1 contains a list of some familiar ones. Some of the skills involve your ability to gather data and information from many sources as accurately and thoroughly as possible. For example, when listening to a political discussion, most of us hear the points that support our political views and tune out or discount contradicting information. A strong critical thinker would equally consider both sides of the argument. Other skills in Figure 9.1 deal with your ability to analyze and evaluate the data and information you have received. Identifying trends in traffic accidents and cell phone usage would be an example of this. Yet other skills involve taking effective action on the data. You would be using these skills if you were predicting sales volume of a new product, based on past sales trends of similar products.

- *The ability to assess your own thinking:* This is also called "meta-thinking." To be a great critical thinker, you must be able to separate yourself from your own thinking to identify what mistakes you made, including where you let your emotions get

---

Figure 9.1: Thinking, Reasoning and Decision Making Skills

Here is a partial list of skills and abilities you will need to develop to enhance your critical thinking, problem solving and decision making. You may want to add others to your list.

✔ *Data and Information Gathering Skills*
- Reading and listening accurately
- Separating fact from opinion
- Separating fact from emotion
- Recognizing
- Questioning, especially open-ended questions

✔ *Data Organization Skills*
- Classifying
- Schematizing
- Diagramming
- Sequencing

✔ *Analysis Skills*
- Compare and contrast
- Recognizing contradictions
- Distinguishing relevant from irrelevant facts
- Noticing similarities and differences
- Recognizing trends

- Recognizing patterns
- Seeing analogies
- Differentiating
- Inferring

✔ *Evaluating Skills*
- Validating sources
- Prioritizing
- Ranking
- Selecting
- Statistical validity

✔ *Implementing Skills*
- Explaining
- Summarizing
- Generalizing
- Justifying
- Hypothesizing
- Deducting
- Interpreting
- Estimating
- Predicting

---

in the way of sound judgment. Other things you want to discern in your meta-thinking include assumptions you need to verify, starting premises and their correctness, the soundness of your logic process, your hidden biases and whether or not you have sufficient evidence to support your conclusions. You may be thinking, "If I knew I was making mistakes, I wouldn't have thought that way in the first place." Hopefully, that's true! Good critical thinkers are constantly evaluating their thinking by considering new data that conflicts with what they think they know, looking for outcomes that contradict expected results, and assessing emotion vs. facts.

Along with practice, here are some other tips to help enhance your critical thinking:

- *Accept the fact that everyone makes mistakes.* The problem isn't making a mistake; the problem is not being able to admit when you're wrong. Learn from your errors and strive not to repeat them.
- *Gain confidence as an independent thinker.* Effective critical thinkers often view the world differently from those with less effective skills. That doesn't mean they can't be liked and accepted by others.
- *Similarly, embrace ideas that differ from yours.* You don't necessarily have to agree with them, but you can learn by exploring different points of view.

Conversely, here are some obstacles to effective critical thinking you want to avoid.

- Believing that what you "know" is true and never exploring any other possibility
- Overly trusting authority figures
- Confirmation bias—selectively remembering things in a way that supports your beliefs and/or seeking facts that support what you want to be true
- Lazy thinking—not bothering to test accuracy, consistencies or other flawed inputs because it's too much work
- Fear or resistance to change
- Insecurity—lacking the confidence to admit when you are wrong or being unable to handle criticism
- Lack of knowledge or background information, which inhibits the ability to make good decisions
- Habit—it doesn't occur to you to think any differently
- Wishful thinking
- Environments that foster conformity

You will see many benefits from enhancing your critical thinking skills, both at work and in your personal life. An obvious benefit is that you will avoid the embarrassment of making a lot of bad decisions. Yes, you'll still make a few, but you will have more confidence to admit the mistake and learn from it so you don't repeat it. As you improve your skills, you'll find that you can deal with change more quickly and effectively, because you have the intellectual skills to assess the impact and resolve any difficulties resulting from the change. You may also find that you get along better with other people on work teams or in your circle of friends as you improve your critical thinking ability. You will be better able to understand and respect different points of view, react less emotionally when you have different opinions, and communicate your ideas and positions more clearly. All these benefits taken together can give you more self-confidence and self-satisfaction, and help you to live up to your full potential. So, is it worth it to commit to the long and difficult task of improving your critical thinking skills?

The Need for Knowledge

Both creative and critical thinking depend not only on the associated set of skills, but also on a depth of content knowledge. In other words, the more you know about a problem domain, the more outstanding the outputs of your creative and critical thinking will be. Breadth of knowledge is also key. Breakthroughs are often made when an expert in one domain sees parallels in another, which lead to analogous solutions. Daniel Willingham provides a fascinating illustration of this in his article, *Critical Thinking: Why is it so Hard to Teach* (*American Education*, Summer, 2007, citing Chen, Z., Mo, L., and Honomichl, R. (2004). "Having the memory of an elephant: Long-term retrieval and the use of analogues in problem solving," *Journal of Experimental Psychology: General*, 133, 415-433.)

His example shows how students of different cultures respond to a problem statement:

"A treasure hunter is going to explore a cave up on a hill near a beach. He suspected there might be many paths inside the cave so he was afraid he might get lost. Obviously, he did not have a map of the cave; all he had with him were some common items such as a flashlight and a bag. What could he do to make sure he did not get lost trying to get back out of the cave later?

The solution is to carry some sand with you in the bag, and leave a trail as you go, so you can trace your path back when you're ready to leave the cave. About 75 percent of American college students thought of this solution— but only 25 percent of Chinese students solved it. The experimenters suggested that Americans solved it because most grew up hearing the story of Hansel and Gretel, which includes the idea of leaving a trail as you travel to an unknown place in order to find your way back. The experimenters also gave subjects another puzzle based on a common Chinese folk tale, and the percentage of solvers from each culture reversed."

TAKE THE INITIATIVE

To be a high-quality thinker, you have to be motivated to become one. You can't be mentally lazy! Nor can "good enough" be a part of your vocabulary. Both creative and critical thinking make some people uneasy when it pushes them out of the comfort zone of their thinking, challenging what they've always believed to be true. You

---

Steps to Improve Your Thinking

To become more creative:

1. Play with creativity
2. Practice the exercise in this chapter
3. Schedule time to be creative
4. Keep challenging yourself to try new things
5. Collaborate
6. Learn to detect barriers to new ideas and innovation

To think more critically:

1. Listen to opposing views to the way you see the world
2. Play devil's advocate
3. Catch your confirmation bias
4. Pay attention to your emotions
5. Find the middle ground in arguments
6. Detect barriers to critical thinking in others, then yourself

see this throughout history, with people who clung to the idea that the universe rotated around the earth or that the world is flat. Politics is full of voters who blindly accept the party line because it reinforces what they want to believe and makes them feel good. This chapter alone can't teach you how to become a high-quality thinker.

But if you're up to the challenge, here are some steps you can take to start you on your way.

Take the Initiative to Become More Creative

1. Learn to play with creativity

The creative process should be fun. Turn off the electronic entertainment. TV, video games, surfing the web and similar activities are mind-numbing. At first you may be bored. That's not bad! Let the boredom inspire you to come up with new ways to have fun. Don't judge what you come up with—that's a quick way to stifle your creativity. Dare to be silly! Besides the possibility of coming up with some really great ideas, you may discover another benefit: a more youthful, flexible mind as you get older.

2. Practice the exercise described in this chapter

Randomly pick two words out of the dictionary and see how you can put them together.

3. Schedule time to be creative—and use the full allotted time.

4. Keep challenging yourself to try new things

New experiences give you more ideas to draw from. Even if you end up not enjoying everything you try, new things offer you more possibilities and keep your perspective fresh.

5. Collaborate

Use your friends' and coworkers' ideas as a springboard to other ideas. Draw on their database of knowledge.

6. Learn to detect barriers to new ideas and innovation

Start by noticing when people around you put up barriers. Listen for the telltale phrases listed in Figure 9.2. Once you can spot resistance in others, look for it in yourself.

Figure 9.2: Barrier Phrases to Creativity

We've always done it this way.

Management would never approve.

That's silly.

What a stupid idea.

That's too risky.

That would never work.

Impossible.

There's no way.

That's not our culture.

This is good enough.

Let's get back to reality.

Don't rock the boat.

I don't see how that relates.

I'll think about it when I'm not busy.

Take the Initiative to Think More Critically

1. Listen to opposing views to the way you see the world

Listen to a radio or TV station that tends to lean in the opposite direction from your beliefs. Challenge yourself to see how different viewpoints might have merit. Try walking in the shoes of people who think differently from you.

2. Play devil's advocate

Actually, this can be pretty annoying to family and friends, so you might want to tell them what you're doing. Even if you agree with the speaker, challenge assumptions and "facts." You all might learn something. Play devil's advocate with yourself.

3. Catch your confirmation bias

Confirmation bias occurs when you seek out or notice data that confirms a belief you hold, and tune out or discount data that challenges or disproves what you want to be true. This behavior reinforces the preconception, which could be incorrect. It does not help you to see all sides of the issue and get closer to reality. When seeking data to support your positions, look for an equal number of facts that challenge them. You may not change your mind, but you will open your mind to the possibility.

4. Pay attention to your emotions

Learn to sense an emotional response to a situation, and then try to detach and deal only with facts. By the way, emotions can be valid inputs to decision making, but need to be recognized as such.

5. Find the middle ground in arguments

Go for "win-win" solutions, where everyone benefits. To do this successfully, you need to understand points of view other than your own and persist in finding a resolution that meets everyone's needs. A true "win-win" solution is not just a weak compromise.

6. Detect barriers to critical thinking in others, then yourself

Just as with creative thinking, people—usually unintentionally—are fairly set in the way they think about the world. It can take a lifetime to become a good critical thinker. Putting up barriers won't get you there. Look for the obstacles listed in Figure 9.3. Try removing them, one at a time.

Figure 9.3: Barrier Phrases to Critical Thinking

You don't understand.

If those people said it, it must be wrong.

If those people said it, it must be right.

You don't really believe that, do you?

We don't have time to study this.

Who would think such a thing?

I know what I'm talking about. I've been doing this for years.

I know I'm right.

No one in their right mind would ever think this.

SUMMARY

Truly great thinkers are hard to find. To become one requires literally years of disciplined thinking. The more you practice, the better you get. Sounds like a lot of work—but the effort is well worth it. Every organization values its best problem solvers. They keep the organization in business and give it its edge. They are the last to go (if they leave at all) in a downsizing situation. Think of what you get when you don't have good creative and critical thinkers: mediocrity, at best. Poor thinking usually wastes time and money, and produces low-quality results.

FAQs

Q: *I'm always coming up with new ways to do things, but my boss is never interested in hearing about them. What should I do?*

A: It could be that your boss is one of those people who are uncomfortable with change. If that is the case, you'll have to slow down a little with your suggestions to allow him to warm up to your ideas. Start with one recommendation. Explain how it could be implemented. Be specific about what steps are needed and what the benefits of the change will be. Offer to do some of the work yourself—possibly on your own time to test the concepts. The point is to take as much risk out of your proposal as possible and to make your boss as comfortable as possible with the new idea. After you're successful with one change, your boss will probably be more comfortable letting you try the next. But don't go too fast! And if your boss is especially resistant to change, you may have to try this approach more than once.

Another reason your boss might be resisting the change is a perceived lack of time. When people are under a time crunch, they usually prefer to follow a tried-and-true approach, rather than risk a failure that will only take more time to correct. If that's the case in your workplace, you might offer to try your recommendations on your own time. No one likes to give up free time, but if the ideas are really good, with a good chance of success, giving up a few hours of free time now might be a great investment in your future.

To be honest, it could also be that your ideas aren't as good as you think. Creativity and excellent critical thinking skills require a strong knowledge base, which as a new person you may not have had time to acquire. The ripple effect of your ideas may not be apparent to you—financial implications, contractual constraints or even organizational psychology impacts. Don't give up on coming up with ways to do things better. But before you offer your next suggestion, try to think through who and what would be affected by the change. Use your critical thinking skills to determine how good the idea is: Do the pros really outweigh the cons? If so, try the other suggestions in this answer.

Q: *I hate making decisions when I don't have all the information I need. But around here, everyone seems to make snap decisions. Why is this?*

A: Those decisions being made around you may not be as "snap" as they appear. Your more experienced coworkers probably have more information about the business than you, so they have more knowledge to bring to the decision than you do at this point. They may have seen similar situations in the past, so they have a good idea how things will turn out. Or they may know the people impacted by the decision— management, the next employees in the process or clients— better than you, so they have a better idea of how they will react or what their needs are.

Your coworkers may also have gotten used to making decisions based on ambiguous, partial or changing data. In many work environments, it's impossible to have all the information needed to make a decision, so you have to do the best with what you know at the moment. If you were to take the time to assemble all the information you need to make a decision, you might find that you're never done collecting the data, because the facts associated with your situation keep changing. The next time you see an employee you respect make a "snap" decision, it might be worth your time to ask her how she came to that decision. Also, spend time really learning about the job you're in—not just what you have to do, but how it fits into the bigger picture of your department, your company and your industry.

Q: *My business isn't very creative. How do I practice being innovative?*

A: Your organization may be in a field that is not generally considered as creative as an arts-related business, but that doesn't mean there aren't opportunities to be innovative. There may be an opportunity to create a new feature in the products and services your organization offers, if not to create brand-new offerings. You might be innovative in the way you deliver products and services to your customers, perhaps expanding your online interface with your customer community. If you read Chapter 4, *Business Acumen*, you know that one goal shared by all organizations is to reduce expenses and increase revenues. Is there a way to improve your processes so that the outputs are produced faster, cheaper or with higher quality?

Remember that innovation is not just for the workplace. Most likely, you encounter all kinds of personal challenges—in your personal finances, housing, relationships or career planning. All can benefit from creative thinking.

Q: *It seems like the decisions around here are based on emotion, not logic. They're terrible! Can I change things? Should I change things?*

A: Your perception that most of the decisions in your workplace are based on emotion may or may not be true. Your supervisor and coworkers may have a bias toward emotional responses, but emotion may not be the only source of the decisions. An example of this is a layoff situation. First-line managers aren't always involved in the decision-making process, but they are often the ones who have to communicate the bad news to the impacted employees. It is an extremely emotional experience for both the manager and the people who are let go. In the process, emotional rather than logical reasons may be expressed. However, the actual decision to conduct layoffs and the process for deciding who will be impacted are usually far less emotional, based on practical, legal and other constraints. Most employees would not be privy to the decision process and might only see the emotional side.

On the other hand, you may be absolutely correct that your organization lacks good critical thinking skills. You can't force your boss or your coworkers to make logical decisions, but you might be able to influence them in that direction. Try asking questions about the issue to help drive them toward more well-reasoned decision making. For example, you might ask about the root cause of the problem or the factors that were considered when making the decision. When you ask the question, you must be careful to demonstrate genuine interest in the answer. If you come across as a know-it-all who is asking questions to point out the weaknesses, you won't succeed. You can also model better decision making in the areas for which you are responsible. If you produce better results from a more logical approach, and are able to clearly and accurately communicate your outcomes (without emotion!), you may find others trying to emulate your style.

CHAPTER 10

Problem Solving Part 2: A Process

> **In this Chapter**
>
> - What exactly is a problem?
> - Key steps toward solving any problem
> - Problem solving requires both creativity and critical thinking

"A problem is a chance for you to do your best."

~ Duke Ellington ~

WHY YOU SHOULD CARE

The previous chapter introduced you to two types of thinking required to be an effective problem solver: creative thinking and critical thinking. Developing these skills isn't enough; you also have to be able to apply them. This chapter describes a process you can use to consistently find great solutions to any type of problem.

Why is it important to become a great problem solver to succeed on the job? Work is basically a series of problems to be solved. Consider two examples:

- Just as a telecommunications company is about to start a large critical upgrade, the project lead is injured in a skiing accident and will be out for several weeks. Should the company delay the upgrade (and risk losing customers)? Or, should it proceed with a less experienced project lead who might not be as successful?

- Despite a multimillion-dollar facility improvement, a hotel can't attract enough conventions, weddings and other large parties to stay in business. Why not? Should management look at its personnel and the quality of service offered? Or, is there a problem with location or marketing?

If you want to be a highly valued employee, you'll need to be a valued contributor to solving your organization's problems. Plus, the better you are at problem solving, the more interesting and important the problems assigned to you will be. That means a more rewarding work experience for you. If, on the other hand, you're responsible for a solution that fails, you'll probably feel embarrassed and may have to spend several weeks repairing your reputation. You could even lose your job if the failure could easily have been avoided, wasted a lot of company resources, or lost valuable customers.

Take the case of Jake, a new employee who was assigned to get his company's cell phone costs under control. When the company first issued cell phones to its employees, it failed to record who was assigned which phones, resulting in all kinds of problems. For example, the company was unable to identify which employees were abusing their phone usage minutes. Even worse, the company didn't even know if all employees who were assigned phones were still with the company! Without much thought, Jake came up with a quick solution. He told the company's telecommunication provider to shut off everyone's cell phones. Jake reasoned that only valid employees would request to have their phones turned back on, and the company would then be able to record who was assigned which numbers. Unfortunately, it turned out that the company president was traveling overseas at the time of Jake's solution, relying on his company cell phone as his primary means of communication during his trip. He suddenly found himself without the ability to conveniently do business via phone as he traveled. He was furious! When the president got back in his office, he demanded to know why he had lost his phone usage. Within twenty-four hours, Jake found himself unemployed. If Jake had given his assignment more thought, would he have come up with a better solution that wouldn't have cost him his job? Let's hope so.

Problems in the workplace are generally different from those you faced in school. Depending on your area of study, you may have been used to problems with a single solution (for example, some math problems). Most problems (and solutions) in school were fairly well-bounded. In other words, input to the problem may have been limited: an assigned set of readings, for example. Your solution was probably well defined: an analysis paper had to be ten typed pages, double-spaced with one-inch margins, using a ten or twelve point font. In the workplace, problems are usually a little more ambiguous. In fact, sometimes problems aren't even identified—part of the job is to figure out if a problem exists! Most problems will have several different solutions. The best solution may depend on current (and changing) conditions—like the changing price of raw materials, or evolving information technology. Your job will be to define what the problem really is, determine the best way to approach it, figure out where to find resources, evaluate alternatives against a set of criteria (that you may have to define), and, finally, decide when you're done solving the problem.

WHAT IS A PROBLEM?
WHAT IS PROBLEM SOLVING?

You can find many definitions of the word "problem," but one that seems to work well is that a problem is an obstacle to achieving a goal or desired outcome. For example, a grocery chain whose goal is to keep prices low (with the larger goal of attracting customers) is challenged by higher supplier costs. A local school board, whose goal is to provide high-quality public education without raising school taxes, suddenly doesn't have enough classroom space because of a dramatic increase in the township's school-age population.

Problems, by definition, are undesirable conditions—and depending on the situation, that may be a gross understatement! Therefore, when problems arise, many people are inclined to jump into implementing a "quick fix" that works only if they're lucky. Another common reaction is an emotional solution—one that feels good based on personal bias but doesn't necessarily make the situation better. Quick fixes and emotional responses often just delay finding an effective solution, and may even make the problem worse.

To solve problems more logically and thoroughly, try using the following steps:

Define the Problem

The most important step! Make sure you address the right issue before you start work. Include some description. Avoid jumping to causes or solutions.

Identify the Root Cause(s)

Use creative thinking to fully explore possible contributing factors to the problem.

Select the Most Significant Cause(s)

Use critical thinking to evaluate which causes contribute most significantly to the problem.

Generate Solutions

Use creative thinking to brainstorm as many possible solutions as possible. Challenge yourself to go beyond the obvious. Avoid judging your ideas.

Select Best Solution

Use critical thinking to define your evaluation criteria and apply them to your list of possible solutions.

Plan & Implement

Follow the process in Chapter 6, *Planning Your Assignment*, to plan and implement your solution.

Evaluate Results

Check that the solution worked and did not create any new problems. If so, use the process again. Think critically to determine how to improve your solution.

Einstein once said, "If I had an hour to solve a problem I'd spend fifty-five minutes thinking about the problem and five minutes thinking about solutions." Smart man! Too many people are either so eager to start problem solving that they don't study the problem first, or they don't think they have time to study it. The very first step is to clearly define the problem so you solve the right issue. Stating the problem in your own words will help get confirmation from your supervisor that you are, in fact, working on the right problem. Hearing the problem stated differently might also help your supervisor clarify the problem.

One way to describe a problem is in terms of the goal your organization is failing to achieve. The more you can quantify the problem, the better. For example, rather than say, "Our art center isn't attracting the number of students we hoped for," a better statement would be, "Our budget is based on a goal of ten students per class, but we are only averaging seven per class." Another way to describe a problem is in terms of "too much" or "not enough" of something, for example, "too much time" or "not enough money." A problem stated in these terms could look like: "Not enough of our engineers are following our company's stated design procedures, which means that we could lose our certification and, consequently, our contracts with our key customers."

When defining the problem, it is also important to provide information that helps describe the problem as completely as possible. You should include:

- **_Elaboration:_** Why is the current situation a problem and how does it adversely impacts your organization? For example, in the case of the art center described above, elaboration of the problem could include more details on how much money the center is losing, or whether diminishing class size is a sudden problem or a gradual trend over several years.

- **_The criticality of the problem:_** How badly do you need to solve it?

- **_Any constraints:_** Are there limitations due to: time, funding, legal issues, contractual terms, etc.?

- *Assumptions you've made:* What assumptions have been identified and have some been missed? (This is hard to do, but you'll find it easier if you're practicing good critical thinking skills, as described in the previous chapter.)

At this point in the process, avoid identifying both causes and solutions. Your goal is to define the problem as objectively and completely as possible. You want a strong and unbiased starting point for your problem solving.

Figure 10.1 contains a problem description for a real company we'll call The XYZ Corporation. XYZ faced staffing problems. It was particularly unsuccessful in recruiting top-quality graduating college students. XYZ created a team of young employees to solve the problem.

Assigned Problem: Within the constraints of federal regulations governing the business, what can the organization do to improve our standing as an employer of choice with top-rated college graduates?

Restated Problem: Our company is not able to attract and hire enough talented college graduates.

Current Situation:

- Top millennial graduates are needed to staff the growing business and replace retiring baby boomers.
- The needs of millennials are vastly different from those of previous generations.

Assumptions:

- "Improve our standing" means succeed at hiring more top college graduates.
- Compensation (for example, sign-on bonuses) is restricted by government regulations.
- The organization is competing against many different industries for targeted graduates.
- Generational differences are leading to problems in recruitment and retention.

Figure 10.1: The XYZ Corporation Staffing Problem Statement

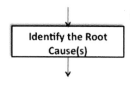

Once all interested parties agree on the problem statement, you can think more creatively about possible causes of the problem. As discussed in the previous chapter, the "obvious" cause of a problem might not be the most significant cause.

Take, for example, Ryan, who seriously injured his shoulder when he took a bad fall down a flight of stairs. When the pain failed to subside after several weeks and extended to his chest, his doctor sent Ryan for an MRI. The test revealed that the chest pain had nothing to do with the shoulder injury. Unbeknownst to Ryan, he had a large tumor on his esophagus that coincidentally started causing him pain at the time of the fall. Happily, the tumor was benign, and Ryan is now fine.

In this step, you want to fully explore all the possible causes of your problem. In the workplace, there are often many contributing factors. One way to find them is to use a procedure called "The 5 Whys." If you have young family members or have babysat little kids, you've probably seen this in action. Just ask the question "why" each time you come up with a possible cause, trying to dig down at least five levels of "why." Another procedure you can use if you're working in a group is simple brainstorming, described in Appendix A. If you get stuck at any point, try looking at the problem from different angles. Try asking the following questions:

- ✔ When did this problem arise? Did it come about gradually or suddenly?

- ✔ What changed inside the organization that might have contributed to the problem?

- ✔ What changed outside the organization?

- ✔ What are the financial dimensions of the problem? (For example, did the economy change? Does something cost more? Were budgets reallocated?)

- ✔ What are the technical dimensions? (For example, are competitors using more cutting edge technology? Does your workforce know how to use new technology? Do your customers?)

✔ What are the human dimensions? (For example, have customers' tastes changed? Do generational differences factor in?
Do global differences?)

If you do a good job with this step, you'll come up with many possible causes—maybe an overwhelming number. Sort the potential
causes into categories. They will be more manageable if they're organized. However, do not start combining causes into broader and
broader, more abstract concepts. It will be harder to evaluate and
later solve the problem if the causes you identify are too general.

Figure 10.2 contains just a few of the causes the XZY Company's team
came up with for its college recruiting problem. The real list had over
100 ideas on it.

Some obvious ideas:

- Poor or untrained recruiters
- Salaries are lower than the national average
- Business isn't appealing to new grads
- Location isn't appealing to new grads
- Products aren't very interesting

Some more original ideas:

- Not enough spirit wear
- Too few social activities after work
- Not advertising on websites visited by college students
- Recruiters aren't on the beach at spring break
- Not offering phones, laptops, etc., to recruits

Ideas that show promise:

- Not enough on-campus presence so college grads could get to know
  the company
- Not marketing some of the company benefits that would appeal to
  younger employees, such as flexible work weeks
- Professional cyber presence was missing
- No activities or policies that indicate that the company respects
  work-life balance

Figure 10.2: Sample List of Solutions for XYZ Company's Problem

This step returns you to critical thinking. If the problem you're working on is large, with many causes, you may not have the resources to address every one of them. You have to decide which causes contribute most significantly to the problem and work on them first. Just addressing the biggest causes may be enough to reduce the problem to a manageable level. Conversely, why waste time working on a cause that only makes a small dent in solving the problem?

If your problem is easily quantified, finding the cause with the most impact should be fairly easy. List the causes and their impact, and choose the greatest contributors. To illustrate, let's say a company thinks its IT expenses are going out of control. The company could apply a ten percent reduction across the board, which might cut some highly critical resources and not cut enough excess in "nice-to-have" services. Alternatively, the company might have heard that "everyone" is slashing mainframe processing costs, and direct its IT department to do the same. If the company's mainframe processing is only a tiny part of its budget, reducing or even eliminating those costs isn't going to make much of a difference in the overall budget. The best approach might be to list all the elements contributing to the IT budget: mainframe processing, network expenses, personal and laptop computers, telecommunications, etc. Next, calculate what percentage of the total budget each individual element expends. Finally, focus attention on reducing the size of the big-ticket contributors. There's no point in spending a lot of time and energy reducing the cost of mainframe processing if it turns out to be only two percent of the entire budget. Reduce those costs after the major cost reductions have been made.

Many problems are not easily quantifiable, especially when they involve people and their motivations or choices. For example, what motivates teenagers to buy one brand of clothing over another? (Or, what motivates them not to buy your brand, if your problem is declining sales?) The motivation is rarely the price!

When causes are not quantifiable, you'll have to rely on your critical thinking tools. Finding trends and similar situations might help. If you have the time and money (and the problem warrants it), polls, surveys and focus groups can provide useful information. For smaller problems, your own judgment, coupled with input from an experienced coworker or two, will probably be sufficient.

Figure 10.3 shows an abridged example of how the XYZ team used a process called "multi-voting" to select which causes contributed most significantly to their company's recruiting problem. This team had to rely heavily on their own judgment. Since the team was composed of recent college graduates, they probably had a better idea of the impact of the causes than their more experienced coworkers. Knowledge of the problem space significantly improves problem-solving outcomes, as long as those with more experience don't let their thinking get locked into what they've always seen or done in the past.

Item	Round 1	Round 2	Round 3
Poor or untrained recruiters	2	0	0
Salaries lower than average	6	2	0
Business not appealing to new grads	1	0	0
Location not appealing to new grads	2	0	0
Vague product descriptions	1	0	0
Not enough spirit wear	2	0	0
Too few social activities after work	4	1	0
Not advertising on websites college students visit	4	2	1
Recruiters not on the beach during Spring break	0	0	0
Not offering phones, laptops or high sign-on bonuses	3	1	0
Not enough college presence	8	8	3
Not marketing benefits that appeal to younger employers (e.g. flexible hours)	6	7	3
Professional cyber presence missing	4	1	0
Not demonstrating respect for employee work/life balance	7	8	3

Figure 10.3: XYZ Root Cause Selection Outcome

Generate Solutions

This step is where you can be your most creative. You want to generate as many possible solutions to your problem as you can. Appendix A describes a process for brainstorming as a group, but you can adapt this to working by yourself. There are two keys to success when brainstorming as a group. First, you want to go for as many ideas as possible. Second, you need to avoid judging the ideas, since prejudging tends to shut down the brainstorming process. Studies have shown that the first set of ideas generated contains the obvious solutions, which may not be particularly creative, and have probably been tried before. Go with one of these solutions, and your result will probably be "good enough," but not very innovative or exciting. When you get past the obvious solutions, the next set of ideas tends to be silly or ridiculous. Go with one of these solutions, and you probably won't be taken seriously. The real "gems" tend to be found in the next set you generate. Remember from the previous chapter that creativity is the process of combining two concepts that haven't previously gone together, to produce something interesting or useful. At this point in your brainstorming, you are combining the boring, obvious solutions with the ridiculous solutions to come up with truly innovative and workable solutions. Don't stop brainstorming until you reach this point!

Figure 10.4 contains a list of possible solutions that the XYZ team generated for one of the causes to their recruiting problem. Could you have done better?

Select Best Solution

We're back to critical thinking. Before you choose your best solution(s), you need to define the evaluation criteria against which you will assess your solutions. In the workplace, some common criteria include:

- **Cost to implement:** Is the solution affordable? Does the solution cost less than the cost of the problem? (Don't laugh—people really forget to consider this.)

- **Time to implement:** Can you put the solution in place soon enough to solve the problem?

Some obvious ideas:

- Support more career fairs
- Put ads in targeted school newspapers
- Put ads on radio stations college students listen to
- Recruit on campuses twice a year
- Build stronger relationship with career centers

Some more original ideas:

- Set up spring break hospitality tables
- Sponsor parties at target schools
- Get a company link on target schools' websites
- Pay young employees to recruit a friend

Ideas that show promise:

- Offer more summer internships
- Set up a program for XYZ employees to tutor/mentor local university students
- Fund student projects
- Mentor student projects
- Support on-campus professional societies

Figure 10.4: Sample Results of XYZ Company's Brainstorming Session

- ***Availability of resources:*** Resources can cover a wide variety of inputs. Do you have enough skilled staff to implement the solution? Do you have the right equipment? Sufficient computing power?
- ***Risk:*** What are the chances the solution might fail? What could go wrong? What would the impact of a failure be?

These are just a few factors for you to consider. Do not limit yourself to these. Think about what is important to your organization and its customers. There may be human factors, like resistance to change, that you will need to consider.

Appendix A describes how an "impact matrix" can help identify best solutions. Figure 10.5 shows how the XYZ team used an impact matrix to choose their final recommendations.

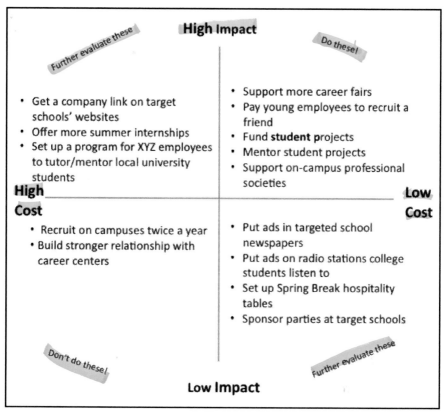

High Impact

Further evaluate these

Do these!

- Get a company link on target schools' websites
- Offer more summer internships
- Set up a program for XYZ employees to tutor/mentor local university students

- Support more career fairs
- Pay young employees to recruit a friend
- Fund **student** projects
- Mentor student projects
- Support on-campus professional societies

High Cost

Low Cost

- Recruit on campuses twice a year
- Build stronger relationship with career centers

- Put ads in targeted school newspapers
- Put ads on radio stations college students listen to
- Set up Spring Break hospitality tables
- Sponsor parties at target schools

Don't do these!

Further evaluate these

Low Impact

Figure 10.5: XYZ team's impact matrix analysis of the possible solutions to their recruiting problems

Plan & Implement

If you followed the advice in Chapter 5, *Understanding Your Assignment*, you know if your task was to recommend a set of solutions to your supervisor or if you're supposed to proceed with implementing the solution. You also know what reviews and approvals you need along the way. If your assignment includes implementing the solution(s), Chapter 6, *Planning Your Assignment*, describes a process that will maximize your success.

Evaluate Results

You're not done problem solving until you see that your solution actually worked. The result may be immediate, or it might be several months until the result is known. For longer-term solutions, you may at least be able to see if the problem is starting to improve. Besides making sure your solution really fixed the problem, you need to figure out if you created any new, unexpected problems. For example, what if the XYZ Company's recruiting solutions were so successful that its human resources staff couldn't process the resulting flood of job applications quickly enough? The introduction to this chapter says work is a series of problems. Start the process over again and figure out how to help the human resources staff process all those applications.

TAKE THE INITIATIVE

Most new employees are motivated by solving problems that are important to their organization. Sometimes, recent grads are overly eager to work on critical issues and get frustrated when these challenges are assigned to more experienced coworkers. Regardless of your ambitions, every job entails some degree of problem solving.

> ### Steps to Improve Your Problem Solving
>
> 1. Learn as much as possible about your job and workplace
>
> 2. Develop your problem definition skills
>
> 3. Practice the problem-solving paradigm described in this chapter
>
> 4. When you think you're pretty good at problem solving, tackle a small but meaningful problem in the office

Here are some steps you can follow to enhance your skills.

1. Learn as much as possible about your job and workplace

Problem solving requires a combination of both original creative ideas and good judgment. To exercise good judgment, you need knowledge about many dimensions of your workplace. An elegant automated solution may not be well received by a no-so-technically comfortable customer base. To recognize this, you would need to know about both the technology required for your solution and your customer's comfort level with that technology. For example, a doctor's office decided it could eliminate staff and associated expenses by providing only electronic interfaces for routine questions and appointments. Good idea? It lost many patients who preferred to talk to a real person about their medical matters. Did the savings from the technical solution make up for the amount of business lost?

It's impossible to list every dimension of your job that you need to become familiar with, but you can start with:

- **The "technical" skills** required in your workplace, including both knowledge and tools.

- **The processes** (work flow) used to get things done. These occur at low and high levels. Know what they are and how you fit in.

- **The people** you work with—their responsibilities, their strengths and weaknesses, and their style preferences.

- **Your organization's products and services**—what they are, their features and benefits.

- **Your customers** (internal and external). Find out their expectations of you, their hot buttons, their goals, their personality styles and their preferred ways to communicate.

2. Develop your problem definition skills

You won't come up with a good and acceptable solution if you've solved the wrong problem! Try defining any problem in terms of "too much" or "not enough" (as described earlier in the chapter). If you're dealing with a very complex problem, try dividing it into smaller, contributing problems. Then try defining the smaller problems in terms of "too much" or "not enough."

3. Practice the problem-solving paradigm described in this chapter

Start with a small problem in your personal life. For example, you can't find enough time to exercise, or you can't seem to find ways to save enough money for the new car you want. Write down your answers to each of the steps. Even if you just jot things down on a scrap of paper, the process of writing forces you to follow the steps. Evaluate your results. Getting better?

4. When you think you're pretty good at problem solving, tackle a small but meaningful problem in the office

You should probably ask your manager's permission before you start, especially if it will take time away from your other responsibilities. Remember to use good communication skills (see Chapters 11 and 12 on effective communications) to report progress.

SUMMARY

You're in a terrific position to be an asset to your organization as a problem solver. As a new employee, you have a fresh perspective and haven't become set in your ways about how to do things. However, you need to keep in mind that you have limited knowledge about your business, what has worked before and what hasn't—and why. Remember also that your new ideas might be threatening. Most human beings don't like change. But don't let that stop you! Practice the skills described in this chapter, and look forward to making a positive difference in your new organization.

FAQs

Q: *I don't have time to follow this process every time a problem comes up. Can I skip steps?*

A: Here's a question to ask yourself: If you skip steps and do a poor job solving the problem assigned to you, will you have time to do the work again? In an emergency, or when you have a short deadline, it's easy to believe that the best thing to do is jump into a solution. Often that's a mistake and things don't work out. Instead of skipping steps, shorten them. Rather than an exhaustive brainstorming of root causes and possible solutions, your situation may warrant "good enough" ideas. If you haven't yet gained extensive knowledge of your problem area, you might shorten the critical thinking steps by getting help from more experienced coworkers. In all cases, use good judgment in scaling your problem-solving process to the size and criticality of the problem. It would be silly to spend several hours problem solving a paper jam in the copier machine.

In all cases, be like Einstein and think about the problem before acting on a solution. The most critical step you cannot skip is a good problem definition. Sometimes, a good understanding of the problem is all it takes to come up with a speedy solution.

Q: *I want to work on important problems that really make a difference to my organization, not some of the low-level work assigned to me. Is there something I can do to get more challenging assignments, or should I look for a new job where I have a more important role?*

A: There are two things you need to do to participate in solving your organization's most critical problems. First, you need to gain a deeper and broader knowledge of your business. The academic knowledge and skills you developed in school are not enough. Your organization's critical problems are likely to also require knowledge of work processes, customer requirements, customer personalities, financial plans and impacts, government regulations, and resource availability—just to name a few possibilities. As a new employee, you're not likely to have this knowledge. If there's a particular aspect of your business that especially interests you, start diving in there. Read, research and talk to people. Sit in on meetings when you can. Make it known that you want to learn as much as possible about this area. Your boss should be happy with your interest and motivation.

The second thing you need to do is develop a track record of being a good problem solver. Associated with big problems is big risk. Putting yourself in your management's shoes, would you risk the company's reputation, a large portion of your budget, or a key customer account on an unproven talent? Most managers would not. But that is not to say that you can't find a role that continues to grow. Produce great solutions to the smaller problems assigned to you, and continue to grow your knowledge. Volunteer to take on low-risk problems that earn you some visibility. It won't be long before you're working on the more critical issues.

Q: *I see problems everywhere in my business, and my boss agrees. But he isn't very interested in addressing most of them. What's his problem?*

A: Organizations and individuals only have so many resources. We're limited on time, money, talent, energy and other things we need or want. Every organization has an ongoing set of problems that are solved, are overcome by events, or remain a tolerable annoyance. Your boss has consciously, or unconsciously, prioritized the issues in your work area and is only addressing the most significant ones he can resolve with his available resources. There could be a good reason the problems you're identifying are lower on his priority list. If that's the case and you think you have the capacity to work on one or two, volunteer. Your boss will appreciate your initiative and will be happy when those problems are gone. Just make sure the higher priority work in your job jar gets done, too. On the other hand, with your fresh perspective and recent academic education, you may see that a problem has more severe ramifications than your boss realizes. In that case, use good critical thinking skills to make a logical argument for why the problem needs to be addressed now—and volunteer to help.

SECTION IV

Interpersonal Skills

Interactions with coworkers, managers and customers sometimes play an even larger role than technical competency in defining workplace success. While some professions require more interaction than others, no one works in a vacuum. Decision making requires sharing information and ideas to persuade individuals or groups to act on your recommendations. Section IV presents an overview of the skills necessary to get your ideas heard and to develop effective relationships with coworkers, managers and clients.

Chapter 11: Written Workplace Communications—Can you write a concise message with clear objectives, in various formats? This chapter introduces you to a basic communications model, and identifies the pitfalls and pointers for successful communication, from email to formal reports.

Chapter 12: Spoken Workplace Communications—Most business communication takes place in spoken forums, from informal conversations to meetings and presentations. Poor oral skills limit your effectiveness, as well as limit your career. Building on Chapter 11, this chapter identifies barriers to effective oral communication and provides tips for improving your listening and speaking skills.

Chapter 13: Managing Office Relationships—Getting along with people at work differs greatly from college relationships, and is far more important to your success than it was in school. This chapter provides a framework for building relationships with coworkers, teammates and supervisors.

Chapter 14: Managing Customer Relationships—Take your customers for granted, and they may take their business elsewhere. The model in this chapter will help you develop the skills you need to establish lasting relationships with your customers.

CHAPTER 11

Written Workplace Communications

"Unclear writing comes from unclear thinking. If you can't put an idea down on paper, chances are you don't have an idea."

~ Andy Rooney ~

WHY YOU SHOULD CARE

Joan works for a large electronics firm as an electrical engineer. Her supervisor asked her to write a position paper outlining her recommendations on how a new technology for testing circuits might be used to improve the company's productivity. The paper she produced gave a long dissertation on the evolution of the technology and how it works. Joan had always prided herself on being a good writer, so she was surprised when her supervisor expressed disappointment with her work. Why? While well-written, Joan's paper didn't provide her supervisor with the information he needed to make a decision whether or not to pursue the new technology.

Writing for business purposes differs from the writing you did for your academic assignments. In school, writing was intended to demonstrate your knowledge of the subject matter, typically to an audience of one—your professor. Business writing addresses a broader audience, with the intention of producing a specific action, such as approval of a funding request or acceptance of a recommendation. In this type of writing, understanding your reader's motivations and needs becomes as important in crafting your message as the subject itself.

U.S. businesses often cite written communications as their employees' weakest skill. If you cannot get your message across clearly and concisely, you risk appearing unprofessional. The risk to your company is lower productivity, lost contracts, and possibly safety hazards. As you advance in your career, the types of written communications you use will become more varied and of greater impact. Since communicating is an integral part of the workplace and critical to your advancement, the time to start practicing is now!

THE BASIC ELEMENTS OF WRITTEN COMMUNICATION

Common definitions of communication include the "imparting or interchange" of thoughts, opinions, or information by speech, writing, or signs. In the workplace, written thoughts, opinions, and information are exchanged among coworkers, as well as up and down the management chain. Organizations also communicate in writing to the outside world—to customers, suppliers, vendors and investors. These written communications take many forms from email messages, memos, letters, reports, manuals and other documents to websites and texting. It is wise to remember that, in our digital world, all written communications should be considered public and accessible to just about anyone at anytime.

There are three elements involved in every communication: the sender, the message, and the receiver. The success of your communication depends on how well you manage these elements.

Figure 11.1: A Basic Model of the Elements of Communications

Element 1: The Sender

Effective communication starts with knowing your purpose. What are you trying to achieve? Is your intent to:

- *Inform?* You may be sharing facts: "The shipment was sent on November 22."

- *Request?* You may be asking for information: "Please send me a price list and specification for …"

- *Persuade?* You may be recruiting someone to a position: "Please consider the low cost and high quality of our product…"

State your purpose up front. This may seem obvious, but a surprising number of new and inexperienced employees fail to do this. Your purpose for communicating drives every other element of your communication: its recipients, urgency, medium, length, tone, and language. If you are unclear about your purpose, don't send the message! Otherwise, you risk communicating your confusion and leaving a bad impression with those who receive your message.

Element 2: The Receiver

Once you know your reason for communicating, you have to decide who will receive the message. Ask yourself these questions:

- *Who needs to receive this message?* Is this the right recipient or set of recipients for the intended outcome?

- *Why does the receiver need this message?* What response do you expect from the recipient? Is it a specific action? An immediate response? General learning? Does your expected response fall within the recipient's area of responsibilities?

- **What does the receiver need to know?** Communicate only information relevant to the recipient's position and area of expertise. For example, an architect doesn't necessarily need the same schedule and budget information as his or her project manager. The architect probably needs to know aspects of the schedule and budget that relate to his or her work, but not information that relates to every member of the project team.

- **What additional material does the recipient need in order to respond as expected?** Are there supporting facts? Background information? A relevant chronology of events? Other important circumstances that motivated you to send the message?

Finally, make sure your reader understands, or is able to "decode," the message. Some questions to ask are:

- **Does your receiver understand:**
  - ✔ **Your Words?** Your receiver could have a different educational level or speak English as a second language.
  - ✔ **Your colloquialisms, acronyms or jargon?** Your receiver might come from a different region or a different company or industry, where people use different colloquialisms, acronyms or jargon.
  - ✔ **Analogies and examples?** If your receiver is not a sports enthusiast, he or she might not understand a baseball analogy.

- **What is your receiver's attitude toward the topic of your message?** If just mentioning the topic makes your receiver angry, you might want to keep your message brief, so he or she can quickly grasp the message and be done with it. If the subject is a favorite of the recipient, you can afford to expand a little on the message with interesting relevant information.

- **How does your recipient prefer to receive data?** Detailed or summarized? Audibly or visually? In graphics or in words?

Your message will be more effective if it is presented in your recipient's preferred style.

Element 3: The Message

The final and most obvious element in writing is the message you want to convey. Unlike conversations, where you can read non-verbal or visual cues (for example, facial expressions, body language or tone of voice), written communications are essentially one-way. This makes it harder to know if you got your message across.

Be aware that your written message becomes a permanent record that may be read in the future by someone other than your intended reader. For example, it is not unusual in corporate legal investigations, like the Enron case, for old email messages to be retrieved from company back-up and storage devices and used as evidence in a court of law.

For these reasons, take care in crafting your written message. Here are some things to consider:

- **Have you stated your message clearly and completely?** Is your purpose for communicating easily understandable? Did you avoid extraneous and possibly distracting information or opinions? Did you convey all relevant data?

- **Have you stated your message concisely?** Reread your message before sending it to make sure that sentences don't contain unnecessary words and paragraphs don't contain unnecessary sentences. Did you avoid pretentious words and complex sentences? Does your message get to the point or does it ramble?

- **Is your message logically organized?** The message should easily lead your reader to your point. Does the information flow in an order that makes sense, or do you bounce from topic to topic?

- **Is your language appropriate?** Does it have the right level of formality? Did you use jargon precisely? Is the emotional tone appropriate? First person (using "I" or "we") sounds more

> ## An Outline for a Basic Informative Message
>
> **I. Introduction** (state the purpose of the message)
>
> **II. Background Information** (if necessary)
>
> **III. Main Message** (may be organized chronologically, in a prioritized list or any other logical sequence that clarifies the message)
>
> **IV. Conclusions** (summary of key points, proposed next steps, request for reader action)
>
> **V. Signoff** (how to reach you, thanks for assistance, invite readers to contact you with questions or concerns)

personal and immediate than third person ("The ABC Company"). Industry jargon, acronyms and colloquial phrases also add an element of informality.

- **Did you convey the intended shade of meaning?** Words have connotations. The specific words you choose will communicate your position on your topic. Consider these sentences:
  - I can *accommodate* your recommendation.
  - I *agree* with your recommendation.
  - I *support* your recommendation.

  These statements convey the increasing strength of the writer's accord with the recommendation. Be aware of the effect your choice of words has on the reader.

- **Does your visual format aid comprehension?** Use fonts and graphics that add to the reader's understanding and are not distractions.

- **Have you chosen the best transmission medium?** Your choices may include email, a memo or a formal document.

Organizing Your Thoughts—A Checklist

✔ **What is the purpose of my message?**

- What outcome do I hope to achieve?
- When is this outcome needed?

✔ **Who is my audience?**

- Why do they need this information?
- What are their primary concerns?
- What information do they need (facts, background information)?
- What 'language' does the audience speak?

✔ **What is the best way to present the information?**

- Chronologically?
- In priority order?
- Other organization scheme?

✔ **After creating the message: Did I achieve my objectives?**

Consider the urgency of your message, the level of formality and whether all intended recipients can access the message. In some environments, an email message could imply urgency, while a paper document could signify more time for a reply. A handwritten memo suggests that the message is still in draft form; a typed message denotes formality.

Inhibitors to Effective Communication

Even if you've carefully addressed the three basic elements described above, there are still many ways in which communications can be blocked. Here are some possible barriers.

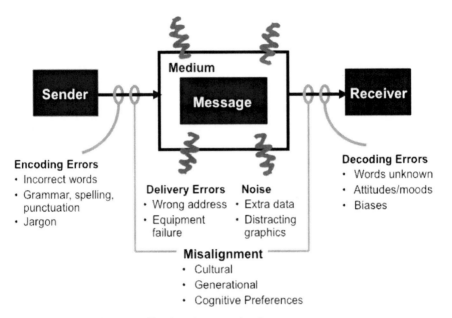

Figure 11.2: Barriers to Effective Communications

Encoding Errors

Even if you have clearly communicated your reason for writing, you may inadvertently introduce "encoding errors" that garble the message. Incorrect words, misspelled words, punctuation errors and grammar mistakes are simple examples of encoding errors. Surprisingly, many senior-level managers and executives are especially distracted and annoyed by mistakes like these.

Delivery Failure

No communication medium is guaranteed to work all the time. Email can go down. Documents can get lost. A note may not be seen in a cluttered office. If your message is important, take the time to touch base with the receiver to make sure it arrived; a simple phone call, email or face-to-face visit shows you take responsibility. Consider a back-up transmission for critical messages; for instance, follow up an email transmission with a phone call.

Noise

In communications, noise is unrelated input that interferes with the reception of the message. In written communications, noise may be extra, unnecessary facts or opinions that confuse the reader, or pointless and distracting graphics that take attention away from the purpose of the message.

Decoding Errors

The most obvious source of decoding errors is misunderstood words, jargon and analogies. The receiver's mood, attitude toward your topic, or existing knowledge of the subject can also color his or her perception of the intended meaning. For example, an enthusiastic or optimistic receiver may put a more positive spin on your message than you intended, while a receiver who is in a bad mood or negatively predisposed to your topic may hear the message with a more negative slant.

Misalignment

No two minds work alike. Everyone receives and processes data differently. Researchers believe that the neural connections in our brains produce different capabilities and preferences in our thinking style. For example, some people think abstractly and look at the "big picture," while others work best with lots of details. Thus, a stockbroker who talks in terms of numbers and uses detailed investment jargon may lose the attention (and business) of a client who prefers to know about market trends and high-level investment strategies.

Another way that people differ in their thinking is in their ability to handle change. Some people are excited by new opportunities and can readily envision new ways to do business. Others need more time to adapt, by carefully evaluating the result of each step before considering the next. A flamboyant marketing manager, who uses language full of promises and possibilities, might fail to persuade a more conservative, sequential-thinking engineering manager to make a needed product change. The engineering manager may not even hear the true need if he or she feels intimidated by the aggressive message of change, or thinks that the marketing manager is out-of-touch with reality and therefore not worth listening to. (You can imagine how the reverse situation could play out, as well.)

The culture and religion we are raised in, our age and our life experiences, and our family's values and style all shape the way we react to the world around us. An acceptable topic for discussion in your culture or family may be offensive and raise defenses in another. A young receiver might respond differently to a message than someone of an older generation. If you and your message recipient are not "coming from the same place," there is a potential barrier to communication.

The key to dealing with misalignment is to recognize and respect each person's individuality. (See Chapter 13, *Managing Office Relationships*, for more on managing differences in the work place.) As Steven Covey wrote in his best-selling book, *Seven Habits of Highly Successful People*, "Seek first to understand, then to be understood."

Pitfalls of Written Business Communications

Anytime you communicate in the office, regardless of the degree of formality or the medium, you must consider the three critical factors—sender, receiver and message. Here are some additional pointers and potential pitfalls to avoid when using specific types of business communications.

Notes and Messages

These short, informal types of written communication provide brief bits of information to the receiver. Notes and messages may be written on a scrap of paper, or they may be sent quickly via e-mail, instant messaging or texting. A note or message might look like this:

Sue,

Ed called at 1:37 with questions about the budget. He'd like you to call him back at x9090.

Bob x5678

Pitfalls and Pointers

1. **Write legibly.** Nothing is more frustrating than deciphering illegible handwriting.

2. **Include your name and phone extension.** Even close associates might not recognize your handwriting. Save them the time of looking up the number.

3. **Leave notes where they can be easily seen:** on a clean desk area, a door or a computer terminal. If the note is personal (for example, a phone message from the person's spouse), leave it in a more discreet place, such as on the person's chair, where casual passers-by will not accidentally read it.

4. **Use notes to convey ordinary, day-to-day types of information.** Do not drop a note on your manager's desk informing him or her that a critical shipment that affects an important contract will be delivered two weeks late. The importance of the message dictates the way it should be conveyed.

5. **Never write anything you don't want others to see.** You never know who else might read your note. A note containing your candid criticism of how a meeting went could accidentally drop to the floor or get stuck to other papers. Similarly, email messages can be forwarded to someone other than your intended recipient. Do not assume that the recipient will protect your confidentiality. Employees read private messages printed on public printers. When you leave a note, consider how it will reflect on you if ANYONE reads it.

6. **Don't leave a note when your message should be delivered in person.** Bad news and emergencies are best conveyed quickly and face-to-face.

7. **Don't leave a note that requires a timely response and think that you have done your job.** If there is any possibility that the recipient will not see the message in time to respond, check back (before the deadline is near) to make sure it was received. If it still hasn't arrived, you may need to personally contact the intended recipient or ask a coworker for help.

Memos and Letters

Memoranda (memos, for short) and letters are more formal means of communicating than notes. They are used when a significant amount of data needs to be conveyed; when the situation requires formality, such as communicating to a superior or customer; or if the information needs to be referenced or saved for later use. While many offices still distribute memos and letters in hard copy, email has become the norm because it is easier and faster to distribute.

Pitfalls and Pointers

1. *Select a subject line (title) that concisely conveys the contents of the memo.* This will help a busy reader prioritize his or her mail and find the memo more easily if it needs to be referenced later.

2. *Understand your reader before you start writing.* How much does he or she already know about the subject or circumstances of the memo? How much attention will the reader be able to pay to details of the memo? Adjust the contents to the reader's level; you don't want to leave him or her mystified, bored or impatient with your writing.

3. *Find out if your memo must be reviewed or approved before you send it.* Many managers do not allow any communication to be sent before they review it. Your manager may want to maintain a consistent office style, determine the thoroughness of the message, make sure you understand the level of the reader, or even ensure that the contents are legal. Communications outside the company, in particular, will probably require approvals. If no approvals are necessary, have a more experienced person review your first few memos anyway to ensure you meet office standards.

4. *Include an alphabetized distribution list.* This is a courtesy if your memo is going to more than one person, so all recipients know who else received a copy.

5. *Remember, people not on your distribution list may also read your memo.* Keep this in mind if your memo conveys negative

opinions, personal information or company-sensitive material. Many companies have special procedures or envelopes for use in these circumstances.

6. **Mark DRAFT across the top of each page of your working copies.** That way, early versions of your memo, which may contain spelling errors and incomplete sentences, will not be mistaken for your final submittal. (Remember to remove "DRAFT" from the final copy.)

7. **Proofread everything you write before distributing it.** Typos, misspellings and incorrect grammar detract from your message and leave the impression that you are careless or have poor writing skills. Electronic spelling checkers and dictionaries will minimize, but not eliminate, errors.

Documents

Documents are the most formal type of written communication. They are usually created for "official" purposes, such as capturing contractual agreements, documenting procedures, conveying contractually required data to a customer, or responding to an auditor's request. Like memos and letters, documents are often transmitted by hardcopy, although electronic transmittal is also common.

Pitfalls and Pointers

1. **Find out if an office document template exists with the preferred style and format for the document you must produce.** If so, adhere to it strictly. You may know a more concise or logical way to format your information, but this official format may be required by the customer or for legal reasons.

2. **Documents usually go through a formal review and approval cycle.** In addition to your immediate manager, higher-level managers, the legal department and others may be involved. Be sure to ask if the approvals must be obtained in a particular order. For example, the president of the company may not want to sign off on a document until the legal department has completed its review.

"Your report was a bit unfocused, so I trimmed
it down from 300 pages to one strong paragraph."

3. *Leave enough time to complete a review process, if one is required.* Many employees fail to do this, which puts due dates in jeopardy. Remember that others in the cycle are busy, too, and need time to read and sign the document. If a reviewer requests changes before signing, it can cause the entire review process to start over again! Plan enough time for changes to be made; ask others in your group how long a review cycle typically takes.

TAKE THE INITIATIVE

For most of us, becoming an effective communicator is a lifelong effort. Even if you have mastered the basics, changes in your work environment can force you to adapt your style. For example, a new management team or a new key client may require a change in the tone or method of delivering your message. A new job responsibility may involve more face-to-face communication or written communication than you are used to. Your organization's growth into global operations could mean new misalignment barriers to study and over-

---

A Timeline to Becoming a Great Writer

(Now!)

>   1. Assess your basic writing skills

(0-3 months)

>   2. Determine which types of communications are most critical in your current assignment

(3-4 months)

>   3. Assess your effectiveness in your top-priority types

(3-9 months)

>   4. Improve and practice your delivery of the top types

(9+ months)

>   5. Go back to step 2 and decide what to improve next

---

come. You can learn to become a great communicator by breaking the challenge into smaller, more manageable tasks.

Here is a timeline to follow in your first year.

1. Assess your basic writing skills

Remember how you learned to drive? You began by learning the mechanics of driving: how to start and stop the car, how to accelerate and slow down, and how to turn. Only when those basic steps became second nature could you turn your attention to driving safely and enjoyably getting to your destination. Similarly, you have to master the mechanics of writing before you can start using them to effectively convey your message. The first step to becoming a great communicator is assessing your basic communication skills and making improvements where necessary. You need to be proficient in the following mechanical skills: grammar, vocabulary, spelling and punctuation. You'll find a list of resources at www.HittheJobRunning.com which can help you assess and improve your skills. Take the time to complete this step; it will quickly become worth it.

2. Determine which types of communications are most critical in your position

After you've been on the job for a few months, you'll find you use some types of written communication more often than others. Define which types are most critical to success in your assignment. You'll want to focus on improving these first. Why waste energy becoming a great proposal writer if your job doesn't involve writing proposals?

Start by identifying the types of communications that you use regularly. You may use some types so routinely that you don't recognize their importance to you. Here is a brief list of possibilities; don't limit yourself to these choices.

Once you have your list, select the one or two types that are most critical to your success and make them your priority to work on.

Types of Written Business Communications

- Informal Notes and Messages

- Memos and Letters

- Status Reports

- White Papers, Technical Documents

- Training or Operations Manuals

- Contracts

- Proposals

- Other Documents

3. Assess the effectiveness of the communications you use the most

Your next step is to assess your effectiveness with the top-priority methods you have just identified. Evaluate honestly if you are getting the desired results from your communications. Here are some of the results you are looking for:

- *Are your readers taking the actions you want in response to your messages?* Are they giving you the information you ask for? Are they acting on your requests? Are they coming around to your point of view? Are they responding directly to you (or do you have to get your boss involved in order to get an answer)?

- *Are your readers taking timely action in response to your messages?* Is the requested information forwarded quickly? Are action items completed when requested?

- *Do your readers respond without a hassle?* Or do they sound annoyed or even complain to your boss or coworkers about your requests?

- *Can you complete your message with a minimum of rewriting?* Do reviewers approve your messages with little editing? Do you require few drafts to complete a final product?

If you answered "no" to any of these questions, you need to zero in on why you are not communicating effectively. Look at the list of barriers to communication and see which apply to you. You may have to go back and reassess your writing basics (Step 1). Do any of the *Pitfalls of Written Business Communications* apply to you? If all else fails, ask for feedback. Talk to your boss, a trusted coworker or, if you dare, one of your message recipients. Ask specifically what you can do to be more effective.

4. Improve your top-priority communication skills

Once you know what you need to improve, do it. Familiarize yourself with how your office uses various types of business communications. Look at what different styles of writing are used within your department, between departments, and in communicating outside the company. You may simply need to adapt your style to the particulars of your work environment. If your weaknesses are more fundamental, there are many ways you can learn better skills and begin practicing them.

- *Find a course* on effective business communications and see if your organization will send you to it. Several good writing skills courses are available face-to-face or online.
- *Buy a book* on effective communication and study on your own at home.
- *Follow the advice in this chapter* as conscientiously as possible.
- *Just take the time to think more* about your messages before you send them.

5. Continue to assess how you can improve your written communication

Once you feel confident that you communicate effectively in your top-priority area, go back to Step 2 and identify the next type of writing you want to master. Follow the same steps for improving that style, then go back down the list and work on other types of writing. If your job responsibilities change or if you get a new job, determine which writing types are important in your new role and work on using them effectively.

SUMMARY

Written communication is only one type of business communication, but a critical one. Never stop striving to improve your communication skills. Your effectiveness will make a decided impression on those receiving your message and ultimately influence your long-term success in the workplace.

FAQs

Q: *I am a manager with an employee who floods me with various types of communications—endless memos, status reports, emails, and messages left on my voice mail. How do I get him to communicate with me in a more manageable and meaningful way?*

A: Your employee is either seeking attention or hasn't developed the judgment to know how much information to share with you. If the employee needs attention, consider spending more face time with him until he gains the self-confidence to work more independently. If the problem is his judgment, discuss the reason for so many messages. Ask him what outcome he expects. Is he looking for action on your part, or does he just want to make sure you know everything? Explore whether the purpose is reasonable. (Do you have enough time to deal with his requests? Are they in line with your position and authority?) Help the employee achieve his purposes more effectively. For example, one well-written, weekly status report summarizing key events is more effective than many reports with lots of details. Helping this employee may be frustrating, because basically you are teaching common sense, which doesn't come easily to everyone.

Q: *I'm not allowed to send anything to our clients without my manager's review. Usually, she makes me redo my memos several times. What a pain! Why is this such a big deal?*

A: This is a big deal because you represent and reflect upon your organization every time you contact your clients. If you send poorly written memos, your clients could conclude you and your organization are incompetent, show poor judgment or lack integrity. What mistakes does your manager correct? Is it your spelling, grammar and punctuation, or your organization and logic? Make it your goal to correct these mistakes. You'll gain your manager's confidence, reduce your overall frustration and find that your manager stops editing everything you write.

Q: *I can't believe employers have nothing better to do than read my Facebook page! How real are the media reports?*

A: The media reports are very real. Checking you out before and after the hiring decision is becoming the norm. Methods include internet searches, in addition to reading social network pages. Remove any damaging information and restrict access to only known and trusted friends immediately. Make sure your friends do the same, especially those party photos! The bottom line: privacy is a thing of the past.

CHAPTER 12

Spoken Workplace Communications

> **In this Chapter**
>
> - Elements of effective spoken communications
> - Barriers to the effective spoken word
> - Pitfalls of spoken business communication
> - Timeline for becoming a great speaker

"The most important thing in communication is to hear what isn't being said."

~ Peter Drucker ~

WHY YOU SHOULD CARE

The way you speak—what you say and how you say it—reveals information far beyond the words you use. For example, consider your reaction to a presentation by an extremely animated speaker. Depending on the situation, his or her energy either infected you with enthusiasm or turned you off, if it didn't appear genuine. Perhaps he misused words (such as "irregardless"—it's not a word!) or mispronounced words (for example, saying "excetera" instead of "et cetera"), so that you were distracted from the message he was trying to convey.

How good are your oral skills, and how do people react to the way you speak? Do you listen to others when they speak, or are you already thinking about what you will say next and constantly interrupting them?

Most communication in the workplace is spoken, ranging from casual conversations with coworkers over a cup of coffee to a formal presentation requesting funding for a project. Poor oral skills—including listening to others—can:

- **Make you appear immature** or incompetent
- **Create a barrier** to establishing and maintaining relationships with managers and coworkers
- **Lead to embarrassment,** reduced productivity and safety issues

Effective oral communication is essential in the workplace. Commit yourself to developing effective speaking and listening skills as a lifelong learning experience.

The Basic Elements of Spoken Communications

In the previous chapter, you read about the basic communication model, which consists of three elements: the sender, the receiver and the message. Spoken communication uses the same model, and introduces a fourth element: more immediate feedback.

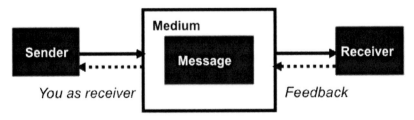

Figure 12.1: A Basic Model of the Elements of Spoken Communications

Element 1: The Sender

As with written communications, your starting point is your purpose for communicating. It may be hard to focus on your purpose when you're speaking extemporaneously or as you switch roles from sender to receiver in a conversation. If you sense that a conversation is rambling or never going to end, you've probably lost your sense of purpose. In a casual conversation, that might be fine. In a more formal business discussion, you may be wasting time. Remember to ask yourself, "Is my intent to inform? Request? Persuade? Entertain? Show support? Other?"

Element 2: The Receiver

Once you know your purpose for communicating, put yourself in the receiver's shoes and try to speak his or her language. Ask yourself these questions:

- *Why does my audience need this message?* What am I expecting them to do?
- *What does the receiver need to know?*
- *Does the recipient need more context* to understand and react as expected?
- *Does my receiver understand* the words, analogies and examples?
- *What is my receiver's attitude* toward the topic of the message?
- *How does my recipient prefer to receive data?*

A listener's ability to understand your message is influenced by how he or she hears you. If the listener is not a native English speaker, you may have to slow down your delivery and avoid the use of idioms they may not understand. If the listener is partially deaf, you may have to speak more distinctly.

Your listener's mood is also important. If your audience is tired, distracted, under a lot of stress or not feeling well, they may not absorb much of what you say. Fortunately, when you are speaking face-to-face, you can tell from body language and other cues whether your listener is bored, getting angry or fascinated by your topic. If your message is important but you aren't getting through, try to reschedule your discussion for a later time.

Element 3: The Message

In the workplace, coworkers, managers, customers, vendors and suppliers constantly exchange ideas and information in person, on the phone, in meetings and in presentations. You can ensure the success of the message—*what* is conveyed—by answering these questions:

- *Have you stated your message clearly, succinctly and completely?*
- *Is your language appropriate?*
- *Did you convey the intended shade of meaning in your message?*
- *Does your visual format aid rather than hinder comprehension?*
- *Did you choose the best transmission medium?*

When you speak, your message must be clear and complete. This is especially critical when your listener has only a short time to listen. In that case, you must also get your points across quickly and succinctly. Unfortunately, the impromptu nature of most spoken communication doesn't always give you time to compose your words in advance. It might be better for you to postpone a critical conversation to a time when your listener can pay more attention or after you've had a chance to identify your key points and can deliver them concisely.

Element 4: Feedback—You as the Receiver

Communicating orally is more complex than written communications for many reasons. When you speak, you transmit your message using more than words: facial expressions, eye contact, your posture, as well as the volume and pitch of your voice, add to your message.

Be sensitive to the fact that telephone conversations, although they do include intonation, still lack other non-verbal cues to meaning.

Also, when conversing, you simultaneously send your message and receive immediate feedback (both verbal and non-verbal), requiring you to constantly shift roles between message sender (speaker) and message recipient (listener). As a result, your listening skills are just as important as your speaking skills. We all have a tendency to hear and remember what we want. An effective listener tries to actively understand what he or she hears. Here are some ways to improve your listening skills:

- *Paraphrase* (repeat in your own words) what you hear to ensure you correctly understood the message.

- *Ask "open-ended questions"* that require more than a one-word or "yes" or "no" answer. The response to an open question offers you clarification and a deeper understanding of the message. A closed question like "Did you like the report?" can be reworded as an open question: "What did you like best about the report?"

- *Listen between the lines.* Is the speaker dancing around the real issue? He or she may be implying more than the face-value message through shades of meaning or emphasis on particular points.

- *Pay attention to non-verbal messages.* Pay attention to facial expressions, gestures, posture and tone of voice for the underlying message masked by words.

- *Distinguish between facts and opinions* by requesting examples from the sender or asking open-ended questions.

- *Check your own barriers to effective listening,* whether physical, decoding, or attitudinal.

- *Show interest* by providing appropriate non-verbal feedback. Small head nods, a smile or raised eyebrow, or oral affirmations, and an open posture encourage the sender to speak openly with you.

- *Don't interrupt or make judgments* until you have heard the entire message. You risk jumping to conclusions prematurely.

Barriers to Effective Oral Communication

Many of the barriers to effective written communications apply to oral communications, but speaking and listening also have their own set of challenges.

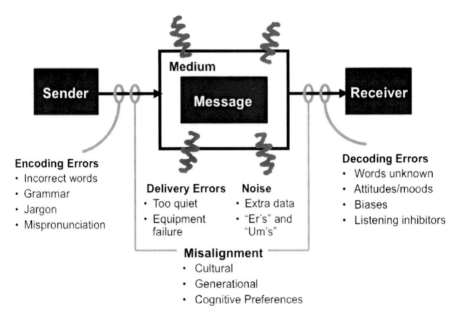

Figure 12.2: Barriers to Effective Oral Communication

Encoding Errors

Encoding errors are mistakes that garble the message, such as incorrect or mispronounced words and grammar mistakes. Gestures and other visual cues can send the wrong message. Consider the speaker who smiles or laughs nervously at an inappropriate time. Have you ever listened to someone who repeatedly mispronounces a particular word? Did you find you started listening for that word more than listening for the purpose of the message? Identify encoding errors (and their ramifications) in the communications around you. Work hard to eliminate those errors from your own communication!

Delivery Failure

Even in spoken communications, things can go wrong. A microphone or projector can fail during a presentation or you could forget your slides. The telephone system can go down, or your listener could have stuffed-up ears from a bad cold or allergy. If your message is important, back it up with a written version. Sometimes you can reschedule a conversation to a later time, when your listener is more receptive.

Noise

Noise is any sensory input that interferes with the reception of the message. It may be literal noise—the sound of a jackhammer pounding on the pavement outside a conference room. It may also be extraneous data that distracts from or confuses the intent of the message. When speaking, this extraneous data can take the form of:

- *Unnecessary facts or opinions*
- *Pointless or distracting presentation graphics*
- *Nervous habits or other inappropriate gestures*
- *"Ums" and "ers" when speaking*
- *Excessive use of idioms, or casual speech patterns such as the word "like"*

Aside from literal noise, most communicators are unaware of the "noise" they make. To identify your noise, record yourself speaking, or ask a trusted colleague to give you feedback.

Decoding Errors

Just as there can be sender encoding errors, there can also be receiver decoding errors. Be careful when you use jargon and idioms. In spoken communication in particular, they can be incorrectly decoded. For example, if the environment is noisy, the receiver may literally hear the wrong words. The receiver may be partially deaf and not hear the entire message. Your receiver may not understand your accent or may have trouble processing very rapid speech. Many decoding errors arise simply because the receiver is a poor listener.

Misalignment

Misalignment errors arise when the sender and the receiver approach a topic from two different frames of reference. We all perceive data based on our own value system and life experiences, as well as how our brain is physically connected.

Generational differences are most obvious in speech patterns and catch-phrases. For example, a young person's use of the word "like" (as in, "He has, like, a gazillion friends.") may sound juvenile and even illiterate to a member of an older generation. Conversely, an older employee may sound old-fashioned and silly using the term "hip." More subtle generational differences can create more substantial communication barriers. For example, a person who spent her entire career with one company may not understand why an applicant has worked for five companies in four years.

Cultural differences also inhibit communication. For example, the physical space considered acceptable between a speaker and listener varies between different cultures. A person from a culture where people stand fairly far apart may perceive a message as hostile if it is delivered by a person standing extremely close. Different hand gestures mean different things in different cultures. A gesture used commonly in one culture may be considered obscene in another. The way Americans shake their head from side to side when they mean "no" can mean "yes" in other cultures. Learn something about the culture if you are visiting another country or working with employees from a culture other than your own.

Cognitive processing differences are the least obvious, yet can cause some of the biggest obstacles to communication. Some people prefer to receive data visually and find it difficult to process information if it is not delivered in writing. Conversely, an auditory learner responds best to the spoken word. (To help determine your own preference, think about which courses you liked best in college; how much listening did you do in those classes versus reading?) In presentations, some receivers learn best from charts made up primarily of words, while others find graphs and colorful pictures more useful. When listening to a persuasive speech, some people respond best to logical arguments, while others are more likely to support an emotional appeal. There is no right or wrong in our cognitive preferences; there are only differences.

Misalignment barriers between a message sender and a message receiver are often difficult to identify, and equally difficult to overcome. Your goal is NOT to change the other person to be more like you. Instead, adapt your style by recognizing and respecting each person's individuality, and doing your best to "talk their language." (See Chapter 13, *Managing Office Relationships*, and Chapter 14, *Managing Customer Relationships*, for more on managing these differences.)

Pitfalls of Spoken Business Communication

Most spoken business communication is two-way. That means that you will play the role of both the message deliverer and the message receiver (or listener). Here are some typical ways we communicate at work, along with pointers and pitfalls to avoid.

Conversations

Conversations are dialogs between two or more people in both formal and informal settings. You might have a casual conversation with friends or coworkers, or when a manager invites you to be informal because he or she wants to encourage a less hierarchical relationship. The topic of an informal conversation can range from work to personal matters. Formal conversations, where you communicate with the utmost professionalism, are usually about business; that includes personal business, such as a banking matter.

Pitfalls and Pointers as a Message Sender:

1. *Modulate your voice appropriately when talking.* Avoid yelling, speaking too softly or whining.

2. *Maintain eye contact with your audience.* People who avoid eye contact may appear distracted, overly nervous or evasive. However, in some cultures, averted eyes are a sign of respect so knowing cultural expectations is important.

3. *Be sensitive to how busy your listener is and whether your conversation is too long.* It's time to end a conversation when:

   - Your listener begins shuffling or reading papers on the desk
   - Your listener gives abrupt responses to your questions
   - Your listener begins edging away from you

4. *Be sensitive to what is important to the listener.* This is especially true in formal conversations. What details of your topic interest your listener, given his or her own responsibilities? Does your manager or customer need a lot of detail or just a summary of your issue?

5. *Don't discuss your problems with listeners who can't help.* It only wastes their time.

6. *Have an agenda.* This is especially helpful in a formal conversation, where you can make all your points succinctly and logically.

7. *Avoid subjects that may be controversial or offensive.* Upsetting someone in a casual conversation can jeopardize your working relationship. As the saying goes, don't discuss religion, politics, and sex. And never ask a woman if she is pregnant unless you know for sure that she is.

8. *Confidential and personal conversations can be overheard.* Remember: restrooms, partitioned offices and hallways are not private places.

9. *Once you tell even one person something, you no longer*

control who else might receive your words. Gossip, judgmental statements, and sarcastic or angry remarks can be repeated, or your comments misquoted out of context.

10. *Don't assume you can be informal with management or customers in your attempt to establish rapport with them.* New employees should use the level of formality set by the senior person in the conversation.

11. *If you need time to compose your message, say so, rather than blurt out an illogical statement.* Say something like "Let me think about that for a few seconds." Then do just that. A few moments of silence may seem like an eternity to you, but it is better to pause and think.

Pitfalls and Pointers as a Listener

1. *Show the same courtesy to people speaking to you as you expect from them.* Don't read or work on your computer when someone is trying to talk to you. If you are very busy or trying to meet a deadline, politely say so, and reschedule the conversation for a later time.

2. *Use body language to communicate interest and understanding.* Eye contact, facial expressions and head nods indicate you are listening.

3. *Avoid reacting to what you hear before the message is completely delivered.* A premature emotional or angry reaction can hinder effective communication.

4. *Don't assume you understand what you have heard without getting clarification.* Paraphrase and elaborate on the speaker's comments. Ask for more details or examples if you are not sure of the meaning. Sometimes these types of misunderstandings prevent coworkers from working effectively together.

5. *Know the difference between confidential and public information.* If you are unsure, ask. You will be known as a gossip if you blab.

Telephone

Phone conversations are a special type of spoken communication, with their own rules. While a phone call is a two-way communication (unless, of course, you are talking to an answering machine), it is obviously not face-to-face, so these special pointers apply.

Pitfalls and Pointers as a Sender

1. **Identify yourself immediately when you initiate a phone call.** If the receiver does not recognize your voice, you may embarrass him or her if you launch into a discussion.

2. **Have all materials you need to reference near the phone before you make your call.** You will waste the listener's time if you have to keep putting the phone down to get something.

3. **Since you cannot see the other person, be especially sensitive to interrupting.** Ask if it is a good time to talk or whether you should call back. Arrange a specific time so you don't interrupt again.

4. **You can't always tell if the person you've called is on a speakerphone, so be aware that someone else could be listening.** If you use a speakerphone, be sure to tell the other person on the other line if others are in the room.

5. **Be careful of your tone of voice.** Remember that your listener hears your voice without seeing your body language. Your voice will reflect that you are upset about something, even if it is unrelated to the phone call, and your listener may assume that your emotion is directed at her.

6. **Don't eat while talking on the phone.**

7. **Don't make your telephone conversation longer than it needs to be.** Some signs that your listener is ready to get off include short answers to questions, the sound of typing in the background, and hints about wrapping up.

8. **When calling from a cell phone, make sure you are in a zone**

with good coverage, so your message is static-free and does not cut off abruptly.

9. **When answering a cell phone in public, be sensitive to what others are hearing.**

10. **Voice mail messages, like other permanent communications, cannot be assumed to be private.**

Pitfalls and Pointers as a Listener

1. **Find out if there is a common greeting when answering the phone at your company.** Some companies prefer that you answer by stating the company's name and your department; others want employees to state their name and position. Remember that you represent your company whenever you answer the phone in the office.

2. **Take a complete and accurate message when picking up calls for someone who is not available.** Getting the caller's name, phone number, time of call and reason for calling will help your coworkers be more effective.

3. **When you answer the phone, don't keep on working just because the caller cannot see you.** You can be betrayed by the sound of your keyboard clacking away or if you fail to respond to a question. Focus your attention on the call.

4. **Don't be held hostage by a phone caller.** If the caller rambles, keep your responses to the business at hand. If you are interested in the information, but too busy to listen, arrange to continue the conversation at a more convenient time.

5. **If you are busy, let disruptive phone calls roll over to an answering machine.** In particular, if you are holding a meeting in your office, arrange for phone coverage so you can focus on the meeting. If this cannot be arranged, keep the calls as brief as possible out of respect for those in the meeting.

6. **Use the mute button when you are listening on a conference call to prevent noise on your end from interrupting the discussion.**

Meetings and Teleconferences

There are rules to communicating effectively in a meeting—which is defined as a situation where more than two people get together, face to face or virtually, to exchange opinions and make decisions. Teleconferences are subject to similar pitfalls and pointers as regular telephone conversations, plus some others described below. Here are pointers to follow if you are either the person running the meeting (the facilitator) or a participant.

Pitfalls and Pointers as the Meeting Facilitator

1. *Establish the agenda before the meeting.* Put items in order of importance. Assign each topic a time limit for discussion, and use your agenda to keep the meeting on track.

2. *Distribute the agenda, reference materials and background information to participants ahead of time.* This helps everyone come to the meeting prepared.

3. *Distribute the list of meeting attendees ahead of time.* This indicates of the type of meeting planned and allows participants to coordinate their items ahead of time.

4. *Ensure a conference room is available and reserved BEFORE you notify people of the meeting.* It is inconvenient and embarrassing to have to reschedule your meeting because a conference room is unavailable.

5. *Start the meeting on time so you don't waste the participants' time.* Arrive ahead of time to check the room setup and to make sure any needed equipment and material (computer, projector, flip charts, markers, etc.) are in the room and working.

6. *Be flexible, but keep the meeting focused on your agenda topics.* You might want to stray from the agenda if someone brings up new information that contributes to the purpose of the meeting. But if you don't see the connection, ask for an explanation. Tangents that interest only a few attendees are topics for other meetings, not yours.

7. *If you are sharing information online via computer, do not*

share your entire desktop. Share only the application with the information. You must control what is seen by others at all times. Instant messages, for example, just might contain very controversial or improper material.

8. **Distribute meeting minutes in a timely manner.** Include the list of attendees, a summary of topics covered and any decisions made.

Pitfalls and Pointers as a Meeting Participant

1. **Let the meeting facilitator know as far in advance as possible if you will be late or cannot attend a meeting.** Don't just fail to show up! The meeting may be counting on you for a particular piece of information. If you can't attend, find out if you can send an alternate.

2. **Be on time for all meetings.** It wastes other people's time to go over information because you weren't there to hear it the first time.

3. **Come prepared to participate at any meeting to which you are invited.** If materials are distributed ahead of time, read them before the meeting. If you were assigned to complete specific tasks before the meeting, have them done. Being prepared minimizes wasted time and avoids having to schedule a second meeting.

4. **Keep your focus on the business at hand.** Sure, there are times when your attention will wander—that's normal. However, conversations on tangent topics or side discussions waste time and may make you unwelcome at future meetings.

5. **Avoid personal attacks or putting people on the spot if they do not share your views or are not as knowledgeable as you are.** Such attacks reduce your coworkers' sense that they can trust you. Contribute your alternate views constructively, or discuss your disagreement in a conversation outside the meeting.

6. **Use the mute button if available to reduce background noise.**

7. **Set your cell phone to vibrate or "off".**

Presentations and Briefings

Presentations and briefings are a hybrid of spoken and written communications. Perhaps that is why they are so difficult! Usually, they combine written slides, prepared in advance, with an oral presentation. You can find *Tips and Tricks for Presentations* in Appendix B. If you are the presenter, pay equal attention to both the written and spoken facets of your briefing. If you are a listener, your behavior can influence the success or failure of the presentation.

Pitfalls and Pointers as a Presenter

1. *Find out how to operate any needed equipment ahead of time.* Come early to the presentation and learn how to use microphones, projectors, and other equipment.

2. *Know in advance who will attend your presentation.* Be sure you know by name and face any key people related to your topic.

3. *Speak slowly and distinctly when you give your presentation.* If you are nervous, you will probably rush your speech, so consciously slow down.

4. *Don't read your charts.* Your audience can do that without you. Use your charts only as road map for your presentation.

5. *"Grease the skids" on controversial topics.* If you think your presentation could provoke an adverse or hostile reaction from some of your listeners, talk to them beforehand to work out differences or at least get them to agree not to disrupt your briefing.

6. *Make sure diagrams, graphs, cartoons and other visuals add to your presentation, not distract.*

Pitfalls and Pointers as a Listener

1. *Don't arrive late to a presentation.* It is rude and can be disruptive to walk in midway through a briefing. If you

"My multimedia presentation is voice-activated.
If it hears a yawn from the audience, it automatically
switches to heavy metal music and throbbing dayglo colors."

absolutely cannot avoid coming in late, slip in quietly and take a seat close to the door.

2. **Don't leave in the middle of a speech.** This, too, is rude and can be disruptive. If you know in advance that you'll be leaving early, choose a seat close to the door so you can slip out with minimal distraction.

3. **Remember that you give the speaker nonverbal feedback with your body language.** He or she can see if you are yawning or listening attentively.

4. **Don't carry on conversations with your neighbor.** Side conversations are distracting to others trying to listen. If you have a question about the presentation, share it with everyone. Chances are that someone else in the audience has a similar question.

5. **Set your cell phone to vibrate or "off".**

TAKE THE INITIATIVE

The process for becoming a great speaker and listener is the same as that for becoming a great writer. Speaking and writing share many of the same skills.

A Timeline to Becoming a Great Speaker

(Now)

    1. Assess your basic communications skills

(0-3 months)

    2. Determine which types of communication are most critical in your current assignment

(3-4 months)

    3. Assess your effectiveness in your top priority types

(3-9 months)

    4. Improve and practice your delivery in the top types

(9 months and beyond)

    5. Go back to step 2 and decide what to improve next

We recommend integrating these two timelines.

1. Assess your basic communication skills

Just as with written communications, your first task in becoming a great speaker is to assess your basic communication skills and make improvements where necessary. You need to be proficient in the mechanics of effective spoken communications so they become second nature. The mechanics of spoken communications include your:

- *Language mechanics:* correct grammar, vocabulary and pronunciation

---

Types of Business Communications

- Informal conversations

- Phone Calls

- Meetings (participant)

- Meetings (leader)

- Teleconferences

- Briefings and Presentations

- *Speaking mechanics:* appropriate volume, intonation or inflection, and accent
- *Non-verbal mechanics:* appropriate eye contact and body language
- *Listening mechanics:* ability to paraphrase, hear the entire message and read nonverbal cues

The list of additional resources on www.HitTheJobRunning.com can help you both assess your skills and make needed improvements. Make the time to complete this task. It will quickly become worth it to you.

2. Determine which types of communications are most critical in your assignment

After you've been on the job for a few months, you can figure out which types of communications you use most frequently and which are most critical to success in your assignment. These are the communications you want to work on and develop.

Start by listing all the ways in which you regularly communicate at work. You may use some types of communications so often that you don't realize their importance to you.

Once you have your list, select the one or two types most critical to your success. Focus on these areas first.

3. Assess your effectiveness in your top priority types of communications

Now assess your effectiveness in using the communications that you prioritized in the previous step. Are you getting the results you want from your communications?

- ***Do your listeners appear interested and engaged?*** Do they respond with favorable body language and contribute to your discussion?

- ***Do your listeners take the actions you desire in response to your messages?*** Do they give you requested information? Do they do what you request? Do they come around to your point of view? Do they respond directly to you, or do you have to involve your boss in order to get a response?

- ***Do your listeners take timely action in response to your messages?*** Are phone calls returned promptly? Is requested information forwarded quickly? Are action items completed when requested?

- ***Do your listeners respond to your messages without hassle?*** Or do they act annoyed? Do they complain about your requests to your boss or coworkers?

- ***As the listener, are you confident you heard the entire message with minimal bias?*** Is your response in sync with that of your coworkers?

If you answered "no" to any of these questions, you need to work on making your oral communications more effective. Go back to the start of this chapter and see which of the barriers to communications may apply to you. Then review the common pitfalls of spoken communications. If all else fails, ask for feedback. Talk to your boss, a trusted coworker or one of your message recipients. Ask specifically what you can do to become more effective.

4. Improve your top priority communication skills

You may simply need to adapt your communication style to your specific work environment. If you need more help, here are ways you can learn better skills and begin practicing them.

- **Find a course** on effective business communications and see if your organization will send you to it. Good courses are offered face-to-face or online.
- **Join an organization** like Toastmasters® to improve your presentation skills.
- **Buy a book** on effective communications and study it at home.
- **Watch and listen to good speakers**—learn from their methods.
- **Review and apply the advice presented in this chapter.**
- **Just take the time** to think before you speak.

5. Assess again where you need to improve your communications

Once you are confident that you have mastered your top priority areas, go back to Step 2 and pick the next type of oral communication you want to improve. Follow these steps whenever your responsibilities change significantly or if you get a new job.

SUMMARY

Effective communication is a challenging, but critical skill. This chapter and the previous one are only an introduction. Never stop striving to improve your communication skills. Your ability to communicate effectively will impress those receiving your message and affect your future success.

FAQs

Q: *My manager is a person who never listens. She usually does all the talking. Even when I manage to talk, she interrupts me and contin-*

ues to dominate the conversation. There are important things I need to tell her and ask her. How do I get through?

A: How frustrating—but not uncommon. When dealing with someone like this, it is especially important to know your purpose for communicating. You need to be ready to deliver your key points when the opportunity arises *and* deliver them quickly and concisely.

There's no easy solution for dealing with an overly talkative or domineering person, but here are some things you can try:

- Prior to a face-to-face discussion, send your manager an email describing briefly your reason for the meeting and key points. This quick message draws your manager's attention to the matter at hand, and she may even "hear" your message. After the meeting, you may want to follow up with an email summarizing what you've agreed to.

- When face-to-face, demonstrate confidence and assertiveness. "Push back" a little—politely, of course. Don't immediately stop talking when your manager interrupts. Assertively get into the conversation when your manager takes a breath.

- Try leading the conversation by asking Socratic questions—that is, questions that lead your manager down a certain path of logic. For some reason, talkative people are more likely to listen to questions than statements.

- Try starting the conversation with a polite but direct statement like "I have something important to tell you; please hear me out." Then be sure to proceed logically and succinctly.

- If you have a good relationship with your manager, raise the issue with her in a conversation scheduled solely on this topic.

- Bring a piece of paper listing your key points with you. Sometimes, this visual reminds a talkative person that you have an agenda.

- If all else fails, ask someone who seems to get through to your manager for his or her secrets to success.

Q: *I have a coworker who is basically unresponsive. Not only does he say very little, but he shows little to no reaction to things I have to say. We have been assigned to work together on a new project. I don't see how we can be successful if this guy won't talk. What should I do?*

A: Communicating with an unresponsive person feels like dealing with a black hole: All your thoughts go in, but nothing comes back out. There are many reasons why someone may appear unresponsive: He or she may be shy, naturally reserved, embarrassed to speak, depressed or preoccupied with another matter. Unresponsiveness can indicate hostility toward something annoying you did. Your first step is to try to figure out why your coworker is unresponsive. The reason will suggest ways you can behave to get him to open up with you. One clue is how he responds to other people in the office. If another coworker gets a better reaction, figure out why. Most of us aren't trained psychologists, so you may never know the reason for his attitude. Here are some steps you can take:

- Ask open questions that draw your coworker out. Be patient in waiting for a response.

- Show interest in and respect for your coworker's ideas through words and body language.

- Try various ways to communicate with him. Maybe he works better via email than face-to-face, or vice versa.

- Keep the communications flowing from your end, even if it feels one-way. If you react in kind to your coworker's silence, you'll just contribute to the problem.

Q: *I get nervous giving presentations or even just speaking at a staff meeting. How can I feel more relaxed?*

A: Most people get nervous speaking in front of a group. The more often you do it, the easier it gets. Here are some things to do that might calm you down:

- If the presentation is formal, rehearse several times before the real thing. Get comfortable with the order and flow of your speech. Practice speaking slowly and clearly.

- When speaking extemporaneously (for example, at a staff meeting), jot down your key ideas and use that as an outline when you talk.

- Remember, almost everyone gets nervous speaking publicly. Your audience is likely to be supportive and sympathetic to your situation.

- Seek opportunities to speak publicly. It will get easier and easier, and you'll become more comfortable (as well as effective).

Q: *I'm uncomfortable speaking on the phone. I have an accent, and I fear people make fun of me. What should I do?*

A: Speaking with an accent can be stressful, because it makes you feel different and can make it difficult to get your point across. It's even harder when you're on the phone and can't use body language to clarify your message. Make sure you speak slowly and distinctly on the phone. Try to identify which words are hardest for your listeners to understand, and work on pronouncing those correctly. Where it makes sense, meet with those people whom you speak to frequently on the phone to establish rapport and alleviate your stress. Finally, be assured that, as the world "globalizes," we're all becoming accustomed to hearing different accents. Relax! Your accent may not be the big deal you think it is and, in some circumstances, may even provide you with an advantage.

CHAPTER 13

Managing Office Relationships

In this Chapter

- Classmates vs. office mates
- Diversity is physical, experiential and cognitive
- The paradox of the Golden Rule
- Assessing your relationships
- Developing a mentor

"Personal relationships are the fertile soil from which all advancement, all success, all achievement in real life grows."

~ *Ben Stein* ~

WHY YOU SHOULD CARE

There is hardly a job (if any!) in which you can work totally independently of others. Businesses, institutions and agencies all depend on the cooperative efforts of individuals to achieve their desired results.

Smooth relationships aren't only necessary to get the job done. Your success in establishing good working relationships can enhance your personal performance, as well as your job satisfaction. People who like you are more likely to look out for you, share information with you and give you constructive feedback. As a result, you are likely to perform better and to feel like an accepted member of the team.

Getting along with other people in the workplace is a lot different—and potentially more challenging—than getting along with people in school.

- At school, few relationships had any bearing on your grades, other than perhaps an association with a professor or class-mates sharing a project. At work, on the other hand, your appraisals, raises and opportunities for advancement all depend on the quality of your relationship with your boss, others in your work unit, a project lead, administrative assis-tants, clients and executives—just to name a few!

- At school you could pick your friends. At work, you're "stuck" with whoever else was hired.

- At school, the people you hung around with were probably similar to you in age, life experiences, intelligence, and gen-eral interests. At work, you'll see much greater diversity among your coworkers.

- At school, you were probably always surrounded by the same people. You may have established a study group with others in your major that lasted over several semesters, while any organizations you joined probably kept the same members year to year. At work, you'll find that the people around you may change often, due to hiring and resignations, promo-tions, organizational restructuring, project start-ups and pro-ject completions.

- You'll encounter more types of relationships at work, ranging from true friendships that extend outside the office, to acquaintances with high-level executives which are governed by an unspoken set of rules. You're expected to know the dif-ference and behave accordingly.

Whether you are an introvert or an extrovert, you will have to put some energy into making your office relationships work. This chap-ter will give you some insight to help you succeed.

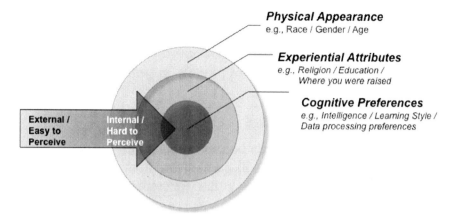

Figure 13.1: Layered Diversity Model

WHAT IS DIVERSITY?

The Golden Rule teaches us to treat others the way we want them to treat us. Here's the paradox: Not everyone wants to be treated the same way. For example, think about how you and those you know react to stress. Some people deal with stress by getting together with others and talking it out. Others want to go off by themselves and think things through. Now, imagine how the person who wants to be left alone feels if the people-person won't leave him or her alone? How about the reverse?

No two people are alike. People differ in a wide variety of ways. To get along with different types of people you need to see each one as an individual—to get beyond stereotypes and find a common understanding. The layered diversity model in the Figure 13.1 can help. The outer layer—physical differences—is the easiest and quickest to perceive, while the inner is usually the hardest. In fact, many people are not aware of their own cognitive profile. Understanding yourself in terms of this model is a good first step toward establishing effective relationships with others.

Physical Differences

The most easily discernible differences between people are physical factors, like race, gender, age and weight. Unfortunately, when most people talk about diversity, they are referring to physical differences that, in themselves, have no bearing on how well people get along. What really gets in the way are preconceived judgments and stereotypes about people, based on their physical appearance.

Experiential Differences

Experiential differences usually become apparent as you get to know a new person. They are details like where and how you were raised, your career path and your stage in life (for example, single or married with kids).

Our experiential differences drive our perceptions of others, our reactions and biases, and our fears and values. That's why they can be a source of conflict. For example, a person whose life experiences fostered an aggressive, outspoken personality may have problems getting along with more casual, easygoing coworkers. However, if you are open-minded, learning from other people's personal experiences can help you grow as an individual and as an effective employee.

Cognitive Differences

Everyone's mind is unique! Different minds take in, organize, process and recall data differently. That's why people have aptitudes for varying types of work. Some of your coworkers will be very good at detailed numerical work. Others will shine at developing strategies from seemingly disparate facts.

Our cognitive differences also lead us to prefer different styles of working. If a coworker likes to learn about a subject by reading, you may want to send him a memo with key points and facts before discussing an important topic. Another coworker may be an audio learner, so you would have a discussion first, and then follow up with an email.

It is often hard to identify cognitive differences, but that doesn't mean you should ignore them. If you're having trouble working effectively with a coworker, try a different approach. Listen for cues. If your boss says, "Don't give me the details, just give me the bottom line," she probably means it. Because you have your own aptitudes

---

Some Cognitive Differences

- Learning by doing vs. learning by watching
- Concrete vs. abstract thinking
- Decision-making based on feeling vs. logic
- Visual vs. audio processing
- Introversion vs. extroversion
- High-level vs. detailed orientation

---

and style preferences, it may be hard for you to shift gears. Make the effort, and you'll find that your working relationships will become more versatile and more effective.

TAKE THE INITIATIVE

1. Assess your own behavior

You can't control other people's behavior, but you can control your own. Keep in mind the diversity model at the beginning of this chapter. Because we are all different, not everyone will respond to your actions and opinions the way you want them to. You can get along with others, regardless of differences, if you always exhibit courtesy, good manners, and an understanding of your group's norms, so you don't violate them. If you haven't read Chapter 2, *Look and Act Like a Professional*, and Chapter 3, *Learning the Ground Rules*, now is a good time to review ways you can make a positive impression on people and learn how your group operates.

Take it a step further: Examine any biases you may have that lead you to judge your coworkers before giving them a chance to show who they are. It's hard to examine yourself so critically. If you suspect you're not being totally honest with yourself, ask a close, trusted friend or family member to help you identify your prejudices. Even once you know your prejudices, it may still be hard to let go of them. Try your best to find the positive in everyone around you.

A Timeline for Effective Office Relationships

(1-2 Months)

   1. Assess yourself for offensive or unprofessional behavior and examine your biases.

(2-4 Months)

   2. Assess and improve your relationship with your boss.

   3. Wait to establish close friendships with coworkers.

(3-6 Months)

   4. Assess and improve relations with coworkers, and improve on your teamwork.

   5. Learn the rules for interfacing with other positions.

(9-12 Month)

   6. Develop a mentor.

---

2. Assess your relationship with your boss

One of the first people you'll get to know and work with is your boss. This relationship is important because it can impact:

- Your short-term career opportunities (including training and assignments)
- Appraisals and raises
- Your overall job satisfaction and comfort level in the office.

Your supervisor will have certain style preferences and behaviors that you need to adapt to. Take the initiative to figure out how he or she operates. The checklist on the following page can help. While your own observations may be sufficient, try to corroborate your impressions with those of an objective coworker.

Understanding Your Supervisor

✔ *My supervisor is most available...*

- First thing in the morning
- Around lunchtime
- At the end of the day
- Other (describe)

✔ *My supervisor does not like to be disturbed...*

- First thing in the morning
- Around lunchtime
- At the end of the day
- Other (describe)

✔ *My supervisor likes to communicate...*

- Face-to-face
- Via the phone
- Via written messages
- Via electronic mail
- Other (describe)

✔ *My supervisor likes to receive information that is...*

- Detailed
- Summarized
- Contains back-up analysis
- Contains just conclusions
- Other (describe)

continued

✔ *Regarding employee autonomy, my supervisor likes to...*

- Get involved in everything
- Get involved only when an employee asks for help
- Never get involved
- Other (describe)

✔ *Regarding office hours, my supervisor expects employees to...*

- Arrive early to work
- Arrive no later than the official start time
- Work late
- Work on weekends
- Take work home
- Never take a long lunch
- Work at any time, as long as assignments get completed
- Other (describe)

✔ *The aspect of my job that my supervisor considers most critical is* _____

✔ *My supervisor's biggest hot button is*

_____

Some people get along so well with their boss that they stay with them for years. Others find it difficult to get along with their boss. If you're one of them, start by asking yourself how you could be contributing to the problem.

Many employees, both experienced and inexperienced, don't fully understand their supervisor's abilities and responsibilities. Sometimes, a manager can only influence and not control expected outcomes. Yes, there *are* a lot of bad managers out there. In some cases, they really are incompetent, selfish and even abusive. However, most often, a difficult manager is responding to pressure from his or her own responsibilities and priorities, which may have nothing to do with you. Sometimes, a manager can only influence and not control expected outcomes. A typical manager is expected to:

- *Ensure that all work assigned to the team gets done on schedule, within budget and with quality results.* If the team fails to perform well, the manager is usually the first to take the heat—no matter whose fault it is.

- *Perform personnel and administrative duties,* such as hiring and firing, writing performance appraisals and managing budgets. This part of a manager's job is often time consuming, tedious and a distraction from "the real work."

- *Respond to employee issues.* Depending on the team, this can be frustrating and exhausting. Many employees don't see the complete picture, but it's the manager's job to deal with each employee's behavior, complaints and demands. Many "professionals" become surprisingly whiney and unreasonable behind closed doors with their boss. A good manager will respect their privacy and not reveal this unpleasant behavior to others in the office.

- *Accomplish projects assigned by his or her supervisor.* No matter what level of the organization they are on, managers have their own assignments to do, ranging from technical tasks to leading the United Way Campaign.

Being a manager is a difficult job. Not everyone does it well. Your manager may not have sufficient skills to cope with these pressures and to effectively lead your group. How does your boss want—and need—to be treated? The key to getting along with even the most difficult boss is to try to understand him or her, show respect, and accept your manager for who he or she is. Find some common ground—a shared work goal or a hobby—and build a relationship on that. You may be pleasantly surprised that even the most difficult boss lightens up if you show support and respect. Establishing a rapport, will open the door to discussing any difficulties you have with your boss and resolving them. You may discover things you can do to lessen your manager's stress, and ultimately open up future opportunities for yourself.

Myths about Managers

- All supervisors are out to get you—therefore you can never trust any of them.
- Managers know—or should know—more than you do about all aspects of your job.
- Your supervisor has infinite time to pay attention to you—whenever *you* decide it's time.
- Managers can fix every problem.
- Managers have limitless resources for making improvements, buying new equipment, paying for training, hiring more employees, etc.
- Managers should never have a bad day or be in a bad mood.
- Managers should never make mistakes or bad decisions.
- Managers can read minds.

3. Don't establish close relationships with coworkers too quickly

It might sound a little cold-hearted, but it's in your best interest to take some time to observe your coworkers' behaviors and standing in the office before establishing close relationships with them. Initially, you don't know who the troublemakers are (if any), so why risk adopting their attitudes or being "guilty by association"? Be friendly to everyone, get to know a broad set of your coworkers, and choose your office friends after you've observed their behavior. In the end, you may still choose to befriend the office troublemaker, but you've made the decision consciously.

4. Assess your relationships with your coworkers—and your performance as a teammate

Inevitably, after working with your office mates for a while, you will begin to see their social and personal sides. Developing personal

**"I've been making an effort to be less critical.
If you weren't so self-absorbed, you'd see that!"**

friendships with coworkers can make the job easier and a whole lot more fun.

However, as with everything else, there are pitfalls to avoid as your social and personal side comes out. Be conscious of how much of your personal life you bring into the workplace. Some sharing—like talking about buying a new car or a great movie you just saw—is positive, fostering camaraderie and common interests. Every office expects a reasonable amount of this type of conversation over lunch or at the coffee machine. However, some people take it too far, spending too much time talking about personal matters or discussing topics that are too personal for the office. No one wants to hear about every play you made in your softball game last night, nor do they want to learn all the details of your love life. At the least, you'll bore your coworkers with this talk. You may also leave the impression that you're not busy enough at work or not focused on your tasks. Save these discussions for close friends.

Socializing is fun, but one of your most important roles is to be a good teammate to your coworkers. Think of ways you can support your team and how your behavior might detract from its success. Here are the behaviors of good team players.

- *Understand your team's goals—and put them before any personal agenda.* Understand your role and your teammates' roles in achieving those goals.

- *Meet your commitments.* Report your outcomes on time, and produce quality results. Attend team meetings—and be there on time. Give the appropriate people a heads-up if you will not be able to meet a commitment.

- *Don't shy away from problems.* Confront the facts of the situation and offer possible solutions. Maintain a positive, can-do attitude, even in difficult times.

- *Welcome diverse opinions.* Ensure all viewpoints are explored. Communicate ideas openly, honestly and thoroughly, and encourage teammates to do the same. Avoid defensiveness. Challenge ideas, not people.

- *Support the success of your team leader and your teammates.* Compliment good performance. Respond to dispirited teammates with patience, empathy and encouragement.

- *Contribute to team cohesiveness.* Demonstrate loyalty to your team leader and teammates. Support team decisions. Avoid creating cliques with inside jokes. Respect authority.

- *Be a person others enjoy being with.* Demonstrate self-reliance, competence, enthusiasm and a willingness to go the extra mile for your team. Observe confidentiality.

5. Comply with the "rules" for interacting with other positions in the organization

One important element of diversity in your workplace is the different types of positions you work with: executives, administrative assistants, "represented workers," vendors and consultants. Some organizations have formal policies that govern how people in these different positions should interact with each other. Breaking these rules can result in financial penalties for your organization.

In other organizations, the rules for interaction may be real, but undocumented. For example, some corporations strongly discourage managers from socializing with their employees—even having lunch!—to avoid the appearance of favoritism. In other workplaces, anything goes. Here, it's hard for a visitor to distinguish the top executive from the lowest person in the office pecking order. Use the techniques described in Chapter 3, *Learning the Ground Rules*, to learn the rules and common conventions that govern various levels of interaction in your organization.

6. Develop a mentor

Having a mentor isn't essential to career success, but it certainly doesn't hurt. What is a mentor? Typically, a mentor is an older, more experienced person who acts as a role model, advisor or coach to a less experienced employee. While good managers provide coaching, a mentor is typically outside the employee's immediate management chain. Mentors can help jump-start a career by providing advice, sharing experience and perspective, and expanding opportunities for development. Initially, mentoring relationships tend to be one-way, with the more experienced person helping the less experienced employee. The most effective mentoring relationships evolve over time so that the relationship becomes two-way, and both members contribute in some way to the other's success. Mentoring relationships can become very close, but they remain professional in nature. Mentors can also change over time, depending where you go with your career and the needs of both parties.

While it's valuable to have a mentor, you can't just ask someone to be yours. Some companies make it easy by assigning a "mentor" when an employee is hired. Like your first college roommate, the match may not be ideal, but take advantage of it. Other companies don't formally assign mentors, but do provide the opportunity to interact with more senior employees, including upper-level management, on "extra-curricular" assignments like college recruiting. This is often the ideal way to find a good mentor, but you'll have to take some initiative to develop the relationship. You'll have to work the hardest at getting a mentor if neither of these opportunities is available to you.

Regardless of your situation, here are steps you can take to find the best mentor for you.

- **Set your goals for having a mentor.** Why do you want one? What do you hope this person can do for you? Perhaps you want a person with similar interests or career aspirations who can help guide your way. Perhaps you want someone who is very different from you and will help expand your perspective or thought process.

- **Knowing your goals, look around for candidate mentors.** Who makes the most sense from your list? Is the candidate at an appropriate level in the organization (not too high or low)? Are there any problems accessing your candidates on a regular basis, such as geographic distance? Can you make the initial contact? Think outside the box. Sometimes a service project or non-work-related activity is the best way to make contact with a potential mentor.

- **Initiate the relationship in a way that will put you in the best light.** You want to make a good first impression. Often, it's best to start by doing a favor for the prospective mentor. You might volunteer for a job or share knowledge that's useful to him or her. Your objective is to get noticed as a valued contributor, not as a person seeking to advance your career. If doing a favor doesn't fit your situation, you might arrange a meeting to ask advice on a specific, narrowly focused issue, like how you can improve your skills in your prospective mentor's area of expertise. Generally, experienced people are happy to share their knowledge and insights.

- **Behave in ways that foster the relationship:**

  1. *Demonstrate interest in learning more about your job and improving your performance.* Ask genuine questions and act on the answers.

  2. *Be receptive to the coaching you receive.* Listen carefully to feedback and evaluate whether it makes sense and if you can follow the advice. Thank the person for the input.

  3. *Only request help for things that really matter.* Show good

judgment in making requests of your mentor, and demonstrate a degree of self-reliance.

4. *Continue to find ways to give back to the mentor in meaningful ways.* Few relationships are successful and lasting when one party does all the giving and the other does all the taking.

5. *Perform as well as you can on the job.* Mentors give up their personal time to coach their "mentees." They want to see a return on their investment.

SUMMARY

Enjoy and respect the differences you observe in other people. What a dull world it would be if everyone were alike! The differences you observe can be fascinating and offer you a great opportunity to learn and grow.

Differences can contribute to stronger performance. Teams made up of diverse members who respect each other's differences often produce more creative, higher quality results than more homogeneous teams. You'll have no trouble managing your office relationships if you observe these two key points:

1. *Understand the other person—then have patience and respect for him or her.*

2. *Understand how your opinions and behavior affect those around you.*

Successfully managing all your office relationships is as important to your on-the-job success as accomplishing assigned tasks competently. Invest the time and have fun!

FAQs:

Q. *I just started a new job, and I think I'm going to be miserable. Even though everyone is nice to me, there isn't anyone my age who shares my interests. I won't have any friends. Should I look for a new job?*

A: If you recently left a college environment, you are probably used to hanging around with friends who are close to you in age and interests. The crowd you're in may even define a big part of your identity. While work can be fun, your reason for being there is to get a job done, not to socialize. Since you will spend many hours with your coworkers, it is important that you establish a good rapport with them, but you'll find it isn't necessary to be best friends outside of work. In fact, many people like to maintain a strict separation of their professional and personal lives to give themselves a break from work, and maintain some privacy when in the office. Look for close personal friends in your recreational activities, your apartment complex or your old gang of friends.

At the same time, don't write off these people in the office who are different from you. Everyone has something to offer: an unexpected sense of humor, a fascinating personal experience or an enviable talent. If you allow yourself to get past your differences, you are likely to enjoy and even learn from the diversity. You'll also discover that "friendship" has more dimensions than what you've experienced in your friendships with your peers.

Q: *I absolutely cannot get along with the person I share a cubicle with. He is loud and offends me with jokes about politics and religion. Should I complain to my manager about this guy?*

A: You don't want to ask your supervisor to mediate every problem you encounter at work. Chances are you'll either look like a whiner or like you are incapable of resolving issues yourself. Try dealing directly with this guy. The next time he acts up, try a non-judgmental but straightforward statement like, "John, I can't concentrate on my work when you're joking around. Can you save it for later?" Or, "We seem to have a different sense of humor. I find your jokes about religion offensive. Please share them with someone else." Hopefully, your cube mate is a professional and will get the message. A few friendly reminders may be required before he cleans up his act.

Some people can't or won't change the way they behave. If this guy's behavior is so obnoxious that it prevents you from getting your work done, chances are that you're not the only one who is bothered by him. Your boss has probably noticed, too. A short, private conversation with your boss may be in order. Outline what you want to say beforehand, focusing on the behavior, how it interferes with your work and what steps you've already tried to remedy the situation. Don't attack your coworker's character, and be sure to curb your emotion. Listen carefully to any suggestions your manager has. If you respond with a statement like "that will never work," you might look like you are part of the problem. After your conversation, try out whatever was suggested and be patient. Your manager may take action that you are not privy to, and it could take "the system" a while to respond.

No one says you have to like everyone you work with. Be friendly to everyone, and politely keep your distance from the people you don't much care for. You never know who will be working for whom in the future.

Q: *I'm really attracted to one of my coworkers, and I'm pretty sure he feels the same way about me. Is it OK to date people in the office?*

A: Dating a coworker is dangerous business! Certainly people do, since many married couples will tell you they met at work. The more closely you work, the riskier dating is. And it's never acceptable to date a married coworker.

Before you date a fellow employee, make sure there isn't a company policy prohibiting it. Why risk losing your job over someone who may turn out to be a jerk? Next, think hard about how your past relationships have ended. Since most relationships don't lead to marriage, you may end up working with someone you broke up with or worse, someone who dumped you!

If you decide to risk it anyway, keep your relationship strictly private. Public displays of affection or adoration are unprofessional and unacceptable. Confiding in an office mate or two may make you the topic of office gossip. Jealous employees may attribute your office accomplishments to favoritism if you're dating someone more senior to you. Finally, all eyes will be on you when your probable breakup occurs. Proceed with caution . . . and discretion!

Q: *I am very shy to start with. With all the people in my office knowing so much more than me, I'm really intimidated. What can I do to feel comfortable with my coworkers?*

A: There are a few fairly easy things you can do. First, have faith that the vast majority (if not all) of your coworkers are good people, who will readily accept you as part of the team. Show interest and effort in doing a good job, and you'll find that most people are quick to reach out to help you. Finally, start to feel more comfortable in social settings by asking questions that demonstrate your interest in getting to know your coworkers. Most people love to talk about themselves, especially if they have an interested audience. Try asking a few appropriate questions: "Tell me about your family." "I heard you are an English-as-a-second-language tutor. How did you get started?" "I noticed a photo of Paris on your desk. Did you go there recently?" Personal items in your coworkers' work areas are great clues to what is important to them. Show some interest, and you're sure to get a good conversation going that will soon lead to comfortable relations.

CHAPTER 14

Managing Customer Relationships

In this Chapter

- Internal vs. external customers

- Understanding customer needs

- Delivering results that meet expectations

- Building and maintaining the relationship

"There is only one boss—the customer. And he can fire everybody in the company from the chairman on down simply by spending his money somewhere else."

~ Sam Walton ~

WHY YOU SHOULD CARE

Regardless of your job in the organization, you have customers. Most employees think of customers as the people who buy the products and services your company offers. However, besides these "external" customers, you also have customers inside the organization. Your "internal" customers are your immediate coworkers, other departments and subcontractors, as well as management. These internal customers either fund the work you do or rely directly on its results.

Whether internal or external, your customers have specific expectations of what you can do for them. Their perception of how well you meet those expectations affects your success and job security.

Everyone at some time has been on the receiving end of bad customer service. Think about how you reacted in that situation. You probably felt a range of emotions: disappointment, frustration, anger, or even rage. The experience may have turned you off so completely that you avoided working with this person or company again. Well, that is exactly how your customers will react if you don't meet their expectations.

It's not only what you do that matters. Customers are people, too, and they want to be "treated right". The rules of office relationships in the previous chapter also apply to your customers. How you treat them, and your attitude, determines their satisfaction with your work. Treat your customers rudely or take them for granted, and you may find someone else is soon doing your job.

A CUSTOMER RELATIONSHIP MODEL

Relationships with your customers do not develop overnight. It takes time to build credibility. Every interaction with your customer is an opportunity to either make or break the relationship. Your credibility can be lost in an instant with one bad interaction, and it can take months or even years to regain it. Managing relationships with customers involves the three elements shown in the diagram .

Figure 14-1: Customer Relationship Model

Understand Customer Needs

Customers have specific *expectations* about the quality and consistency of the products or services they want. They also come to you with their own priorities, as they balance cost, schedule and quality—in other words, cheap, fast and good. For some customers, cost and affordability are a primary concern, while others will pay "top dollar" to get something sooner, or for features like higher quality, a customized solution, convenience or ease of use. To understand your customer, you have to know not only what they want, but also what motivates their choices. Here's an example that illustrates this point.

Assume you are taking a car trip and are on a tight schedule to reach your destination. You choose to stop for lunch at a fast-food restaurant. Being in a hurry, you would be upset if the service was slow, no matter how good the food. Now imagine taking a leisurely trip. You might stop at a full-service restaurant, where you expect to relax and enjoy the meal. If the server hurried your meal and rushed you out the door, you would be annoyed that the experience did not meet your expectations or desires.

Deliver Results

In addition to knowing what your customer expects, it is important to *commit* to doing your job in a way that meets or exceeds their expectations. However, before you make the commitment, are you sure you can deliver? Do you have the necessary *skills* and *competency*? Do you have the *capacity to* deliver at the required time? Making a commitment you know you cannot meet is a sure way to destroy a customer relationship. If you lack the necessary skills or capacity to deliver, you can still satisfy your customer by "managing" his or her expectations. Top performers will discuss what they *can* do for their customers and offer alternative solutions to meet their needs.

For example, suppose your car needs repair. When you call to make an appointment, the service manager knows the parts are not available so the repair might not be done by the end of the day. Instead of having you come in and possibly be disappointed, he can explain the situation and suggest that if you bring the car in first thing the next morning, he can order the parts and complete the job in less than an hour.

Most customers also expect *consistency* in quality, cost and timeliness. They dislike surprises, because any variation from what they expect can cost them additional work and expense. Think about how you feel when you show up for a doctor's appointment on time and have to wait more than an hour. The delay may force you to reschedule or even cancel other appointments, inconveniencing more people and making you appear inconsiderate. Remember, if you vary from their expectations, you can erode the trust essential to a solid relationship.

Eliminating the variability that erodes customer loyalty is the primary goal of a concept called Six Sigma®. If you work for a major corporation or government agency, you have probably been involved in some way with Six Sigma®, a rigorous, statistically oriented analysis aimed at eliminating defects in business processes. Companies have used Six Sigma® in a variety of applications, from manufacturing high-tech circuitry and satellites to serving hamburgers. The government has even used it for Homeland Security and the War on Terror. Its name comes from the statistical term, represented by the Greek letter sigma, which measures the variation in a process from its statistical mean. Achieving a Six Sigma® level of quality requires 99.9997 percent accuracy, or 3.4 mistakes per million. By using the Six Sigma® methodology, an organization creates a culture based on measurement and teamwork that strives for continuous improvement. The result is lower costs, less waste, greater reliability, faster delivery and, ultimately, more satisfied customers.

Build Loyalty

Even in a business relationship, your customers are real people, not an anonymous organization. In order to build and maintain customer relationships, you must treat your customers decently. Use the effective communication skills presented in Chapters 11 and 12. Your action should demonstrate these qualities:

- *Attitude*—believe that your customers are important and you want to make a difference to them.
- *Trust*—demonstrate that you have your customers' best interests at heart by competently delivering what they need.
- *Credibility*—demonstrate your competence by consistently delivering on your promises.

- *Integrity*—keep your word and abide by the standards of professional conduct in your industry.

Your approach to customers is similar to what medical professionals call "bedside manner." Being abrasive or abrupt demonstrates lack of caring. Similarly, being condescending makes customers feel inadequate. In other words, when your customers have a problem, you have to deal with their emotions, as well as their problems. If you don't, they will not complain to you; they may simply find someone they feel more comfortable working with.

TAKE THE INITIATIVE

1. Who are your customers?

This question seems obvious, but if you do not consciously identify your customers, you will not always focus your energy on the right people. Most people have more than one customer. For example, a teacher's customers include students and their parents, as well as the department chairperson and school administration. An accountant's customers include internal management, shareholders, the board of directors and even the Security and Exchange Commission for public companies. The

---

A Timeline for Managing Your Customer Relationships

(0-3 Months)

    1. Identify your internal and external customers

    2. Make a personal connection with them

(3-6 Months)

    3. Determine their needs and expectations

(6-9 Months and beyond)

    4. Analyze how well you meet their needs

    5. Develop a plan to fill any gaps

more you know about your customers as individuals, the better service you can provide. Let's start with your external customers.

External customers are the people who choose to buy the products and services your organization provides. The operative word is "choose," because if customers are not satisfied with what they get from your organization, they can switch to the competition. Sometimes, the level of service you provide can give you an edge, even if your competitor has a better product or lower price. Identifying who your customers are depends on your type of business and services.

- *Consumer-oriented:* If your organization sells directly to consumers, as do banks, retail stores, or airlines, identifying your customers is simple: They come to you. Your goal is to provide them with an experience that creates repeat business.

- *Business-to-business:* In this case, other corporations purchase your organization's products. Remember, there is a person behind the decision to buy, and sometimes more than one, if the user has a purchasing agent.

- *Service and Support:* Sometimes a company sells its products through another organization, such as a retail store or distributor, but continues to provide service and support after the sale. In this situation, your customers come to you, but you may only interact with them once, so there is no way to develop a relationship. In this case, you might assess your customers by various categories. For example, a computer support person would treat technically sophisticated customers differently than those with less technical knowledge.

Internal customers: A business's success depends on how well the various internal departments interact with each other to accomplish results. These interactions, called processes, create a customer relationship between employees in different areas. The success of these interactions ultimately affects your organization's relationships with external customers. To identify your internal customers, ask yourself:

- ✔ *What happens to the output you produce?*
- ✔ *Who receives it, and how do they use it?*
- ✔ *Who would care if you suddenly stopped doing your job?*
- ✔ *Who would be affected if your work were late or incomplete?*

2. Make a personal connection

Start by knowing your customers by name and recognizing them when you see them. Next, find some common ground to make a personal connection. Anything, no matter how trivial it seems, can serve the purpose. It could be a hobby, travel experiences, a favorite author or sports; it might be something as simple as your hometown. Do some research to learn more about your customer. Try searching on the web, but make sure you find the right person. Talk with other people who know your customer, to learn about his or her interests, likes and dislikes. Use

© 2001 by Randy Glasbergen.

Customer Service Department

"No, I'm not angry at you, sir. I'm angry at the random act of fate that directed your call to my extension."

your communication skills (see Chapter 12, *Spoken Workplace Communications*) to get your customer to talk about him or herself, but avoid overly personal topics, especially in the early stages of the relationship. The effort will pay off by making your customer feel more comfortable about opening up to you on business-related issues. It might even be the start of a friendship.

3. What are their needs and expectations?

The answer to this question depends on the nature of your business. If your customers include individual consumers, look at them as a generic group and study their general needs. This involves researching demographics, as well as the social and economic trends that motivate this group. Once you understand the needs of this broader group, talk with individual customers to get their unique perspective.

If you are in a business-to-business relationship with customers, look at trends in the customer's industry. Research their company and industry to identify the issues they face, including changes in government regulations that affect them. Search online for industry or trade journal articles about the organization. Talk with your customers to understand the thinking behind their requests. Listen carefully. Is increased competition causing their revenue to drop, making cost and affordability an issue? Perhaps a major project has fallen behind schedule, and they need an innovative approach to get it back on track. Use this as an opportunity to "think outside the box" and uncover creative ways to meet your customer's needs that add value.

To understand the needs of your internal customers, study your organization's culture and politics. Are they facing budget or head-count reductions? Has there been a change in management? Have they put in a new system that is causing problems? Consider these factors when dealing with others in your company, and show empathy for their situation.

4. Analyze how well you are meeting expectations

Are you meeting or exceeding your customers' expectations? Are you building customer loyalty? To analyze how well you are doing, listen to feedback from your customers. If you do not receive any, ask for it. Apply some of the techniques in Chapter 7, *Performance Feedback*. Remember, it is your *customer's* perception of your performance that counts, not yours. Using this checklist, compare your self-assessment to your customers' perceptions. Where do you agree or disagree?

- ✔ *Attitude:* How is your "bedside" manner? Are you apathetic, grumpy and rude, or do you display genuine interest in a way that invites customers to come back? Are you condescending, arrogant, abrupt or abrasive? Does your attitude show that you care more about your customers' needs or your own?

- ✔ *Ownership of problems:* Do you hold yourself accountable? Do you admit to mistakes and fix them, or do you blame others? When someone comes to you with a problem outside your area of responsibility, do you shuffle them off or do you hold onto the problem until you can smoothly transition the customer to the right person?

- ✔ *Professional competency:* Do you provide your customers with the level of quality and consistency they require? If not, why not? Is it a question of skills, equipment or, perhaps, your attitude towards your work?

✔ *Trust:* Do you meet your commitments to your customers? Do you admit when you cannot meet customer requests and offer alternative solutions that might satisfy their needs? Do you maintain confidentiality of sensitive information your customers disclose to you? Does your industry or profession have a code of conduct? If so, do you adhere to it?

Problem Resolution Process

When your customer has a problem, try the following process to resolve the issue and keep the relationship on track:

- *Accept responsibility:* Don't get defensive or offer excuses. If it is your fault, admit it. If it's not, accept responsibility to resolve the problem, without placing blame on anyone. This will allow you to move into resolution mode more quickly.

- *Set expectations:* Explain the approach you propose to take to identify the cause and resolve the issue. Listen to the customer's reaction, and adapt your approach based on feedback.

- *Clarify the problem:* Gather any necessary facts that will help identify the root cause. Establish a set of objective criteria to evaluate proposed solutions.

- *Identify possible solutions:* Brainstorm with your customer or others in your organization to develop feasible solutions to the problem. Do not jump on a solution too quickly, or you may miss a better approach.

- *Evaluate alternatives:* Look at each solution and evaluate how well it would work, by using the objective criteria you defined earlier.

- *Agree on a plan of action:* Propose a plan to your customer based on the alternative you have chosen. Get them to buy into it. Implement and monitor the plan to make sure you achieve the desired results.

✔ *Innovation:* Do you ask questions to understand the reasons for a customer's request, or do you simply accept it at face value? Do you try to uncover innovative ways to meet your customer's needs that add value?

✔ *Responsiveness:* Do you get back to your customers in a timely manner to answer questions?

5. Develop a plan to fill any gaps

Once you have evaluated your customer relationships, keep using those actions and attitudes that are working for you. Go down the checklist in the previous step, and develop a plan to address any weaknesses. Do not be afraid to talk with your customers to get their perspective on how you can improve. Identify coworkers who have established good customer relationships, and learn from them as well.

SUMMARY

Top performers—those who receive letters of recognition from their customers or generate high amounts of revenue—work hard to build long-term relationships with their customers. They treat every inter-action as an opportunity to extend the relationship, by listening, empathizing and taking responsibility for solving their customer's problems. In the process, these top performers establish *credibility, trust and integrity,* and earn a reputation as employees who can deliver the results their customers expect and deserve.

FAQs

Q: *I have had several experiences where customers have been hostile towards me. I don't know why they did this, because the problem wasn't my fault. It upsets me when this happens, and I don't know how to handle it.*

A: Some people can be obnoxious when things don't go their way. Remember that it is not personal; you just happened to be there when they needed to vent. The key is to maintain per-spective on the situation and control your emotions. Showing anger or raising your voice will just escalate the situation. Remain calm and show empathy. Let them vent their frustration until they run out of steam—they will, eventually. Once they calm down, use your communication skills to uncover the real problem and find a solution that serves their needs, as well as those of your organization. Talk with other people to learn how they deal with similar situations. Of course, if the person becomes abusive, violent or threatens you, call for help.

Q: *While in training, I was told never to deviate from company policy with customers. Yet, when customers ask to speak to my manager, she ignores the policies and gives in to the demand. How can I avoid looking like a fool when this happens?*

A: Talk with your manager to understand her reasoning. Tell her how you feel, and ask for advice. Perhaps you are taking the policy too literally and actually do have some latitude. Learn the extent of your authority. Check your attitude, as well. Does your body language say that you have no authority or don't care? Have you ever told a customer, "I just work here"? Look for role models in your organization, and watch how they work with their customers, or ask your manager for guidance.

Q: *I have one customer who can never tell me what he wants. He only "knows it when he sees it." This is very frustrating, and causes a lot of additional work for me. What should I do?*

A: Some people have difficulty expressing their needs, while others don't really know what they want. If asking questions doesn't work, try describing some sample scenarios or characteristics, and gauge their reaction. If your customer still doesn't respond, do some preliminary work by creating a prototype or model. Depending on your job, this could involve drafting a document, storyboarding a presentation or sketching a diagram. While this requires extra work on your part, it will help your client visualize his needs and minimize the amount work you need to do later.

Q: *What my customer says she wants is not what she really needs. Which should I deliver? Is the customer always right?*

A: Not always, but you will have to persuade her that *you* are, without making her feel inadequate or stupid. This is not always easy. Start by considering that your customer may be right; make sure you understand all of the facts behind the request. If you still think your customer is on the wrong course, outline the positive aspects of her approach, while also making your concerns clear. Ask strategic, open-ended questions, like *"what if…," "where would…"* or *"who else has…"* That way, you will engage your customer in defining an alternative solution, and allow her to save face. Try to avoid asking "why" questions—they make most people feel defensive. On the other hand, don't ask questions that can be answered with "yes" or "no." They will leave your customer in a passive mode and shut down creativity. Good luck!

Q: *I lost my cool with an internal customer. Should I just wait and hope the situation blows over?*

A: You're only human. It happens, but don't just ignore the problem and hope it goes away. That could make the problem worse. Go to the person, admit your mistake and apologize for losing your cool. This might be sufficient, but chances are you will have to do more to repair the damage to the relationship. If possible, offer some way that you can make it up. In most cases, it is a good idea to let your supervisor know what happened and how you plan to deal with it. That way, your supervisor will not be caught off guard if your internal customer complains to him or her.

Q: *Many of my customers have come to expect "giveaways"—everything from free tickets to a credit on their account—whenever something goes wrong. How should I handle this situation to avoid the appearance of favoritism to some customers?*

A: What is acceptable practice for one company may be unacceptable for another. Certain industries, especially those with the U.S. government as a customer, must meet very strict restrictions and dollar limits set by federal law. Violations could result in a stiff fine or even land you in prison. Your organization probably has a policy that sets limits on what you can and cannot do in these situations. You should also find out if there are limits on accepting gifts or meals from vendors as part of their sales approach. Don't assume anything. Get a copy of the policy or ask your supervisor for help on how to deal with these requests.

SECTION V

Personal Management Skills

For better or worse, your job and personal life are inextricably linked. Dissatisfaction with your job can spill over to your personal life. Similarly, the quality of your life outside the workplace affects your ability to perform your job, as well as your sense of happiness. So far in this book, we've dealt with how to function in the workplace, but for most of us, life is about more than work. This section deals with managing your personal time and money to minimize stress and enhance your ability to achieve your life goals.

Chapter 15: Achieving Work-Life Balance—For most people, work is a major part of their identity which provides a sense of belonging, as well as income. The pressure to have it all (prestigious job, big home, expensive cars, etc.) can lead to a vicious cycle of working longer and longer hours, with less time for other aspects of life essential to your happiness. You can have it all—just not all at once. In this chapter, we'll discuss ways to achieve your personal goals and minimize stress in your life.

Chapter 16: Managing Your Personal Finances—In a country that prides itself on independence, it's ironic that our educational system spends virtually no time on financial literacy, a key element for establishing financial independence. A sense of financial security allows you to keep your options open and maintain your integrity. Excessive worry about money creates stress that can affect your relationships and job performance. In this chapter, we'll discuss some of the key elements of personal money management and suggest ways to develop your financial literacy.

CHAPTER 15

Achieving Work-Life Balance

In this Chapter

- Determining your goals and priorities

- Managing your time

- Maintaining your health

- Dealing with the unexpected

- Creating balance

"Most folks are as happy as they make up their minds to be."

~ Abraham Lincoln ~

WHY YOU SHOULD CARE

Most adults feel pulled in many directions—working hard in the office, meeting family obligations, and squeezing in time for recreation. There seem to be endless demands on our time. Thanks to technology, from cell phones to email, we are accessible to the "outside world" 24/7. To top it off, the media bombards us with images of the "perfect life" we're expected to attain. Whew! No wonder so many people feel stressed out!

To be happy and relatively stress-free requires creating a balance between your work and personal time. Balance allows you to enjoy relationships with family, friends and coworkers. It gives you the energy to do your best both at work and in recreational activities. A balanced life also contributes to your physical well-being. Numerous studies have shown that stress can leave us more susceptible to illness and physical ailments like back or hip problems. An extreme life imbalance and the associated stress can result in lost perspective, burnout and depression.

You can have it all—just not all at once. With awareness, planning and some survival strategies, you can thrive in your new job, not to mention in your life. This chapter introduces ways to determine your priorities, and strategies for coping with the unavoidable periods of stress everyone encounters from time to time.

WHAT IS WORK-LIFE BALANCE?

Time is a precious—and finite—commodity. Once it's gone, you can't create more. Making the most of it, however, doesn't mean cramming every minute with activity. Everyone needs some downtime to recharge his energy level and enjoy life. If you are doing more now and enjoying life less, something is wrong—you've lost your balance.

Creating balance in your life involves apportioning your time in a way that reflects your priorities—those things that matter most to you. The demands on your time fall into three categories:

1. **Things you have to do:** These activities include making a living, paying bills and taxes, and shopping for food or clothing. You can't avoid these activities; they are necessary to your survival.

2. **Things you want to do:** This category covers your recreational activities, such as going on vacation, taking a course at night, or renovating your home. You are doing these activities by choice. Hopefully, this time is fun and rewarding!

3. **Things you think you should do:** It's often difficult to identify the things you're doing to meet someone else's

expectations. You may work in a certain field because family members expect that of you. If they paid for some or all of your education, you may feel obligated to continue this work, even if you don't like it. Or you may feel pressured to take a higher-paying job you don't want in order to afford the lifestyle you think your spouse wants. When you spend a lot of your time meeting other people's expectations, you are likely to compromise your own values and goals. The result: a stressful imbalance.

A key to preserving balance is to know the difference between what you have to do, what you want to do, and what you think you should do—then balance your time accordingly. Top priority goes to the things you have to do. Otherwise, you'll get in trouble and see your stress levels climb.

Next, you need to identify your personal goals and limit your commitments to activities that are the most important to you. Setting manageable goals will give you a sense of direction. Personal goals help you choose how much time to allocate to your various interests and obligations, so your real life is aligned with your ideal life.

Strategies for balancing your work-life commitments also fall into three categories:

1. **Economizing effort:** Finding ways to get things done efficiently frees you up to do other, more rewarding things. Economize the time spent on things you *have* to do but don't especially enjoy, either at home or work.

2. **Preventative measures:** Remember the old adage "A stitch in time saves nine"? Investing time or money to maintain critical resources like your car, your home and your health can avoid costly repairs or extended downtime.

3. **Create safety nets to deal with the unexpected:** You can't control everything that happens to you. Developing a safety net (for example, a financial cushion and a network of supportive friends) lessens the negative impact of some of life's little surprises.

Maintaining your work-life balance takes a little effort, because your life will change over time. A significant life event like marriage can place new demands on your time or alter your priorities. Expect periods of imbalance to occur. To regain balance, try some of the suggestions in the next section of this chapter.

Table 15.1: Many factors prevent balance in your life

Challenge	Description	Coping Strategies
Corporate Culture	Some companies have expectations about working "casual overtime" on a regular basis. Some jobs require extensive travel and time away from home.	• Learn what's important and how your contributions will be measured. Prioritize your time and effort accordingly. • When traveling, make time to phone home, catch up on reading, or take care of other personal matters.
Poor Economy	In bad economic conditions, some people fear losing their jobs, causing them to put more energy into work and spend less time on other things important to them.	• Develop self-confidence in your abilities, and fill in any skills gaps. • Bolster your finances when times are good so you can survive losing your job.
Societal Norms	Our culture equates time with money, pressuring us to feel like we're "slacking off" if we're not continually doing something productive at work or at home.	• Remember that you are human and need time to recharge your body, as well as your spirit. • Take some time to do something nice for yourself.
Technology	Today's technology lets us communicate faster and gives us more flexibility, but it also has drawbacks. Useless information proliferates, and miscommunications occur faster, causing confusion. People can contact us anywhere, anytime, resulting in unwanted intrusions. It also makes it easy to procrastinate and be less responsible.	• Become proficient at using technology. • Turn off your cell phone and email. • Use your voice mail to screen unwanted calls and provide you with some quiet time. • Sign up for the "do not call" list to prevent telemarketers from calling you at home.

Table 15.1: Many factors prevent balance in your life (continued)

Challenge	Description	Coping Strategies
Negative Thinking / Self Talk	When things go wrong, beliefs about yourself or others may lead you to over generalize and build up problems in your mind to be greater than they are in reality. Excessive worry causes mental roadblocks that prevent you from acting sensibly in your best interest.	• Challenge your beliefs about yourself and others by looking at all the facts objectively. • Channel your thoughts in a positive direction. Instead of needless worry, look for creative solutions to problems. • Determine the outcome you want, and take the action necessary to make it happen.

TAKE THE INITIATIVE

1. Know your goals and priorities

Decisions are easier when you've identified your goals and priorities. Without them, it's easy to react to the pressure of problems that seem

---

A Timeline for Achieving Balance in Your Life

(0-3 months)

1. Know your goals and priorities
2. Manage your time
3. Identify your "time bandits"

(3-6 months)

4. Commit to a wellness program
5. Organize your life at work and home

(6-9 months)

6. Prepare for unexpected problems

(9-12 months)

7. Monitor your stress levels
8. Plan and take your vacation!

urgent at the moment. Although solving these problems may make you feel good in the short term, it won't necessarily move you closer to the life you want and deserve.

One way to define your goals is by identifying the most important roles in your life. For example, you may be a professional employee, family member, hobbyist and volunteer. For each role, estimate the percentage of time you both need and want to spend in each role. The total of the percentages should add up to 100 percent. Next, look over all your roles and write down the significant goals you want to achieve within each role in the next 12-18 months. Don't go overboard. No more than three goals is about the right number for most people. If you don't have a goal for a role right now, you may at a future date.

Every month or so, assess how you've actually spent your time against the plan. Any major, prolonged deviations—for example, working excessive overtime—will cause you stress. Make adjustments as needed, to make sure your activities help you achieve your goals.

2. Manage your time in line with your priorities

While you can't spend each day exactly according to your ideal, you can use a variety of tactics to keep on track. Here are some ideas to help you gain control over your time:

- *Use a planner to organize your time.* Whether you use a paper or electronic method, the important thing is to have a planning system and use it consistently. Using the same system for office and home activities makes it easier to integrate your work and personal life. Be realistic—set aside enough time for each task. Give yourself breathing room between activities to switch gears and concentrate on the next task. Book personal commitments as if they are appointments. If you don't, you'll never get to do the things you want—exercise, socialize with friends or spend time with family. Allow yourself some personal downtime!

- *Set limits on your accessibility.* Technology has blurred the line between work and personal time, making it difficult to get away from the demands of the workplace when you're at home or on vacation. On the flip side, try focusing on work while in the office. Try using technology to put up the electronic equivalent of a "Do not disturb" sign. Turn off your cell phone and email when you're not "on call." Let the answering machine record messages, then, return those calls at your convenience. When you go on vacation, have someone in the office handle any anticipated problems. If you must stay in touch with the office while on vacation, limit contact to periods of time that will minimize the disruption.

- *Focus on resolving problems.* Worrying unnecessarily can rob you of energy and waste time. It also won't solve your problem. Instead of worrying, focus your energy on defining solutions and acting to resolve the problem. Chances are you are not the first person to experience this problem. Do some research: Search the web; talk to friends and coworkers; seek expert advice. In the process, you'll feel less isolated and more energized by channeling your efforts in a positive direction.

- *Review your accomplishments at the end of each week.* Don't concentrate on what you didn't get done. Instead, take pride in your successes, large and small. Over a few weeks, identify trends in tasks that didn't get done. If you continually fail to address your high-priority goals, ask yourself whether they really are high priority. If not, let go. If you find yourself avoiding certain must-do tasks, explore alternate ways to

**"Before we begin our Time Management Seminar,
did everyone get one of these 36-hour wrist watches?"**

accomplish them. For example, is there a home repair you keep avoiding? Consider paying someone else to fix it for you.

- **Before leaving work on Friday, take 15 to 30 minutes to identify the personal and work tasks you need to accomplish the following week.** Use your goals to set priorities so you're sure to address the most important tasks first. Rank activities most closely aligned with your overall goals as "A." Give the next most important tasks a rank of "B" and "C." Focus your energy on accomplishing the "A's" and "B's" on your list. Let the "C's" slide until you have more time.

- **Learn to say no.** You can't do everything. At home or at work, consider the impact of additional commitments before making them. At work, one of the worst mistakes you can make is committing to something that you can't accomplish. Ask yourself: "Am I the best person to handle this? Do I have time? Will it prevent me from meeting prior commitments?" If unexpected tasks come up at work, discuss with your manager where they fit in relation to your existing priorities. For activities outside of work, ask yourself, "What won't get done if I say 'yes'? Do I have the money for this activity? Am I even interested in it?" If not, politely decline. There are times when declining a task is not appropriate and could have negative consequences, either at work or in your personal life. Evaluate how saying "no" will affect your relationship with the person making the request. Declining too often could eventually isolate you from friends or coworkers and even limit your career. Having clear goals and priorities helps with these tradeoffs.

- **Leverage relationships.** Consider collaborating with more experienced coworkers to get your job done more efficiently. Network with others and incorporate their best practices into your work routine. If subordinates report to you, delegate tasks that they may be able to do more effectively. This will free you up and also help them develop new skills. Make sure you give credit to others where it's due, so they're willing to work with you in the future.

- *Know your peak performance time and use it wisely.* Use your peak performance hours for tasks that require the greatest thought, creativity and mental alertness. If you don't come alive until after 10 a.m., use early morning hours to return phone calls, clear paperwork off your desk, and perform other tasks that do not require your peak concentration. Conversely, morning people should save these tasks for later in the day, when they start to tire. Also, remember that different activities use different parts of your brain. Constantly switching between various activities can tire you out. Schedule your time in blocks, grouping activities that require similar skills, such as reading email and doing research online.

3. Identify your "time bandits"

A certain amount of distraction can help you relax and be more productive. But allowing yourself to be distracted too often can rob you of valuable time and prevent you from accomplishing your goals. If you don't seem to have enough time to get things done, try keeping an activity log. Write down what you did in 30-minute increments for a week. Review the log daily, and look for "time-bandits"—that is, those activities that eat up a lot of time with no productive results, like excessive web surfing. Develop strategies to keep these in check. Consider these tips:

- *Limit office socializing.* Although it is important to maintain good relationships with coworkers, people often waste the first hour of the day in idle conversation. Bow out in a friendly manner after a few minutes.

- *Keep business calls short and to the point.* Business calls should be limited to a few social amenities before you get to the business at hand. With chatty coworkers, arrange to have lunch or meet after work to socialize, instead of using the office phone.

- *Come in early or leave late.* In addition to helping you avoid traffic jams, coming in early or staying late gives you quiet time to complete important tasks. It's amazing how much you can get done without the phone ringing or coworkers interrupting you.

- **Use your commute time.** The time you spend commuting to and from work can be productive. You can listen to the news on the radio or audio versions of books. If you ride a train or bus, you can read, catch up on paperwork, or even take a short nap. If your commute is too long, consider moving closer to your office, or ask about adapting your hours to avoid traffic.

- **Take advantage of the hours before and after work.** Many businesses open early and close late to accommodate working people. Shop or drop off your dry cleaning before work. Schedule doctors' appointments after work, to avoid taking time off.

- **Use one-stop stores and shopping centers.** Organize your errands around a single stop, if possible. You may pay a little more for items, but you will minimize the amount of time you spend running errands.

- **Limit unproductive computer and TV time.** Take a break now and then, but be careful not to waste a lot of time on addictive electronic entertainment. Try limiting yourself to only your favorite TV shows, and do chores like folding laundry while you watch. Set a timer when you log onto the Internet. Those minutes can vanish before you know it!

4. Commit to a wellness program

A healthy lifestyle helps you overcome the physiological and emotional effects of stress. Being healthy is more than the absence of disease and illness. It's also being able to get through your daily life without feeling fatigued and joyless. Your health depends to some extent on your genetic makeup. However, there are many things you can do to enjoy life more, live longer and be more productive at work and home.

- **Eat healthy.** Eating nutritionally gives us energy and allows our bodies to function properly. It also affects our mood and contributes to mental alertness. Today's frenetic pace promotes unhealthy eating habits. Assess your eating habits, and make adjustments as necessary. Consult your doctor, access reliable online websites, or subscribe to a newsletter or magazine that covers dietary and health matters, if you need information.

- **Benefit from regular exercise.** In addition to lowering the risk of certain diseases, regular exercise helps reduce anger, fatigue, tension and anxiety. Regardless of the activity you choose, the key to physical fitness is to do something regularly. Team sports offer an opportunity to socialize, as well as exercise. Individual exercise can be done at your convenience and can restore your emotional equilibrium after a trying day. Even if you hated gym class, there is a form of exercise out there that you can enjoy: Yoga? Karate? Dancing? Yard work? To maximize your likelihood of success, pick activities you enjoy and set realistic goals for yourself; schedule the activity in your planner; and don't feel guilty if you miss a day. Don't get discouraged. If your routine isn't working, make adjustments until it does.

- **Avoid smoking, heavy drinking and illegal drugs.** In college, you could occasionally go to class hung over without anyone noticing. That's not true at work. Your performance will suffer, and it will be noticed, even if it happens only periodically. You already know about the detrimental effect that cigarettes, alcohol and drugs have on your health. Is use of these substances worth the potential risk to your health, reputation, relationships and career?

- **Get enough rest.** Losing a little sleep can make you cranky. Chronic lack of sleep directly affects your health and can lead to safety, as well as productivity, issues. Severe sleep deprivation slows your reaction time, weakens your memory and decreases your alertness. For most people, eight hours of sleep each night (give or take an hour) is needed to maintain a well-rested feeling.

5. Organize your life

Having too much "stuff" clutters up your life. It makes it hard to find things when you need them. It can be distracting. Too much clutter can even affect your ability to function properly. Follow these guidelines to eliminate the clutter in your life.

At Work: If your desk is messy, you'll have trouble finding things when you need them and will be less productive. Take some time to organize your work area:

- *Purge your desktop, drawers and file cabinets of useless items.* Ask yourself if you really need each item. If not, toss it. Not sure? Then put it aside until you make a final determination.

- *Separate reference materials from those requiring action.* Once you've chosen which items to keep, store them until you need them. Keep materials you need only for reference separate from items you use regularly. Keep frequently used items close at hand, so you don't have to constantly get up to retrieve them.

- *Create a filing system.* Ask coworkers about methods they use for filing, and incorporate their best practices into your system. Everyone has different preferences. Some like to file alphabetically by categories, using hanging folders. Others prefer piling related items on a shelf. Whatever system you use, have one, so you don't waste time looking for things.

- *Keep your desktop clear.* Only keep items on your desk that you need daily (for example, in/out baskets, calendar, pad of paper). Keep supplies (for example, staplers, pens, paper clips) in your desk drawers. When you've completed a task, put away any items you used. This will keep your desktop— and your mind—clear for the next task.

At Home: Clutter accumulates at home because certain items remind us of people or past events, creating an emotional attachment. Sometimes, it helps to remember it's just "stuff" and that getting rid of it won't change the memory. If you're running out of space and tripping over things, don't just stow them away out of sight. You need to get rid of some things. Give away what you no longer want or need. Throw out broken and useless items. Paperwork (receipts, bills, tax forms) may accumulate because you don't know what you need to keep or for how long. Find out what you do and don't need to keep and for how long. Create a home filing system so you can find things more easily. Table 15.2 provides some guidelines.

Table 15.2: Suggestions for getting paperwork under control

Item	Comments	Storage Guidelines
Bills and Receipts	Keep unpaid bills together in order of due date. You can use an automated program to help you establish a bill-paying schedule and remind you when items are due. Pick one day each week to review and pay those that are due. Once paid, write the check number and date on the receipt.	• Use a filing cabinet or an accordion style folder with multiple pockets. • File items alphabetically by category or chronologically by month. • Receipts for bills need to be kept only 6-12 months for reference, unless tax related. • Purge files once or twice a year.
Investment and Bank Records	Review your bank, brokerage and mutual fund statements each month to insure their accuracy. Reconcile your bank statement with your checkbook. When you complete your review, file your statements by account.	• Keep monthly brokerage and cancelled checks at least five years. • Consider signing up to receive bank and investment statements electronically. • Keep confirmations for the purchase or sale of stocks at least seven years beyond the date of their sale. • Mutual fund statements can be replaced each month. Keep year-end statements at least seven years after you sell the shares.
Tax Records	After completing your tax return, you won't need to refer to it until you work on next year's taxes or in the event of an audit. Store it in an out-of-the way place (for example, attic, basement, closet).	• The IRS recommends saving tax records for at least seven years. • Place a copy of your return in a manila folder or envelope and store it in a well-marked, watertight box.
Major Purchases	Many large ticket items (cars, appliances, computers, etc.) come with warranties. Keep them handy in case of a problem.	• Keep warranty materials as long as you own the item. • Store them together in a large manila envelope or pocket folder.

Table 15.2: Suggestions for getting paperwork under control *(cont.)*

Item	Comments	Storage Guidelines
Other Important Items	Documents that prove ownership (deeds for your home, car titles) or identity (birth certificates, passports), or pertain to legal matters (wills, trusts) are difficult and costly to replace. Keep them safe from hazards such as fire, flood and theft.	• These documents must be retained permanently. • Purchase a small, fireproof lockbox or rent a bank safe-deposit box to store them. • Keep a copy of wills and other legal documents with your lawyer.

6. Prepare for unavoidable stress

Some stress just can't be avoided. Daily events can irritate us (for example, traffic jams, arguments with coworkers or family members, unexpected car repairs). Natural transitions that occur throughout life (getting married, moving to a new city, taking a new job, etc.) come with a certain amount of stress. Some jobs require more intense activity at certain times (for example, accountants at month-end or year-end closing) than others. When a number of these events occur in a short time, it can seem overwhelming and give you a sense of losing control. Here are some ways to deal with unavoidable stress:

Maintain a Positive Attitude

- Our minds play a powerful role in dealing with stressful situations. If you think like a victim of circumstances, you will become one. Surround yourself with people who have a positive attitude, build your self-confidence and bolster your courage to do your best, no matter what comes along.

- Too many people stress out over events they cannot control: traffic jams, supermarket lines, plane delays, lost baggage. Focus your energy on the things you can influence, and accept what you cannot.

- Maintain proper perspective. When you have a problem, it's easy to get wrapped up in it and feel sorry for yourself. Helping someone else, like a sick neighbor, is a great way to keep your problems in perspective. You often find out your problems are no worse than anyone else's.

- Stay flexible. Many people stay locked into a routine they can't or won't change, even when problems arise that jolt their normal routine. For example, a family member could get sick and require your time during the day. Be flexible, and think creatively about how to deal with the situation. Can you change your hours at work for a while? Remember that the change is probably only temporary.

- Stay calm. Nothing clouds judgment more than emotions. When problems arise, deal with the emotional aspects, but also try to maintain your sense of calm. This allows you to see opportunities, make better decisions and lower your stress.

Anticipate Problems

Unexpected problems can disrupt your life and prevent you from meeting commitments. You can minimize disruptions and alleviate stress by preparing in advance for certain common problems. Create contingency plans for situations like these:

- If your car breaks down, do you have an alternate means of getting to work?

- If you have to leave town on business, who will take care of your children or pets and collect your mail?

- If you get locked out of the house, does someone have a spare key?

- If you get sick and can't get out of bed, is there someone to check on you to make sure your needs are taken care of (food, medicine, etc.)?

Develop a Support Network

Asking for help does not represent weakness. Don't be afraid to ask for help when you need it, or to accept it when it's offered. Whether it's someone to walk your dog when you're sick, or someone to talk to, we all need help at some point. Family, friends, neighbors and coworkers are all willing to help out in a time of need, if you don't abuse their kindness. Find an appropriate way to thank them. A short note, cup of coffee, a plate of homemade cookies or a simple "thank you" will usually suffice. Be willing to reciprocate if the situation turns around and they need help.

While a stressful situation can be the catalyst for a new relationship between two people, it's best to build relationships ahead of time to establish trust. Recognize that support networks can change over time, due to lifestyle changes. For example, best friends from college may drift apart if one gets married and has children before the other. You can still be friends! You may just play new roles in each other's support network.

Coordinate with Your Boss

At one time or another, almost every employee faces a personal situation, such as marriage or a serious family illness, which demands attention during working hours. Some situations even require frequent or prolonged absences. If you try to hide it, people will probably notice the stress. Supervisors are not heartless; tell your boss when you're facing something big. Your boss will probably cut you a break and even run interference until you resolve the problem.

Do your best to continue meeting your work commitments, within reason. You should be able to find time to work out personal matters during business hours, by coming in early, eating at your desk or staying a little late. Just make sure you observe your organization's rules for using company resources and recording hours. It's usually best to review your approach with your boss so there are no surprises and you get his or her support.

More serious personal problems may require you to take time off. Give your supervisor as much notice as you can. Work together to figure out how to cover your critical commitments. Offer to make up some of your missed time. Your boss and coworkers will appreciate your sense of responsibility and commitment.

Some companies provide paid personal leave benefits when you must be absent from the office for legitimate reasons (illness, personal business, a funeral, jury duty, military leave, etc.). Smaller companies may have less formally defined leave policies. If you have no paid leave benefit, you will have to negotiate time off without pay. If you have been keeping your supervisor informed of a developing personal problem, or if the emergency is sudden, like a death in the family, you should be able to take the time off with no future repercussions.

Save these requests for true emergencies. If you have a track record of frequent unexplained or unplanned absences, you may damage your personal credibility, and your supervisor may be suspicious of your request. Reliable attendance is critical to your professional reputation.

Recognize When You Need Professional Help

There may come a time when work or personal problems are so overwhelming that you need professional help. Many companies now provide confidential, professional counseling for employees to deal with emotional problems, as well as substance abuse, such as excessive drinking or drug addiction. There is no stigma associated with using such services. Companies consider counseling a good investment in a valuable resource—you!

7. Monitor your stress levels

The initial stress of starting a new job will go away once you establish a routine. When you're settled in, see if your level of stress seems reasonable. Become aware of the normal "rhythms" of your job. Certain periods will be more stressful than others (month-end, year-end, pending proposal or project deadlines). Avoid becoming overcommitted elsewhere during those periods.

Do you think you're under too much stress? Network with coworkers and others to compare your situations and reactions. Use this checklist to help identify possible sources of stress:

✔ Do you get along with your supervisor and coworkers, or is there constant tension in the office due to poor communication, low morale or office politics?

✔ Do you feel like you have control over what you do, or are you micromanaged by your supervisor?

✔ Do you understand your responsibilities and what is expected of you? Are the expectations realistic and achievable? Do you have the resources you need to meet these expectations?

✔ Do you have the skills and competency to feel secure about your ability to perform your job and meet expectations?

✔ Do you get the support you need from coworkers and your supervisor, or do you feel like you are left "hanging in the wind" when things get tough?

✔ Do you find your work meaningful and take pride in it, or are you just going through the motions?

✔ How's your social life? Are you feeling lonely or ignored by neighbors and friends?

✔ What about your situation at home? Is there a problem with your family or personal life? Are you having a disagreement with your spouse? Is your child having a problem at school?

✔ Are you financially stretched and having difficulty paying bills?

Answer these questions honestly. Identify the true source of your stress, and take the appropriate action to deal with it.

8. Plan and take your vacation

Before long, you'll be eligible for some vacation time. Two to three weeks' vacation—the typical length for most employees in their first year—is often shocking when compared to having summers off from school. Try taking vacation days in conjunction with company holidays to extend your time off.

Make sure you take your vacation. Enjoy planning your vacation activities; the anticipation can be as rewarding as the vacation itself. When you're away, leave the laptop home and turn off your cell phone so you can enjoy the moment and relax. If you go away for a week or more, brief someone on the status of your projects and anything that might arise while you are away. If necessary, tell your supervisor how you can be reached in the event of an emergency, but place limits on how and when you can be contacted.

SUMMARY

The way your personal life interacts with your work life can have either a beneficial or detrimental effect on you. Balancing the two requires both knowledge and skill. You can achieve balance between your personal life and work life by setting goals, recognizing and relieving stress, maintaining good physical and mental health, and managing your time wisely.

FAQs

Q: *My job has taken me to a new city where I have no friends or relatives. How do I meet people and create a support network?*

A: There are a number of ways to get to know people and develop friends when you move to a new area. Start by attending company functions at work. If you like sports, some companies sponsor athletic events to build a sense of rapport among employees. Outside of work, volunteering with a local nonprofit organization is a great way to meet other people with similar interests and do some good at the same time. Check out your local alumni club for activities; some have activities and social functions geared to young alumni. Also look into activities sponsored by your place of worship. Scan your local newspaper for other ideas. Good luck!

Q: *I have a coworker who comes to my cubicle several times a day just to chat about topics unrelated to work. It's keeping me from getting my work done. I like this person and want to remain friendly. How can I get rid of him when he disrupts my work?*

A: Start subtly. When your coworker has overstayed his welcome, stand up and act as if you are about to leave your cubicle to go to a meeting. Most people will take the hint and leave. If the problem persists, talk with him frankly, but in a way that doesn't offend. Remember, you want to maintain the relationship. Be honest, and tell him how you feel. Explain how his behavior affects your productivity. Suggest carrying on your conversation over lunch, during a coffee break, or after work over a drink.

Q: *I've been on my new job for almost a year and hate it. I receive good feedback from my supervisor, but the work is nothing like I thought it would be, and it's causing me undue stress. I'd like to switch to a career unrelated to my major in college. What should I do?*

A: First, remember you still have to eat and pay the rent. Don't make any impulsive moves like quitting your job, before you know your next move. Jumping to another job or career too quickly and without a plan can land you in an even worse situation. Make sure you've given your job enough time to get a true picture of what the career entails. Keep in mind that every job has some undesirable aspects, especially in the first few years, and many improve as you become more senior.

Get to the root of your dislike. Is your employer the problem? Then explore other companies that could use your skills. If the nature of the work truly is the problem, redesigning your current job might make it more interesting and meaningful. Or, you might transfer to another department within the company that better matches your talents. Finally, a career counselor can help you determine where your career interests really lie. Start with the career center at your alma mater. If they can't help you directly, they may be able to recommend resources that can.

Q: *I seem to be working a lot of casual overtime just to complete my normal work, and it's preventing me from pursuing other interests outside work. I'm really frustrated and want to quit. Help!*

A: Take a deep breath and then evaluate your situation objectively. This may just be a temporary situation. Your company may be temporarily understaffed. The project you were assigned to may be having problems that need to be worked out to get it back on schedule. If so, do what you can to help within your capabilities and wait to see how things go. Consider whether you may be the source of your problem. Are your work habits preventing you from working efficiently? Do you lack the necessary skills to do what you're being asked to do? If so, determine where your problem is and correct it. If the situation has been ongoing since you started, network with your peers to find out if this is normal for your company. If it is, then you might want to find someplace else to work. Be aware that this amount of overtime might be the accepted norm in your field, so quitting to take a similar job somewhere else won't eliminate the problem. In that case, you might want to consider changing careers.

Q: *I have two managers who give me assignments. How to I handle this situation to avoid excessive demands on my time?*

A: This is a difficult situation that comes up frequently, especially in matrix style organizations. Your managers may not be aware of the conflict. Keep them up to date on your activities—regardless of which manager assigned them to you. When conflicting deadlines come up, negotiate with each manager to resolve the conflict. Propose alternatives to see if they are acceptable. In extreme cases, you may have to get them both in the same room to resolve the situation. See Chapter 6, *Planning Your Assignment*, for more ideas.

Q: *I'm having difficulty separating the office from the rest of my life. I bring work home every evening and on weekends. I feel like I don't have any time for myself. What am I doing wrong?*

A: Possibly nothing. Start by analyzing why you bring so much work home. Ask coworkers if this is normal. If so, you may have no alternative, if you want to continue working for your employer. If it's not the norm, look at the factors that might be preventing you from finishing your work at the office (frequent interruptions, poor time management, frequent computer problems, lack of skills, etc.). Identify the cause, and decide how to correct it. The list under "time bandits" in this section has some ideas on how to handle interruptions. If the problem is poor time management or lack of skills, find a course or book to help you become more proficient at completing your tasks. For additional suggestions and recommended reading, go to www.HitTheJobRunning.com.

CHAPTER 16

Managing Your Personal Finances

In this Chapter

- It's all about making choices

- Align your spending with your goals

- Manage and protect what you already have

- Saving and investing choices

- Make the most of your company benefits

- Improve your financial literacy

"No matter who you are, making informed decisions about what to do with your money will help you build a more stable financial future for you and your family."

~ Alan Greenspan ~

WHY YOU SHOULD CARE

You work hard for your money, but somehow it never seems to be quite enough. In reality most people have limited financial resources and therefore are forced to make tradeoffs or choices. Consider these examples:

- **Buying a car:** Should you buy it now or wait until you can pay cash? Buy the new Jag or a used Saturn?
- **Continuing education:** Should you quit your job to attend graduate school full-time or continue working while you study part-time?
- **Living arrangements:** Rent an apartment or buy a condominium? Live alone or take in a roommate?
- **Vacation:** Take a big international trip or go to the local beach?

If your finances are out of control, it affects other aspects of your life. You will experience more stress, which can affect your relationships, as well as your ability to perform your job satisfactorily. Conversely, building your financial security gives you more choices about where you live and where you work. Consequently, you will have less stress and more peace of mind.

WHAT IS FINANCIAL MANAGEMENT?

Financial management involves more than just knowing where to invest your money. It is about taking control of your financial life to advance continually towards your goals and objectives. While you cannot guarantee the outcome, you can improve the odds for success by:

- Leveraging the advantage of time when you are young
- Defining realistic and specific goals in writing
- Improving your financial literacy to make informed decisions
- Committing to regular savings
- Establishing a prudent investment strategy

The Importance of Time

Time, literally, is money and the most important factor in accumulating savings. It works to your advantage when you are young, but against you as you get older. How? Through the power of compounding, that is, earning interest on your interest, you can grow a small amount of savings at an exponential rate. Therefore, to increase the probability of achieving any financial goal, you must start early.

Consider the hypothetical case of Mike and Karen. Assume that they both:

- *Start working at the same company at age 25*
- *Earn $60,000 a year and never get a raise*
- *Contribute eight percent of their gross pay to their 401(k) plan for 10 years*
- *Earn an eight percent return each year on their savings*

However, Mike buys a house and pursues a second degree unrelated to his work. As a result, he waits until he is 55 to contribute to his 401(k) plan. Karen, on the other hand, starts her 401(k) plan contributions immediately, but she stops contributing after ten years at age 35. How much would they each have by the time they retire at age 65?

By starting early and consistently putting the same amount away, Karen's savings would grow to over one million dollars, while Mike's only would reach just over $100,000. If Karen continued to invest until age 65, her savings could grow to more than $1.8 million. No wonder Albert Einstein called the combination of time and compound interest "the most powerful force in the universe!"

Figure 16.1: The sooner you start saving for a goal, the less you have to save each month. Assuming a hypothetical rate of 8% after taxes and compounded daily, the following chart illustrates the monthly savings required to reach a goal of $250,000.

Setting Goals

While it is easy to calculate projected savings, sometimes the pressure from peers and marketers make the choices difficult in the real world. Setting goals and reviewing them periodically, helps you stay on track. There are two dimensions to setting your financial goals: knowing what you want to achieve and understanding how achieving those goals will affect other aspects of your life. Consider a typical situation:

Christine has her eye on a hot sports car. She also wants to buy a townhouse in a "trendy" part of town. If she buys the sports car, she will have less money to save for a down payment on the house—and consequently delay achieving that goal. Should Christine get the car, or settle for a less expensive one and buy the house sooner? The answer depends on which of these goals she considers most important since she currently doesn't have the ability to do both.

Financial goals are very personal and unique to each individual's situation. Nevertheless, Table 16.1 depicts some "big ticket" items typical at various stages of life. While some of these decisions may seem to be far off, remember that planning and saving for them early increases your chances of attaining your goals.

Once you have decided which events are likely in your life, you next need to identify:

- **When they will occur:** Determine how much time you have to save, the rate of savings you need, and where to invest (liquidity).

- **How much they will cost:** Determine how much money you need to save to achieve the goal.

- **Where the money will come from:** Identify all possible sources, including your earnings, loans, and gifts from relatives, among others.

Setting goals lets you plan for them rather than simply reacting to circumstances. Put them in writing and be as specific as possible. Review your goals periodically to stay focused on what is important to you.

Table 16.1: Characteristics and financial considerations at the four major stages of life

Early Adult 20–30	Foundation Years 30–50	Established Years 50–65	Senior Citizen Over 65
This is when you establish independence from your parents and start life on your own. With your first real job, your earnings potential looks bright but you may start off saddled with college loans and needing to make a number of purchases to get established.	During this period, major decisions and commitments are made that establish the patterns and roles for the rest of your life, such as marriage, children, and careers.	The period of maximum earning potential for most people. Simultaneously, your children start moving out, reducing some expenses, your parents are aging and may need care. For some, it is also a time when they really start thinking about what they want out of life (a.k.a., the mid-life crisis).	Healthier life styles and medical improvements are helping people live longer, active lives in retirement. At the same time, corporations are shifting away from traditional defined benefit pension plans based on salary and years of service, requiring individuals to take more responsibility for their financial needs in retirement.

Some major consideration:

• Choosing where to work or live • College loans • New work wardrobe • Buying first car • Renting an apartment / buying a house • Household furnishings • Advanced degree • Emergency funds	• Increased expenses • Single or dual income • Child care • Need for bigger house or apartment • Saving for children's education • Saving for retirement • Life insurance	• Career change • Recreation or hobbies • Travel • Care for aging parents • Weddings • Opening your own business	• Retirement living expenses • Long-term care needs • Providing for your grandchildren's education • Estate planning • Burial expenses

Making Informed Decisions

Knowledge is power. When it comes to financial literacy, studies show that it also can increase your income, and save you money. The complexity of financial products can seem overwhelming, but it does not require a Ph.D. in finance to become a knowledgeable consumer and investor. However, it does take a level of commitment and time. Making the effort can be fun and rewarding. Continually exposing yourself to personal financial topics will help you gradually develop the financial acumen you need.

A Disciplined Savings Plan

If you save your money by investing through your company's 401(k) or 403(b) plan, you defer taxes and earn interest. Some companies will match some or all of your contribution. Having savings withheld automatically from your paycheck each pay period or withdrawn from your checking account monthly will help you become a disciplined saver. If you have no company sponsored savings plan, consult a financial planner or tax advisor on opening an IRA and/or Roth IRA.

Investing Prudently

There are many investment choices available in today's financial markets. The basic choices include money market funds, certificates of deposit (CDs), bonds, individual stocks and mutual funds. Each has unique characteristics and risks associated with it. You build a portfolio of investments by choosing how much money to allocate to each of these alternatives. Your decision should be based on three factors:

1. Your time horizon: When will you need to access the money? Are you investing for retirement that is 30 years away or for a tuition payment that is due in 12 months? The shorter your time frame, the more liquid your investment should be. For example, money held in a checking or savings account is more liquid than money in a 12 month CD. Generally, liquid assets have less risk but also pay lower returns for the convenience of having ready access to your money. See Figure 16.2 following.

Figure 16.2: Liquidity is the measure of how easily you can convert an investment into cash without the risk of losing any of your money or paying a penalty fee. Liquidity and risk have an inverse relationship

2. Your tolerance for risk: Investment risk measures the chance of losing some or all of your money. Greater risk usually means greater *potential* reward, but not everyone has the same capacity for risk. Factors, such as age, income level and stability, and attitude towards risk, determine how much you can handle. Diversifying your money between a mix of stocks, bonds, and cash helps you adjust the risk in your portfolio to match your personal comfort level.

3. Your ability and willingness to manage your investments actively: You need to be involved to some extent in the planning and management of your investments. Your level of involvement depends on the time you can devote to it, your level of interest, and your knowledge. Initially, it may make sense to ask an experienced family member or a financial professional, such as a broker or financial planner, for help with your plan.

TAKE THE INITIATIVE

1. Identify and manage what you have

Sign up for company benefits. Most companies offer employees a variety of benefits to address specific needs economically and conveniently. Find out specifically what your company offers and sign up for those that apply to your situation. Employers often ask that you sign up for certain plans on your first day. Other benefits, such as healthcare, are only available at certain times during the calendar year or after you have worked for the company for a specified time.

A Timeline for Managing Your Finances

1. (0-3 Months) Identify and manage what you have

- Sign up for company benefits
- Determine your net worth
- Know where your money goes
- Create a budget

2. (3-6 Months) Plan for the unexpected

- Sign up for health insurance as soon as possible
- Build and maintain an emergency fund
- Get casualty insurance
- Assess your needs for life insurance
- Create a Last Will & Testament
- Create a Living Will

3. (6-9 Months) Use credit wisely

- Assess your use of credit
- Check your credit rating
- Shop around for interest rates

4. (9 Months and beyond) Grow your savings

- Contribute to your 401(k), IRA and/or Roth IRA
- Determine your target allocation
- Put your money to work
- Improve your financial literacy
- Revisit terms of school loans - consolidate, if needed

Do not be intimidated by all the forms and miss out on important benefits. If you have questions, ask your personnel representative or benefits administrator to clarify the plan. Your family can also be a source of advice for you.

Determine your net worth. Create two columns on a piece of paper. In the left column, list all your assets (that is, the things you own) including cash, savings accounts, investments, and major items such as a car, home or condominium, along with their value. In the right column, list amounts you owe, including credit card debt, car loans, student loans, mortgage, or personal loans. Total each column and then subtract what you owe from what you own. The result is your net worth. If you are like most people just starting out, it is probably a small amount (or even negative). This reality can motivate you to increase your savings or pay off your debt. Do this exercise at least once or twice a year to measure your progress and to help reaffirm your financial strategy.

Know where your money goes. Get a small notebook and write down all your daily expenditures—big and small. Categorize your expenses by "Wants" vs. "Needs". Unless you track your spending, your money is probably not going where you want it to go. Understanding how you spend your money will help you economize, allocate your money between current expenses and future goals, and provide for unexpected events.

Create a monthly budget. A budget consists of your estimate for your income and your expenditures. Creating a budget is not difficult but it does take discipline to manage it.

Balance your budget. Compare your monthly income and expenditures. Adjust your discretionary expenses until your income covers your expenses and savings target.

Once you create a budget, track your actual expenditures against it. If you consistently spend more than you budgeted in a certain area, look for other areas where you can cut back. If your circumstances have changed significantly due to a major life event (getting married, having a child, getting a new job), adjust your budget accordingly.

Personal financial software can make it easier to budget and track expenses. Many financial service providers, including banks, brokers and credit card companies, allow you to download your transactions directly into these software products.

Steps to Creating a Budget

- **Determine your take home pay:** This is the amount left after deductions for taxes, company benefits, savings plans and other miscellaneous deductions are subtracted from your gross pay.

- **Estimate your expenses:** Start with the information you wrote down in your notebook and dividing them into three categories:

  - *Fixed Expenses*—items you have to pay by law or contract, including payments for taxes, rent or mortgage, school loans, insurance.

  - *Variable Expenses*—necessities that you have some level of control over the amount spent. Examples include food, clothing, utilities, and medical expenses. The amount for some of these items (for example, utilities) may vary with the season.

  - *Discretionary Expenses*—entertainment, dining out, travel and vacation are examples of items in this category. They are things that improve your quality of life but can be done without if necessary.

- **Establish a savings target:** A standard rule of thumb suggests starting with at least five percent of your annual gross pay for needs other than retirement. Steadily increase the percentage you save as you receive pay increases. Using a payroll deduction plan helps enforce the discipline of saving.

2. Plan for the unexpected

Sometimes things happen that are outside of your control: unemployment, accidents, death, major illness, or disability. You need to provide an appropriate level of protection to cover you and your family, if they occur. Here are some ways to do that:

- *Sign up for health insurance.* In the event of a major illness, lack of health insurance can prove financially devastating. If offered through your employer, sign up for this benefit as soon as you are eligible. If your company does not provide health coverage, consider joining a professional, fraternal, or academic organization that offers members access to a group plan. Group plan premiums can be lower than premiums for individual plans, but may not cover as much in the event of an illness.

- *Build and maintain an emergency fund.* If you do not have sufficient savings, you can get into financial trouble quickly when life throws you a curve. Establish a fund to cover emergency repair bills or your living expenses for an extended period in the event that you lose your job. As a rule of thumb, financial planners recommend the equivalent of at least six months of your gross pay. In difficult economic conditions, it may take longer to find another job, so you may need more. Build this account up over a two to three year period or sooner, if possible. Make sure that you replenish any money you have to withdraw for emergency purposes.

- *Get casualty insurance.* Your possessions represent a significant amount of money. Replacing them in the event of a fire or theft can be a big setback. If you own a home, your mortgage lender will require you to obtain adequate coverage. If you rent an apartment, be aware that your landlord's insurance policy will not cover your possessions if lost in a fire or stolen. Many apartment dwellers do not realize this until they experience a loss. Shop around for the best deal, but make sure you compare policies with equivalent coverage. You might be able to save money by obtaining both your home and auto insurance from the same company. Ask agents if their companies offer "multi-policy" discounts. Also, consider using a higher deductible amount. This reduces your premium but, in return, the insurance company will reduce its payment for a loss by the amount of the deductable.

- **Assess your need for life insurance.** If you have a family that depends on your income, then you need life insurance to provide for their living expenses, the cost of your funeral, the mortgage, you children's education, etc. The amount of coverage you need varies with your personal situation. A term insurance policy is the most appropriate for most people; it provides a benefit only in the event of death and is the cheapest form of coverage. You can purchase term insurance for as little as one year or up to 30 years. When the owner of the policy dies, it pays the face amount to the beneficiary. Shop around to get the best coverage and price for your needs. Some employers offer life insurance policies as part of a flexible benefit plan.

- **What happens if you die prematurely or cannot make your own health care decisions?** Most of us do not want to think about death. But it can happen unexpectedly, and you need to plan for it. Even if you do not have a lot of money at this point, you don't want the state to decide who gets it. Create a Last Will and Testament no matter how young you are. A will spells out how you want your possessions distributed upon your death. It also names someone to manage your estate, collect assets from any insurance policies, and pay the bills you leave behind. You should also determine who will have custody of your children. Also consider preparing a Living Will, which tells your family and physicians what measure you want taken in a medical emergency when you cannot make your own choices. While standard documents are available for both a will and a Living Will, consult an attorney to ensure they comply with the specific laws in your state.

3. Manage your use of debt

Incurring some debt can help you reach your goals faster, but it can cost more than you realize, if you don't use it wisely. The trick is

> ## *Credit card financing can significantly increase the cost of your purchases if you pay only the minimum balance each month.*
>
> Consider this example:
>
> Compound Interest can work against you if you do not pay off your credit card balance each month. For example, assume you buy a computer for $1000 using your credit card. Your annual interest rate is 18% and your minimum payment is calculated as 2.5% of your outstanding balance. If you pay only the minimum required each month:
>
> - The interest paid would amount to $1,115.41 bringing the total cost of the computer to $2,115.41, more than two times the purchase price.
>
> - The time required to pay off the balance by paying only the minimum amount each month would be 12 years and 9 months. Will you still be using that computer by then?

knowing how much you can afford, while still maintaining a good credit rating.

- *Assess your credit card use.* Do you carry a balance and pay only the minimum amount each month? Unfortunately, the power of compounding interest works against you when it comes to debt. By paying only the minimum each month, you are also paying large interest fees that significantly increase the cost of any item you buy. One simple rule to keep your credit card balance in check: only use it for purchasing major items that will last for several years. Paying for a meal 18 months after you ate it can be very disheartening.

- *Check your credit rating.* If you're having trouble paying loans or other monthly bills, it's a sure sign that you have taken on more debt than you can afford. Reduce your spending by delaying purchases or forgoing them altogether so you can meet your financial commitments. Missing or late payments hurt your credit rating. Maintaining a good credit rating can actually save you money:

- Banks offer lower mortgage and other loan rates to borrowers with a good credit history.

- Credit card companies charge higher interest rates to people with lower credit scores.

- Insurance companies use credit ratings to determine insurance premiums because they consider individuals with bad credit history poor risks.

- Some companies now use applicant credit scores to screen applicants because they consider those with higher credit scores more responsible.

Check your credit score periodically to ensure the accuracy of the information. If you see errors, get them corrected. You may also find out if someone has fraudulently taken credit in your name. If your score is good, contact your credit card company to negotiate a lower interest rate. Go to www.HitTheJobRunning.com for links to get your credit report.

- ***Shop around for interest rates.*** If you need to borrow money, look for the lender who offers the best terms and conditions. Deal only with reputable lenders and always read the fine print on any loan documents to know what the penalty is if you cannot make your payments. Be wary of anyone offering to lend you money regardless of your credit history; it will probably carry a very high interest rate. Ask lenders about interest rates and fees. Before you take out a loan, figure out the amount of interest you will have paid by the end of the loan term. Is the item you are buying worth the extra cost or would it be wiser to defer your purchase until you have the cash? Do the terms of the loan allow you to repay it before the end of the term without a penalty? If you already have a loan and interest rates have dropped significantly, you can refinance at a lower rate if there is no prepayment penalty. Similarly, if you have multiple student loans, you can consolidate them into a single loan with one payment, sometimes at a lower interest rate.

4. Grow your savings

- ***Contribute to your 401(k) or 403(b).*** Many corporations offer a 401(k) plan instead of a defined benefit pension plan. The 401(k) plans makes individuals more responsible for their own retirement income. A 403(b) plan is a similar retirement plan available to schools, hospitals and other non-profit organizations. Even if your company has a traditional pension plan, contributing to your 401(k) plan in addition still makes sense. Taxes on both your contributions and earnings will be deferred until you retire. Many companies match some portion of your contributions which gives your return a strong boost. Ask your benefits administrator to explain the plan's features, such as how much you can contribute, the company's matching policy, and information about available investment options. Start contributing as soon as you are eligible and contribute the maximum percentage the plan allows. If you can't afford the maximum, at least contribute enough to get the full company match if it is available.

- **Choose how much to invest in stocks, bonds and cash.** Most people invest in some mixture of stocks, bonds and cash, also known as asset classes. To decide where to put your money, start by determining your capacity and tolerance for risk. Many financial websites, including those of brokers, have quick tests that can help you make this assessment and recommend the appropriate mix of stocks, bonds and cash. The reference section at www.HitTheGroundRunning.com lists some sites you can use. If you lie awake at night worrying about your investments, you probably have taken on too much risk. Cut back the percentage of stocks and allocate more money to bonds or cash. Periodically rebalancing your portfolio to your allocation targets will help you manage risk by capturing gains and using them to make new investments in a lower priced asset class.

- **Put your money to work.** If you have saved 5% or 10% of your gross pay each period, you should have a few thousand dollars to put to work. For most people with this sum, buying mutual funds makes the most sense as they offer diversity and low cost. If you have not saved very much, do not beat yourself up. Some mutual funds will start an account with an initial investment of only $100 if you agree to make regular contributions through automatic withdrawals from your checking or savings account.

Choosing Mutual Funds

Choose funds that have been highly rated by an independent agency such as Morningstar®. Restrict your search to funds that do not charge a commission (also known as no-load funds) and have low operating expenditures (1.0% or less). You can find this information in the material (a *prospectus*) that you receive from the fund's manager. Morningstar® or your broker can also provide this information when you perform your initial search.

Keeping the number of funds you buy to a small number (no more than two or three) and within a diverse family of funds will minimize the effort of tracking the performance of your investments and simplify accounting at tax time.

- *Improve your financial literacy.* Here are some suggestions to consider:

  - Read widely and with skepticism. The best sources include personal finance magazines, newspapers, and books on investing and personal finance.

  - TV and radio shows dealing with financial issues are abundant. Don't rely on this medium as your sole source or information, as it tends to be "sound bite" oriented.

  - Many helpful websites provide information and calculators to make your job easier. Most are free, but be wary of sites that push specific products.

  - Take a class on personal finance at local college or adult night school. Courses are also available online, many at no cost.

  - Start or join an investment club. This is a good way to develop your investment skills and learn from other people. For information, contact the National Association of Investment Clubs (NAIC).

  - Discuss financial matters with people in different stages of life to learn from their experience. Incorporate their feedback into your financial plan.

  - Talk with a certified professional (preferably either a CFP or CPA) about specific situations that are more complex.

SUMMARY

Personal financial planning is all about envisioning the future so you can do something about it now. It's not difficult to do, but it does take time and commitment. You can increase your chances of reaching your goal by:

✔ Acting early to leverage the advantage of time

✔ Saving regularly

✔ Investing consistently with your personal tolerance for risk

✔ Committing to become more financially literate

✔ Being an active participant in managing your finances

✔ Believing in your financial strategy and committing to it

FAQs

Q: *I need a car in order to commute to work. Is it better to buy or lease one?*

A: Typically, leasing makes sense only when the car is used for a business. The main advantages of leasing are lower monthly payments than a loan and the opportunity to drive a more expensive car than you could afford to buy. If you are intent on driving a new car every two or three years, leasing might make sense. Keep in mind that most leases require a down payment of several thousand dollars. There are also hidden costs, such as an excess mileage charge if you exceed the pre-set limit in the lease agreement. Don't forget, at the end of the lease all you own is the right to purchase the car at a pre-agreed price. If your objective is to save money, purchasing the car and driving it for seven to ten years makes more sense. Want to save even more money? Pay cash and/or buy a used car from a reputable dealer. Paying cash avoids the interest expense (unless the dealer is offering zero-interest loan incentives), while buying a used car reduces the price you will have to pay, although you may not own it as long.

Q: *I make less than $30,000 a year. How can I expect to save enough money to do all the things I want to do when I retire?*

A: Consider the often-cited case of Anne Scheiber. When she retired from her job as a federal tax auditor in 1944, she had $5,000 in savings and a monthly pension of $83. When she died in 1995 at the age of 101 her estate, which she left to her alma mater, Yeshiva University, totaled $22 million. While there is debate over how much she had actually saved before retiring—some reports indicate that she retired with savings of $20,000—her example still stands out as a model for creating wealth: live a modest life style, invest prudently, and hold your investments for the long term. Anne Schieber started late but we all don't live to the age of 101, so start investing now.

Q: *My employer has let me defer my start date for three months after graduation so I can study for the CPA exam. What should I do about health insurance coverage during that time?*

A: Your parents' policy may still cover you. Some providers let you stay on for six months after graduation. It depends on the policy. Ask your parents to contact their benefits administrator or insurance agent to ensure you are covered. If not, you can purchase an interim package from an insurance company by paying a monthly fee until your employer's plan covers you. If you are in good health, it may make sense to get a policy that covers only catastrophic illness. Consider that even a broken arm, should there be complications, can cost as much as a new car. Contact your alumni association. Many now have group plans available to graduates and even make special interim plans available to cover this situation. If all else fails, contact an independent insurance agent for advice.

Q: *My 401(k) plan allows me to buy stock in the company I work for. Should I invest in it?*

A: That depends on the company, its financial situation and growth prospects. Do some research on the company before you decide. Get a copy of the company's annual report and read what management says about its outlook. Also, get a report from Standard & Poors (available at your local library or from your stockbroker) or another independent source to get an outside perspective on your company. If you are comfortable after doing this research, then it may make sense to allocate some of your 401(k) savings to company stock. However, remember what happened to people who put all of their 401(k) savings in Enron and WorldCom stock: when the companies went bankrupt, the investors were left with nothing. Be prudent—don't put all your money into a single investment.

Q: *I don't plan to stay at my company for more than a few years. What happens to my 401(k) account if I leave?*

A: When you leave your company, you have three options:

1. Keep your 401(k) account with your old employer;

2. Roll it over to your new employer's plan; or

3. Roll it over to a personal IRA with a broker or bank.

Become familiar with the specific terms of your company's plan, especially about any company matching contributions. There are also potential tax implications, depending on how the rollover is handled. These rules change so check with a tax adviser before initiating any rollover transactions to make sure you avoid penalties or unnecessary taxes.

Q: *I can't seem to find a way to save any money and my credit card balance keeps growing. What should I do?*

A: You need to get your spending habits under control and live within your means. Start by taking the credit card out of your wallet and keeping it at home in a safe place so you won't be tempted to spend more than you have. Next, figure out what you can afford to spend vs. what you make every month. Cut out any non-essential spending and allocate as much as you can to paying off that credit card balance. When you do make a purchase, only pay cash. If this does not correct the situation, seek the advice of a reputable credit counselor. Your bank's local branch manager may be able to help you find someone in your area.

Q: *My employer doesn't have a 401(k). How can I save for my retirement?*

A: Contact a brokerage firm or a bank and set up an IRA (Individual Retirement Account). You have two alternatives: Traditional IRA and Roth IRA. A traditional IRA provides the double advantage of a tax deduction and tax-free growth until you withdraw your money. Alternatively, a Roth IRA does not provide an immediate tax deduction, but you will not have to pay taxes on any of the earnings, even when you make withdrawals. Both have limits on the amount you can contribute and when you can make deductions. Tax laws change periodically. See your financial advisor for the latest information on limitations and new tax-deferred plans that may be available.

Q: *I'm contributing to a 401(k) plan at work. Should I also put money in an IRA?*

A: It can't hurt, especially if your company does not have a defined benefit pension plan (i.e., one in which your pension benefit is determined by a formula based on your salary level and years of service). Make sure your contributions do not exceed the amount allowed. Check with your benefits administrator or financial advisor to determine the current limits. To make it easier, include contributions to your IRA/Roth IRA as a fixed item in your budget and have payments automatically deducted from your checking account each month.

Q: *How do I know if I'm paying too high an interest rate?*

A: Most local papers will publish rates from banks and other institutions located in your area. You can find them listed in the business section of the paper. Banks will post the rates for mortgages, auto loans and personal loans, as well as the rates you can earn by putting your cash in a money market account or certificate of deposit (CD). Some papers only post the rates once a week, typically on a weekend. Search online for local rates.

What Now?

"If one advances confidently in the direction of his dreams, and endeavors to live the life which he has imagined, he will meet with a success unexpected in common hours."

~ Henry David Thoreau ~

Congratulations! You've made it through your first year on the job. Hopefully, your career is off to a good start as a result of the actions you took after reading this book. You're no longer a rookie and can expect your share of more interesting assignments and additional responsibilities. Perhaps, you will even receive a promotion, which brings new opportunities. So, what do you do now?

First of all, don't become complacent. Those new assignments and responsibilities will come with new challenges. People will raise the bar on your performance and expect more of you. At the same time, managers and coworkers will be less willing to cut you slack for any mistakes you make. Keep applying and honing the skills you learned in this book to:

- Become efficient at performing your job to demonstrate competency and improve your confidence
- Deliver effective results which illustrate your value to the organization
- Listen, evaluate and act on the feedback you receive to improve your abilities
- Practice creative and critical thinking in your problem solving
- Continually work on your communication skills in order to have your ideas heard and understood

- Value and respect the opinions of others to build a cooperative environment, showing your leadership and opening
  more doors to you

Next, keep in mind that the world is ever changing and the pace of
change continues to accelerate. When it occurs, analyze how it affects
you and embrace it by maintaining a positive attitude. The ability to
be flexible and adapt to change is critical to both your survival and
success. Change also requires a commitment to continuous learning.
Expanding your knowledge base opens up new opportunities and
gives you the confidence to pursue them. This book only touches the
surface of the topics presented. You should read more advanced
books on topics you feel you need to strengthen.

Finally, remember the ten most powerful two letter words in the English language: "If it is to be, it is up to me." From performing your job
and planning your career, to managing your finances and achieving
your dreams, you must take the initiative to define your goals and act
on them. No one else can live your life. It is truly up to you to define
and achieve the level of success you imagine.

Best of luck and stay prepared to hit the ground running!

Problem Solving Skills

Creative Thinking

Brainstorming

What: Brainstorming is a process used in problem solving to generate ideas. This process works best with several people because ideas from others in the group help to provide each participant with fresh perspectives and generate more ideas. Quantity is important for obtaining the best results from this process. The basic method can be applied by individuals with good results. The ideal group size is seven to ten.

When:

- To identify a wide-ranging list of potential problems, causes or solutions during a group problem solving activity;

- To gather all points of view on a topic, particularly in a situation where one or a few members dominate the group or where some members are shy about participating;

- To encourage deep and creative thinking about a problem, thus gaining a truly wide range of views to consider.

How:

- Clearly state the topic and make sure everyone understands the purpose of the session. A good way to do this is to state the issue or problem in terms of a question for which the session will generate answers, such as "How can we attract more college graduates to work at our company?"

- Allow the group members to silently brainstorm their individual responses and write them down on a sheet of paper. Allot approximately 10 minutes to this step.

- When all participants feel they can't think up any new ideas, start the process of sharing the ideas one at a time. Participants can either say their ideas randomly, or they can go around the room sharing one idea at a time. Sharing ideas in an orderly manner helps ensure that quiet members are not drowned out by more outspoken members. Appoint someone to record ideas so all can see the list; do not paraphrase or summarize what is said.

- At this point, limit discussion to points of clarification, only. Judging ideas at this stage will only inhibit the creative process. Participants should avoid both positive and negative comments on others' inputs. They should also avoid laughing – it is a form of judgment.

- As ideas are shared, encourage participants to add to their written lists as new ideas occur to them based on others' inputs. The goal is to reach at least 100 ideas. Typically, the first third generated are obvious and not particularly creative. Often groups give up at this point, thinking they've exhausted the possibilities. If pushed to go further, the next third of the ideas tend to be absurd or laughable. Again, groups give up at this point thinking that anything else they think up will be silly. The last third is when the real innovation usually occurs, as groups merge the obvious with the absurd to produce interesting yet workable results.

- Finally, review the list of ideas. Get clarity where needed, making sure all participants understand each idea. Combine or eliminate similar or duplicate ideas. Determine the criteria and approach for moving to the next step in the group process.

Supplies Needed: A means of recording and displaying ideas for all to see: a computer with a projector, old fashioned flip charts or white board and markers. Scratch paper and pens/pencils for each participant.

Critical Thinking

Multi-Vote Ranking Technique

What: Multi-vote ranking helps teams sort priorities and make selections from among a group of ideas or options. This technique is used with groups. It is especially helpful when a large number of choices must be narrowed to just a few.

When:

- To reduce the number of items under consideration (e.g. opinions, solution alternatives) down to a workable number;
- To select the top choices from a large list of items;
- To ensure full participation in a group decision-making process.

How:

- Establish the criteria that will be used to make the selection (e.g. importance, cost, feasibility. Using different criteria will often yield very different lists.). Make sure that all group members understand the criteria, including ensuring that everyone is using the same definition of the criteria.
- Create list of all choices under consideration that is visible to all participants – projected on a screen, posted on flip charts or printed as a handout for each member.
- For round one, grant each participant 5 votes he or she can cast for his/her top choices. Each participant can use the votes for 5 individual items, put all 5 votes on one item, or any other combination of the votes. Record the votes for each item.
- Eliminate from the list all items that received 0 votes. Put the remaining choices in a matrix like the following.

Item	Round 1 Vote	Round 2 Vote	Round 3 Vote
Item 1			
Item 2			
Item 3			
Etc.			

- As a group, discuss each item on the list. Encourage each participant to discuss how he or she thinks each item best meets the evaluation criteria. Also discuss the downside of each choice.

- Conduct a 2nd round of voting. Grant each participant 3 votes to cast as desired. Record the votes in the matrix. Eliminate all items that received 0 votes. Discuss the results.

- Conduct a 3rd round of voting, this time limited each participant to 1 vote. Record the results in the matrix and eliminate all items receiving 0 votes.

- By this point, just a few obvious top choices should have emerged. Depending on the situation, pursue the number of choices (e.g. top item or top 3), according to priority.

- Different variations of this approach may be used: varying the numbers of votes allocated, number of rounds used to select, whether the vote is taken privately or openly, the degree of discussion allowed, etc. Be creative and adapt to your particular situation.

Supplies Needed: A means of recording and displaying ideas for all to see: a computer with a projector, old fashioned flip charts or white board and markers. Scratch paper and pens/pencils for each participant.

Critical Thinking

Impact Matrix Technique

What: The Impact Matrix Technique is a way to prioritize and select solutions from a list of possibilities, based on specific criteria. It may be used with groups or by an individual.

When:

- To prioritize the best solutions to a problem when considering several (10-25) alternatives;
- To evaluate possible alternatives as logically as possible, based on well-defined and accepted criteria. Can be especially helpful in avoiding emotional decisions;
- Participants must be able to identify and agree on key evaluation criteria, and to reasonably evaluate each option against them.

How:

- Define two criteria against which the group will evaluate the options it is considering. Possible criteria include (but are not limited to) cost, time to implement, ease of implementation, potential impact and urgency.
- On a large piece of paper or white board, draw a pair of intersecting axes. Label one axis with one of the criteria, and the other axis with the second. Label the high and low end of each axis (e.g. highest cost vs. lowest cost).
- Select the first option to evaluate. The order of evaluating doesn't matter. As a group, discuss the option and decide where it ranks on each axis. Write the option in the appropriate quadrant.
- Continue evaluating and plotting each option until all are mapped.

- The top solutions are those found in the quadrant defined by the two positive ends of the axes. Consider abandoning the solutions that land in the quadrant defined by the two negative ends of the axes. Solutions in the remaining two quadrants require further discussion. (See example.)

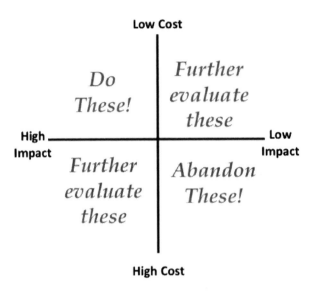

Example of an Impact Matrix

Alternative:

- If you have more than two criteria, you can repeat this process for each additional consideration. Using the results from the first evaluation, assign a '1' to the "Do These!" solutions, and a '2' to the "Further evaluate these" solutions. Eliminate the "Abandon These!" solutions. Create a new set of axes – one represents the new criterion, the other represents the output of the first round (i.e. '1' = high, '2' – low). Plot the solutions again, using the new criteria. Repeat the process as many times as necessary.

Supplies Needed: A large flip chart or white board, and markers.

Tips and Tricks for Presentations

There are many opinions about what makes a good presentation. We provide some additional resources for you on our website, www.HitTheJobRunning.com. Here we have a summary set of "Tips and Tricks" for creating and delivering a successful presentation.

Creating a Presentation

- **Understand the purpose for the presentation.** Is it to inform? Persuade? Present various solutions for a decision? You should be able, in one sentence, to write the message your presentation must deliver.

- **Know your audience.** If you've read the chapters in this book about effective communications, you know that there are many questions you should answer about your audience. Here are just a few:

  ✔ Who is your audience and why do they need to hear your message? In one sentence, you need to be able to state what action you expect them to take as a result of your presentation. Does your audience understand your expectations of them and the desired outcome?

  ✔ How much does the audience already know about this topic?

  ✔ Do they understand the purpose of the briefing or do you have to inform them? Do they know all the needed background for the topic or do you have to create it in "backup" slides or materials?

✔ Do they come with concerns that have to be addressed?

✔ Do they speak the language (e.g., do they know the acronyms, formulas, references) you are using? Do you need to translate to their "language" (finance, legal, marketing).

- **Create an outline.** Yes, your teacher was right way-back-when. Starting with an outline helps keep the presentation clear and well organized. At its most basic, the outline should include:

  ✔ An Introduction or Agenda—orients the audience

  ✔ Background information—enough data to get everyone in the audience on the same page

  ✔ Main Message—contains the bulk of your content. Organize this section based on your content and purpose. For instance, if you are recounting something that happened, a sequential organization is probably best. If you are presenting status, there may be some logical way to walk through the various items, e.g., by due date, by program or by customer. If you are presenting a number of options to consider, you could follow a rank order—most to least preferred (or the opposite).

  ✔ Conclusions—gets the audience to acknowledge their buy-in or consensus

  ✔ Summary—reminds the audience of the purpose and re-states the outcome or next steps succinctly

- **Use well accepted design principles**. Whether you use PowerPoint or some other delivery mechanism, here are good design principles which can help you.

  ✔ **Less is More.** Concentrate on your purpose and message. Keep it simple.

  ✔ **One idea per chart.** Limit the message for each chart to one main idea. The main idea should be described in one or two main bullets, with indented bullets following, which support the main idea with more detailed data or background information.

  ✔ **Keep bullets succinct.** A bullet should occupy one line and not wrap wherever feasible. Bullets don't necessarily have to be complete sentences. In fact, to help you avoid reading your charts, it helps to use partial sentences or phrases instead of complete sentences.

✔ **Limit the number of bullets.** A good rule of thumb is 5–7 bullets per chart.

✔ **Be sensitive to the color blind.** It is estimated that 8% of males and .05% of females have some degree of color blindness. Never convey information using color alone. "Double code" information using color and some other marker (pattern, for example) so the message reaches everyone.

✔ **Use graphics (diagrams, flow charts, matrices, etc.)**—with caution. A picture can be worth 1000 words if it is readable, understandable and conveys the message concisely. However, some people find graphics distracting, especially if they are more decorative than informational in nature. Be sure you know the "culture" of your audience so you're using a style that works for them.

✔ **Avoid overuse of "gimmicks" (animation, cartoons, clip art)** which serve no real purpose and distract from your message.

• **Have someone knowledgeable review the charts.** Is your message the right one? Clear? Understandable to the audience? Is the language known to all involved? Do you stress the right key points? Does the message progress logically? Do you have a spoken or written transition from chart to chart? Are the introduction and summary at the appropriate level?

Delivering a Presentation

• If speaking in public scares you, you aren't alone, says Paul L. Witt, PhD, Assistant Professor of Communication Studies at Texas Christian University, Fort Worth. "It is even scarier than rattlesnakes. The idea of making a presentation in public is the No. 1 fear reported by people in the U.S." (as reported on WebMD, 2006). If you feel this phobia is blocking your career success, join an organization like Toastmasters® where you can practice presenting information in a non-threatening "safe" environment, away from the workplace. Confidence built in these practice sessions may transfer to your work situation.

- Rehearse your presentation where you can be at ease and comfortable—perhaps in front of a mirror, your family, friends or colleagues. Use a tape-recorder, as well as videotape, and analyze yourself. However, do not over rehearse to the point of memorization.

- Never read your charts line by line. Know the content and speak to it. You will lose your audience if they feel you are just droning on with rote recitation. Let them feel your enthusiasm and confidence in the message.

- Try not to speak too quickly or softly—a problem for those who are nervous. Vary your intonation and delivery.

- Smiling too much is another problem which some nervous speakers face. You want to look friendly, but not like you're not taking your subject matter seriously.

- Looking the part may be just as important as sounding like an authority. Dress appropriately for the situation. During the practice video tape sessions, watch your body language and what you do with your hands. Practice looking confident and using meaningful hand gestures, while moving minimally around the stage.

- On the day of the presentation, eliminate all potential distractions. Make sure you know the room and its associated technology. Dry run setting up any special equipment, if needed. Have a backup ready for any failure points (extra bulbs, presentation on thumb drive or other additional media, hard copy handouts, etc.). Make sure your cell phone and/or pager are turned off and ask the audience for the same courtesy—at least suggest they set theirs to vibrate rather than ring.

- Speak to and involve the audience. Watch their faces. Make eye contact individually for no more than 5 seconds and occasionally sweep the entire audience with your gaze. Elicit questions or responses. Adjust to their feedback. Allow some pauses (which many people are not 100% comfortable doing). This gives them time to absorb and reflect on your message.

- Use some gentle humor, IF you're comfortable. Don't force bad jokes into your presentation but take advantage of opportunities to get your audience engaged with some light hearted comments. Jokes that come across as rehearsed usually crash like a lead balloon.

- Try to be flexible. You may have to adjust to the situation and feedback on the fly. For example, if you are one of several presenters in a meeting that is running much longer than expected, you may be asked to shorten your presentation time. Or, a senior manager in the audience who is already familiar with your background information might direct you to jump to the recommendations section of your presentation. Know in advance how and when to eliminate or condense a chart (or charts), identifying the most critical points that should not be skipped and the associated verbiage to stay on track. You need to leave enough time to ensure they absorb the critical conclusions and/or summary chart message(s). End with the singular most important thing you want them to take away from the presentation.

Acknowledgements

We are most appreciative of the time and efforts of all those who contributed to the creation of both this edition, as well as past editions of *Hit the Job Running*. What depth of content you have provided to us and our readers!

Thank you once again, Marlene Prost for your ability to focus on the details of editing, while also seeing the big picture of the flow and tone of the manuscript. Thank you Beth Fazio for your fresh and creative vision in designing the new book cover. And thank you Marian Hartsough for a clean and professional layout. We appreciate and profited from your sharing your vast experience and wisdom. All three of you are a joy to work with!

Thank you, Ray Sarnacki for your many contributions to the first edition of *Hit the Job Running*, on which this edition is based. The depth of your financial knowledge continues to shine through.

Thank you, Scott Vail at L-3 Communications, East for continuing to allow us to refine our concepts through our workshops for your entry level employees and for your Foreword to this book. You are more than a client; you are a friend.

Thanks to the following for various inputs to the creation of the new sections introduced in this edition of *Hit the Job Running*: Nancy Partridge, Linda Dowd, Nick Dowd, Joanne Helfrich, Carlos Bautista, Ryan Clemens, Anthony McClellan and Nick Petti. We remain thankful for the time and effort of the following who reviewed and provided expert feedback on the original content of the book: Mike Arnold, Stephen Belter, Carrie Belter, Ilyse A. Berman, John Bish, Carla Booker, Jim, Breitenback, Tom Breitenbach, Arlene Cohen, Mark, Deese, Andrew DeWese, Colin J. Donnelly, Tom Dougherty, Gena M. Groves, Michael Gunn, Randy Hubschmidt, Janet Mouat, Jamie Perencevich, Daniel R. Sandler, Lauren Sarnacki, Mike Sarnacki, Derek Sciecinski, Carl J. Suppa, and Ruth Thomas.

And finally, thank you family and friends for your patience and support throughout this project.

Andrea Dolph
Lynda Clemens
March 2010

About the Authors

Andrea, Lynda and Ray met as managers at GE Aerospace, where they discovered a shared interest in determining how best to mentor their employees. The impetus for this book's first version was a lay-off in 1992. During the painful process of deciding who would be laid-off, the authors had a pivotal insight: Most employees did not lose their jobs for lack of technical skills, lack of effort or lack of ambition. Instead, most were let go because of poor "workplace skills," such as an inability to adapt to the business culture, poor planning or problem solving, inappropriate interpersonal interactions and lack of time management. The authors have since devoted a significant portion of their careers to helping people benefit from this insight.

Andrea T. Dolph

Andrea has more than 20 years of hands-on experience in strategic business and Information Technology planning, program management, process optimization and planning/managing budgets in the millions of dollars. As a manager/director at GE and Lockheed Martin, she hired and coached entry level to experienced employees, and served as executive coordinator for recruiting at the University of Virginia. Her corporate and subsequent consulting experience spans the aerospace and defense, pharmaceutical, hospital, retail, and insurance industries. She has held numerous leadership positions in various non-profit organizations.

Andrea's BA, Russian Studies from the University of Virginia, and an MS, Computer Science from George Washington University have been enhanced by training in many aspects of leadership development at both GE's Crotonville Management Development Institute and through off-site programs sponsored by GE and Lockheed Martin.

Lynda Clemens

Lynda has more than 25 years experience in Information Technology program management, having led multi-million dollar projects for Lockheed Martin. As a senior manager at Lockheed Martin, she mentored many entry-level to more experienced employees.

Lynda received her Ph.D. in Educational Psychology from Temple University in 1985. She has taught as an adjunct for Penn State Great Valley School of Graduate Professional Studies since 1993, twice receiving the Teaching Excellence Award. She also received training in many aspects of leadership development through programs sponsored by GE and Lockheed Martin.

Raymond P. Sarnacki

Ray gained extensive management experience over a 30 year career, producing demonstrated results in cost reduction, process improvement and alignment of IT initiatives with business objectives. As a manager at GE and Lockheed Martin, he also served as executive coordinator for recruiting at Notre Dame and played an instrumental role in developing Lockheed Martin's IS Leadership Development Program. He left Lockheed to become a managing director for a $60 million venture capital fund investing in retail, food service, and technology companies. He now lectures on management topics in the MBA program at St. Joseph's University. Ray serves as an advisor and board member for several non-profit organizations.

A University of Notre Dame graduate, he holds a BA in Economics, as well as an MS in Operations Research from Union College. He graduated from GE's Financial Management Program and received additional training at GE's Management Development Institute in Crotonville, NY.

Index

CPSIA information can be obtained at www.ICGtesting.com
Printed in the USA
BVOW01s2155010414

349485BV00009B/177/P